COSMIC COWBOYS

COSMIC COWBOYS AND NEW HICKS

The Countercultural Sounds of Austin's Progressive Country Music Scene

TRAVIS D. STIMELING

OXFORD

UNIVERSITY PRESS

Oxford University Press is a department of the University of Oxford.
It furthers the University's objective of excellence in research, scholarship,
and education by publishing worldwide.

Oxford   New York

Auckland   Cape Town   Dar es Salaam   Hong Kong   Karachi
Kuala Lumpur   Madrid   Melbourne   Mexico City   Nairobi
New Delhi   Shanghai   Taipei   Toronto

With offices in

Argentina   Austria   Brazil   Chile   Czech Republic   France   Greece
Guatemala   Hungary   Italy   Japan   Poland   Portugal   Singapore
South Korea   Switzerland   Thailand   Turkey   Ukraine   Vietnam

Oxford is a registered trade mark of Oxford University Press
in the UK and certain other countries.

Published in the United States of America by
Oxford University Press
198 Madison Avenue, New York, NY 10016

© Oxford University Press 2011

First issued as an Oxford University Press paperback, 2016

Library of Congress Cataloging-in-Publication Data
Stimeling, Travis D.
Cosmic cowboys and new hicks: the countercultural sounds of Austin's
progressive country music scene/ Travis D. Stimeling. — 1st ed.
p. cm.
ISBN 978-0-19-974747-4 (hardcover); 978-0-19-061035-7 (paperback)
1. Country music—Texas—Austin—History and criticism. I. Title.
ML3524.S75 2011
781.64209764'31—dc22   2010029052

Publication of this book was funded in part by the Publications Endowment
of the American Musicological Society, supported through the
National Endowment for the Humanities.

Preface

Popular music plays a remarkably powerful role in the definition, articulation, and actualization of individual and collective identities. As George Lipsitz remarks in the foreword to Susan D. Crafts, Daniel Cavicchi, and Charles Keil's extensive study, *My Music: Explorations of Music in Daily Life*, "As creators and receivers, performers and spectators, active and passive listeners, people's musical tastes and interests reveal far more complexity and far more self-directed searching, testing, and experimenting than either music schools or commercial market categories can account for."[1] That is, we use our various interactions with music as opportunities to assume identities, to determine how they fit with our prior self-conceptions, and to explore how other people might react to our new, musically defined identities. As we venture out of our private listening sanctuaries and interact with other people, we often build valuable social relationships with those who share our musical tastes, who are engaged in the same process of identity formation, and who might be interrogating the same issues that we are.

It is from these rather simple human interactions that music scenes develop. Used in casual conversation between musicians, the term *scene* is often used as a synonym for the availability of quality employment opportunities in a given locale. Journalists, too, have employed the term since the 1940s to describe any underground collective of artists, poets, musicians, and assorted hangers-on. This usage, perhaps the most common one, often characterizes the scene as a sort of bohemian commune in which the participants live without regard to money, status, and popularity and focus their energies instead on making art for art's sake. Since the early 1990s, however, the term has been transformed into a key unit of analysis in the study of popular music. Richard A. Peterson and Andy Bennett have described music scenes as "situations where performers, support facilities, and fans come together to collectively create music for their own enjoyment."[2]

The "scenes perspective" is a particularly useful model with which to investigate the sociocultural value of music because it requires that we approach music making from a variety of perspectives and engage with the competing values, practices, and goals of scene participants.[3] Because it requires grounding in the specific circumstances of musical production and consumption, the scenes perspective allows us to understand the slipperiness of musical experience and to appreciate the beauty of this chaos. As applied by the branch of popular music studies that has been informed primarily by the field of cultural studies, the scenes perspective draws attention to the role that rhetoric, fashion, song lyrics, interpersonal relationships, and local music industries play in the formation of individual and collective identities within music scenes and in the scene's ability to take action in support of their ideals.[4] When brought into dialogue with popular music analysis, which employs the tools of musicology and music theory to explore the reasons that music (as sound) exerts such a powerful effect upon us, the scenes perspective reveals that people also decide to participate in a music scene for aesthetic reasons that are grounded to varying degrees in their personal interactions with one another, with nonmusical signifiers of identity, and with music itself.[5] Moreover, by affording musical compositions and practices the same consideration as nonmusical signifiers, we can better understand the ways that musical practices link communities that seem otherwise opposed and divide apparently homogeneous ones.

This study is also informed by the intensely local focus of the scenes perspective. Local case studies—especially those that are ethnographically grounded—challenge us to view the consumption of music as a process that is shaped by local histories and values. While it might be expedient to speak in broad terms about people who listen to or perform a certain type of music (the punks, the Goths, the teenyboppers, and so on), these case studies reveal that people everywhere actively engage with popular music and use it as a potent tool to express their political, social, economic, and aesthetic views within their communities.[6] In addition, the tendency of cultural studies to treat everything as a cultural text is a particularly valuable tool for the study of music scenes as it encourages careful investigation of speech about music and of institutions. Implicit in this approach is the notion that all products of a music scene reveal important information about the core values of scene participants.[7] It follows, then, that messages that are encoded in nonmusical products of a music scene should inform any musical analysis, engaging in a complex dialogue within which musical meanings are created and articulated. Finally, several studies of music scenes have examined the role of specific venues and organizations in institutionalizing the scene's values and the effects of this institutionalization on competing voices within the scene.[8] As with the scenes perspective's emphasis on specific case studies, this approach confounds the tendency to view scenes as relatively stable and homogeneous cultural formations and instead casts the scene as a space within which meaning is constantly contested.

This book is fundamentally about the ways that musicians, producers, venue owners, journalists, record buyers, and concertgoers use music to articulate and actualize their individual and collective identities. In this book, I explore the many and often contradictory ways in which participants in the progressive country music scene that flourished in Austin, Texas, during the 1970s used specific compositions, performance practices, and musical traditions as a medium through which to understand and express their identities as individuals and as a group. To accomplish this task, I offer a model for a music-centered scenes perspective that demonstrates the important role that individual musical compositions and more general musical practices played in shaping individual and collective understanding of the progressive country music scene of 1970s' Austin. It presumes that even a rudimentary understanding of sound informs everyone's consumption of music regardless of whether the listeners can articulate what they are hearing, and, as such, it recognizes that all listeners have aesthetic agency. Moreover, musical compositions and practices are considered here to be gateways into the broader cultural milieu as they are both shaped by their cultural contexts and exert an indelible influence on the world around them. As such, musical analysis serves as an entry point to cultural understanding. Yet, at the same time, this approach recognizes that music is not necessarily homologically related to cultural context. Rather, it proposes a dialectic relationship between the musical text and its cultural context that parallels the relationship that exists between scene participants, music scenes, and the music that is created and consumed therein. As the following analysis demonstrates, the portrait that results offers clearer insight into both the reasons that people wish to participate in music scenes and the processes by which cultural meaning is created within them.

The chapters that follow build on the socioculturally focused insights that have been widely treated in the literature on music scenes by situating music—in the form of specific compositions, performance practices, and styles—at the center of the complicated discussion about the value of Texan culture and the meaning of Texanness that took place within the progressive country music scene in Austin, Texas. The introduction situates the progressive country music scene within the cultural context of contemporary attitudes toward country music. It also proposes that this setting allowed the participants to use music to reconcile their ambivalence toward musical traditions that represented both the conservative values they rejected and a viable alternative to the problems of the modern world. Chapter 1 focuses on the musical, social, ideological, and industrial roots of the Austin music scene through the lens of two important case studies, the emergence of folk-singing as a distinctly countercultural act at venues such as Threadgill's restaurant in the 1960s and the development of the "progressive country" radio format at Austin radio station KOKE-FM in the early 1970s. Chapters 2 and 3 examine a series of musical compositions that provoked and responded to debates about the core values of the progressive country music scene. In a detailed study of the musical construction of two of the progressive country music scene's most prominent icons—the cosmic cowboy and the redneck—these chap-ters also show that a cultural space was created within which scene activities could take place. Chapter 4 investigates the ways that Austin's progressive country musicians composed and recorded music that was imbued with an aura of authenticity because it bore obvious traces of the social and musical interactions of the city's musicians. Centering around a detailed account and analysis of a series of recording sessions that singer-songwriter Jerry Jeff Walker led between 1972 and 1973, this chapter suggests that musicians sought to capture and transmit the relaxed and collaborative social environment of Austin. To do so, they used self-referential lyrics, the preservation of imprecise ensemble execution and intonation in the final product, the inclusion of friends and neighbors on recording sessions, and anti-industrial rhetoric. Chapter 5 interrogates the ways that Austin's progressive country musicians and audiences interacted with the wide variety of Texan musical traditions to create a unified vision of Texas music that they could claim as their collective cultural heritage. Focusing on western swing revivalists Asleep at the Wheel and Alvin Crow, this chapter investigates the cultural value attributed to western swing music and suggests that, by performing music from what they viewed as an idealized Texan past, the scene participants were able to resolve some of the ambivalence they felt toward their own white middle-class Texanness. The conclusion draws the threads of the previous chapters together through an exploration of the central role that Willie Nelson's Fourth of July Picnics played as points of confluence for the wide variety of musical practices, attitudes, and people that characterized the progressive country music scene in Austin.

When the progressive country music scene emerged in Austin, country music was vilified in the liberal and countercultural press as a sonic representation of the ignorance and violence of the Silent Majority. Yet, through their work in this setting, Austin's musicians and audiences reclaimed the sounds of country music to create a safe social space that merged their love of country music and their countercultural lifestyles. The case studies that follow bring into relief the important role that music, as a sonic artifact with culturally specific meanings, plays in the construction of individual and collective identity and the political, cultural, and social work that music accomplishes within music scenes more generally.

Acknowledgments

It is truly a pleasure to acknowledge all of the people who have contributed, directly or indirectly, to this book. This project could not have come to fruition without the careful assistance, gentle advice, and insightful criticisms of a very large and supportive community of individuals who have assisted me in a variety of ways throughout the conception and gestation of this project.

Numerous participants in Austin's progressive country music scene have graciously offered to share their personal recollections of their activities in the scene. Their memories and insights have opened innumerable pathways for my research. Marcia Ball, Ray Benson, Floyd Domino, Joe Gracey, Tommy Goldsmith, Ray Wylie Hubbard, Bob Livingston, Bill Malone, Ken Moyer, Lucky Oceans, Joe Nick Patoski, Mickey Raphael, Jan Reid, and Bobby Earl Smith granted formal interviews, responded thoughtfully to email questionnaires, and provided valuable feedback about my work throughout this process. I am deeply indebted to them for their perspectives on their roles within the progressive country music scene, the composition and recording of key progressive country songs and recordings, the daily activities of the scene, and the complex political and social environs within which the scene emerged and flourished. I am also thankful for the many informal conversations and email communications I have had with Don Cusic, Chet Flippo, the late Archie Green, Martha Hume, Joe Kruppa, and Hazel Smith about their memories of Austin and Nashville during the 1960s and 1970s. Their contributions to this study added immeasurably, and their support of my work has been a constant source of encouragement.

Several people have been responsible for bringing new primary resources to my attention throughout this project. John Wheat of the Dolph Briscoe Center for American History at the University of Texas made available the vast resources of the center's vertical files, several boxes of business papers and tapes of radio advertisements from the Armadillo World Headquarters, documents pertaining to the Kerrville Folk Festival, and his memories of performances he witnessed. Steve Weiss of the Southern Folklife Collection at the University of North Carolina at Chapel Hill also made available several taped interviews with Guy Clark, Townes Van Zandt, Michael Murphey, and Kris Kristofferson from the Jack Bernhardt Papers and the copious newspaper clippings and field notes housed in the Archie Green Papers. The staff of the Austin History Center of the Austin Public Library also provided valuable access to newspaper records and interviews that have left an indelible mark on this work. Aaron Smithers lent me copies of independent newspapers and out-of-print albums from his personal collection and offered insight that only a native Austinite can. Thanks to David Menconi of the *Raleigh* (NC) *News & Observer* for lending me a copy of his master's thesis on the Armadillo World Headquarters and for introducing me to Tommy Goldsmith. Furthermore, I have been especially fortunate to work in the company of outstanding librarians in the Music Library at the University of North Carolina at Chapel Hill and Millikin University's Staley Library, and I am profoundly grateful for their assistance in obtaining books and recordings for this project. Jim Franklin, Ken Moyer, Alan Pogue, and Gilbert Shelton have graciously provided several photographs that have proven to be invaluable to my understanding of the progressive country music scene. I would also like to thank Gary Hartman for granting permission to reprint much of the material that appears in chapter 4, which was published in *Journal of Texas Music History* in an earlier incarnation as "*¡Viva Terlingua!*: Jerry Jeff Walker, Live Recordings, and the Authenticity of Progressive Country Music" (*Journal of Texas Music History* 8 [2008]: 20–33).

I have also had the good fortune of conducting this research and writing this book as part of a remarkably supportive academic community that has been interested in this project from its earliest stages through its completion. The observations, criticism, and support of those in this group have been invaluable to my work. During my doctoral studies at the University of North Carolina at Chapel Hill, Jocelyn Neal's guidance throughout this project instilled in me the desire to discover my authorial voice and stood as a reminder of how to have great fun with one's research while maintaining the highest standards of academic rigor. Jon Finson, David García, Mark Katz, Tim Marr, Phil Vandermeer, and Sarah Weiss were generous with their time and their insights during my dissertation research and writing. Much of what follows was developed in response to their questions and comments. Tracey Laird's nuanced approach to the study of music and place exerted a profound influence on this book, and her comments on the early drafts of this manuscript were invaluable. Chris Wilkinson provided encouragement and served a model of academic excellence and personal integrity for me throughout this project. Matt Meacham was a constant presence throughout this project as well, asking provocative questions that have encouraged me to think in new ways about this field. Furthermore, innumerable colleagues, friends, and students have patiently endured my rhapsodizing about the beauties of country music and have shared important insights from their own research and experiences. Among them are Kevin Bartig, Dave Burdick, Cate Edwards, Andy Flory, Nancy Freeman, Kevin Fontenot, Jason Gersh, Paul Harris, Annie Kennedy, Jj Kidder, Ethan Lechner, Michael Luxner, Alicia Levin, David Pruett, Annett Richter, Steve Shearon, John Stafford, and Katie Sullivan. I would also like to thank Steve Widenhofer and Barry Pearson at Millikin University for their continued support of this project. I am also profoundly indebted to the anonymous readers who commented on the manuscript for Oxford University Press, as their detailed attention to my ideas prompted me to consider new directions, offered clear ways to improve the clarity of the text, and provided valuable encouragement. And, of course, this project would not have come to fruition without the encouragement and assistance of Suzanne Ryan, my editor at Oxford University Press, and her remarkable editorial staff, which answered the questions of this novice author with great patience. I would also like to thank the Publications Endowment of the American Musicological Society, supported through the National Endowment for the Humanities, for offering a publication subvention for this project.

Last, but certainly not least, I would like to thank my wife, Melanie, who has been not only a careful reader of my work but also a steadfast champion of it, and my son, Christopher, who has enjoyed the good fortune of being immersed in this fantastic music since his infancy. Their kindness and patience, especially during the times when I exhibited neither, have made this project much easier, and for that I am eternally grateful.

LYRIC PERMISSIONS

"Gettin' By" by Jerry Jeff Walker. Courtesy of Groper Music. Used with permission.

"Cosmic Cowboy" by Michael Murphey. Courtesy of Bro `N Sis Music, Inc. Used with permission.

"Take Me Back to Tulsa" by Tommy Duncan and Bob Wills. Courtesy of Peer Music International and Red River Music. Used with permission.

"They Ain't Making Jews (like Jesus Anymore)" by Kinky Friedman. © YRU Following Me Music, LLC. Used with permission.

Contents

COSMIC COWBOYS AND NEW HICKS

Introduction

Making Country Music "Progressive"

AT THE BEGINNING OF THE 1970s, "progressive country music" seemed to be a contradiction in terms. Country music was, to most observers, anything but progressive—musically, politically, or culturally. Through the combined and often conflicting efforts of folk revivalists, folklorists, and Nashville insiders, country music had been elevated to the status of American folk music in the 1960s. As a consequence, its public image was transformed from that of an oft-maligned but profitable subgenre of American popular music into a revered, if often misunderstood, link to a premodern American past.[1] At the same time, political commentators from the Right and the Left remarked on the conservatism of country musicians and their songs, an attitude perhaps best exemplified by Merle Haggard's 1969 hit, "Okie from Muskogee," and the support that musicians such as Roy Rogers and Roy Clark lent to conservative political candidates Ronald Reagan and George Wallace, respectively.[2] Moreover, in comparison to the modern synthesizer banks, extended improvisations, and fantasy-laced lyrics of contemporaneous "progressive rock" music, country music's "down-home" lyrical tropes, compact song forms, and string band instrumentation sounded remarkably regressive.

Yet, while many observers believed that country music was decidedly unmodern, it gained increasing currency during the late 1960s and early 1970s among a group of politically and socially liberal young people in one of the most rapidly modernizing regions of the United States, the so-called Sun Belt. For many musicians and audiences, country music had been an important part of the soundscape of their youths, and, despite its conservative political associations, many members of the baby-boom generation had an ambivalent relationship with country music.[3] In the spirit of hating the sin but loving the sinner, several southern musicians—many of them children of the post–World War II baby boom—merged the musical practices of country music with their own rock-influenced musics, creating hybridized styles that were reflective of their own complex and ambivalent experiences of race, class, gender, and geography in the wake of the civil rights movement, women's liberation movement, and Vietnam War. This project resulted in a wide variety of musical styles that can be categorized generally as "country rock," including the Bakersfield-tinged sounds of The Byrds and The Flying Burrito Brothers in Southern California, the blues-driven music of southern rock groups such as Lynyrd Skynyrd, the Charlie Daniels Band, and the Marshall Tucker Band in the southeast, and the strange mélange of western swing, honky-tonk, blues, Cajun, zydeco, and conjunto music, which became known in Texas as "progressive country music."

The progressive country music scene in Austin was a cultural space in which a generation of young Texans redefined what it meant to be Texan in a countercultural age by claiming ownership of distinctly Texan forms of expressive culture, including not only music but also fashion, language, and art. Over the course of the 1970s, progressive country musicians in Austin created a musical style that was informed by the state's wealth of Anglo-American, African American, Tejano, German, and Czech musical traditions and reflected the vibrant and variegated Texan soundscape. On a typical evening at the zenith of the progressive country scene, one could hear a wide variety of Texan musics in the Lone Star capital. The Split Rail often hosted San Antonio native Doug Sahm, whose blend of conjunto and blues sounds reflected his vibrant intercultural experiences in the Mission City, while the pioneering western swing fiddler and former Texas Playboy Jesse Ashlock performed with revivalist Alvin Crow at the Broken Spoke on South Lamar Boulevard. In addition, the centerpiece of the Austin scene, a former national guard armory turned concert hall called the Armadillo World Headquarters hosted artists such as former Nashville songwriter turned countercultural icon Willie Nelson and Michael Murphey, a Dallas-born songwriter who had scored a pop hit in 1968 with the Monkees' recording of "What Am I Doin' Hangin' 'Round?"[4] In these venues, musicians and their audiences—both of whom were predominantly Texan—gathered for the purpose of engaging collectively with musics that represented their unique cultural heritage as Texans and brought them great aesthetic pleasure.[5] Yet, more important, as participants in Austin's progressive country music scene filed into clubs, discussed the latest progressive country records with their friends, and wrote about the music in local, regional, and national media outlets, they articulated the value of Texan musical practices to their individual and collective identities.

This was especially important for young Texans who responded to the cultural turmoil of the late 1960s by turning their gaze away from national and international affairs, seeking an understanding of their own experiences, and viewing the Texan culture that they so dearly loved through the lens of racial injustice against Native Americans, African Americans, and Tejanos.[6] The University of Texas at Austin had long been on the front lines of the civil rights movement, having hosted a particularly active chapter of the Student Nonviolent Coordinating Committee (SNCC) throughout the 1950s and 1960s, served as the scene of numerous sit-ins both on and off campus, and was, in 1946, the defendant in the precedent-setting desegregation case *Sweatt v. Painter*, which set the desegregation of public universities and schools into motion.[7] Beginning in the late 1960s, Austin was also an important center of the emerging Chicano Power/La Raza movement, in which young Tejanos—ethnic Mexicans in Texas—gathered to call for greater attention to the complicated history between Anglo-Texans and Tejanos and to demand equal treatment both on and off campus.[8] Furthermore, students were inevitably aware of the effects of the Vietnam War on their generation, whether they supported the war efforts or not, although there were relatively few antiwar protests in the city. As such, Austin was, like most university towns at the time, a center of grassroots political energy that challenged residents—and especially its youth population—to reevaluate the status quo.

Yet, concurrent with this inward turn was a growing sense, informed by Texas nationalism, that the Lone Star State and its culture offered a presumably better alternative to the mainstream American way of life. Many participants in Austin's progressive country music scene were, therefore, ambivalent about their collective "Texanness" and sought ways to reconcile these contradictory notions. As a sonic representation of the state's racial and ethnic diversity, progressive country music revealed points of racial friction as well as important commonalities that resulted from decades of cross-cultural exchange. Moreover, progressive country's self-conscious engagement with early Texan country music provided an important link between younger progressive country fans and older generations of Texans during a time when cultural politics threatened to tear them apart.

Progressive country music was also informed by a growing suspicion of the national music industry that mirrored the youth counterculture's distrust of institutions more generally. Many leaders of the Austin scene proclaimed that industry executives squelched quality music and traditional musical practices, paid little attention to the artistic needs and desires of the musicians it employed, and failed to take their role as arbiters of taste seriously. For instance, radio personality, concert promoter, and journalist Joe Gracey suggested that Austin's music was "progressive" because it challenged what many perceived to be the "regressive" nature of Nashville's country music industry, which he thought had forsaken its working-class honky-tonk origins in order to create "respectable" music with broad middle-class appeal during the 1960s.[9] Furthermore, many of the musicians who formed the early core of progressive country artists had relocated to Austin in the first years of the 1970s following brief stints as recording artists, session musicians, and songwriters in major music industry centers such as Los Angeles, New York, and Nashville and, as such, provided living proof of the music industry's failures. These musicians flocked to Austin because the city's small-town atmosphere afforded them more freedom to create their music, opportunities to collaborate with other talented musicians, and receptive yet critical audiences. Songwriter and Dallas native B. W. Stevenson remarked in 1974, for example, that he chose to leave Los Angeles because Austin offered him more time to work on his songwriting.[10] It also allowed many aspiring musicians to leave the small towns that they had grown up in for an environment that would support them as they developed their craft. As Marcia Ball, who sang and played piano with Freda and the Firedogs before striking out on a solo career, recalled:

> There was a time when music was a corporate bailiwick entirely. You had to spend money or have money or connections. Productions were done in Nashville, New York, and L.A. It was just big-city stuff and big business stuff. And then the Rolling Stones—these like five scruffy guys with guitars and drums made us all realize that, well, we could do that. Anybody could do that. So a whole bunch of bands of people my age— y'know, eighteen at the time—started being in bands. And then, in the late '60s, if you were going to stay in the South, you didn't want to stay in Atlanta or New Orleans or Baton Rouge or Little Rock or any of those other places. Austin was an oasis for I don't know what reason

except its business was a big university and the state capital. It was like a . . . just a slightly larger version of a cool college town. And that was a really big draw. Plus there were beautiful lakes, and it wasn't a big city. It was cheap.[11]

Also, Lubbock native Butch Hancock, who with Jimmie Dale Gilmore and Joe Ely formed the Flatlanders, remarked, "We didn't feel like we fit in any place in [Lubbock] . . . , so we ended up on each other's back porches. . . . Austin's the same way [as the back porches of Lubbock]. It became the Texas magnet for artists and writers and all kinds of other crazy creative people."[12] Thus, the progressive country music scene in Austin challenged listeners to turn away from overtly mediated musical experiences, including format radio broadcasts and major-label recordings, to join with their local community in the shared experience of live musical performance.[13]

Austin's progressive country music scene may be seen, therefore, as the site of a Texan renaissance in which native and naturalized Texans ranging in age from their late teens to early thirties searched for the roots of their collective heritage.[14] They refashioned these roots to articulate a locally grounded alternative to mass-mediated country music and the national counterculture that allowed them to communicate more directly with each other.[15] Yet, in the summer of 1970, the idea that a regionally (and later nationally) renowned music scene would spring forth from the city of Austin, Texas, would have been met with incredulity by Austinites and national music journalists alike. In December 1968, for instance, *Rolling Stone* contributors Larry Sepulvedo and John Burks observed that, although numerous Texan rock musicians—including Janis Joplin, Doug Sahm, the 13th Floor Elevators, and Boz Scaggs—had achieved at least some national success, problems with infrastructure and rampant racism inhibited attempts to develop a scene in Texas.[16] Even as late as January 1973, Chet Flippo, who would soon become *Rolling Stone*'s Austin correspondent, questioned whether an identifiable and unified music scene was emerging in the city: "This insistence that there be a 'Texas Scene' seems to arise from regional chauvinism more than anything else. The state probably has more musicians now than any time in the past 15 years, but to insist that they fit together in a cohesive scene is akin to lassoing a hummingbird. Tricky."[17]

Unlike Houston, San Antonio, and Dallas (which could boast several major venues, recording industry connections, and a sizeable amount of financial capital to support a local music scene), Austin had

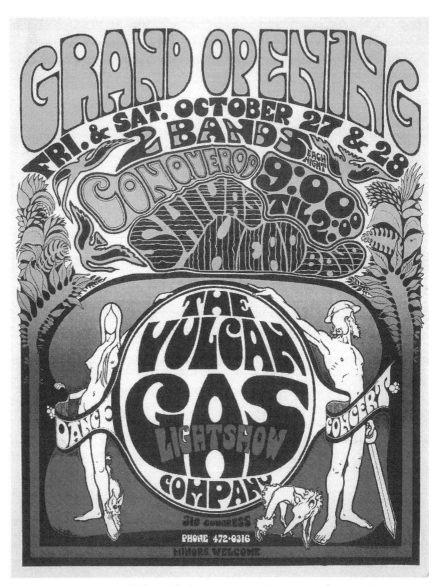

FIGURE 0.1. Artist Gilbert Shelton's poster advertising the grand opening of the Vulcan Gas Co., October 27–28, 1967. Dolph Briscoe Center for American History, University of Texas at Austin. Used by permission of Gilbert Shelton.

little to offer aspiring and professional musicians except a constantly fresh audience, brought to the city because of the state legislature and the University of Texas, that needed to be entertained. Although the city was home to dozens of restaurants, bars, nightclubs, and dance halls that catered to its large itinerant population, in 1970, Austin could boast no concert halls or large venues capable of supporting the development of a citywide music scene. In fact, the city's only large (and arguably adventurous) concert hall, the Vulcan Gas Co., had closed for financial reasons around July 1970.[18] Furthermore, musical life in Austin was extremely fragmented as, for the most part, musicians performed for racially, generationally, and economically segregated audiences in equally segregated venues.[19] For instance, the Broken Spoke, a country dance hall on the southern outskirts of Austin, invited the city's working class to dance to hard-shell country music and was consequently a known danger for long-haired young people until the early 1970s. On the other hand, the Rubaiyat showcased local and touring folk musicians and singer-songwriters for a primarily white, middle-class, and university-aged audience with little interest from the Broken Spoke's clientele or from the blues audiences that flocked to the city's historically black East Side.[20] Thus, while the musical culture in Austin was thriving in 1970, local musicians, audiences, and businesspersons showed little interest in undertaking efforts to expand their impact beyond their established clientele.

It was at precisely this moment, however, that a group of men and women in their twenties began to undertake the first efforts to create a music scene in Austin that was self-sustaining, that reflected the totality of Texan musical culture, and that could unify the city's full-time and part-time residents through shared musical experiences. Beginning with the establishment of the Armadillo World Headquarters in August 1970 and continuing with enterprises such as radio station KOKE-FM, the Kerrville Folk Festival, the Dripping Springs Reunion, Willie Nelson's Fourth of July Picnics, and the television show *Austin City Limits*, dozens of Austin-based entrepreneurs, lawyers, recording and broadcast engineers, politicians, musicians, and fans collaborated on a decade-long project to define Austin as an alternative music center and a welcoming site for creative and industrious Texans and non-Texans alike. By positioning the city as an alternative to Los Angeles, New York, and Nashville, Austin's boosters tapped into the mounting ennui that many musicians were beginning to feel with the music industry. Austin, which gained a national reputation when, in 1971, the *L.A. Free Press* called it a "hippie Palm Springs" for its remarkably low cost of living and small-town feel, also resonated with the emergent "back to the land movement" that was inspiring thousands of young people to move to more isolated regions of the country in search of a more authentic experience.[21] What is more, for many young Texans, Austin was a more than suitable alternative to the conservative climates of both rural

Texas and the state's larger cities. As such, Austin became, in the words of Armadillo World Headquarters cofounder Eddie Wilson, "an oasis in the middle of Texas."[22]

At the same time that Austin's image was being transformed into an alternative, semirural place for musicians and young people to gather, the city was also drawn into the wave of unbridled economic growth that reshaped the Sun Belt states during the 1970s and 1980s. Historic neighborhoods were bulldozed to make way for high-rise buildings, apartment complexes, and housing developments, much to the chagrin of many long-time Austin residents who saw the construction as a threat to the city's unique character and who took to the streets in protest of the city's zoning policies and developers.[23] During the 1970s, Austin became the headquarters of several microcomputing and semiconductor companies, including Texas Instruments and the fledgling Dell Computers, and sprawling industrial complexes that paralleled the skyscrapers, refineries, and factories in Houston and Dallas increasingly taxed the city's then inadequate infrastructure.[24] As a result, the city of Austin witnessed an unprecedented physical expansion and population growth that fundamentally reshaped the city. According to U.S. census records, a little more than 250,000 people were full-year residents of Austin in 1970; by 1980, Austin had experienced a 37.2-percent population increase, bringing the total population to 345,496, as slightly fewer than 94,000 additional people made the city their new home.[25] Simultaneously, the city's student population was also enjoying significant growth. In the fall semester of 1968, the University of Texas was home to 32,155 students, nearly 26,000 of whom were undergraduates. By the fall of 1977, however, the university boasted 32,535 undergraduates—nearly four hundred more than had been enrolled in all of the campus's programs in 1968.[26]

This trend toward urban growth was typical of Texan cities during the 1970s. Houston and Dallas, benefiting from the post–World War II oil boom and the growth of the cities' military populations, witnessed similar population increases and faced many of the same issues that Austin was confronting. City planners and residents struggled to accommodate new residents, to promote economic growth without ruining the land around them, and to maintain local identity in an increasingly national and international economic arena. Austin was different from its sister cities, however, because its new residents were significantly younger than were the residents of Houston and Dallas. The student body at the University of Texas accounted for nearly 10 percent of the city's population, and when combined with the youth population that was not attending the university, young people played an unusually important role in the shaping of Austin's culture in the 1970s, bringing with them an energy and an openness toward all kinds of cultural expression that was unparalleled in Texas and in most other cities nationwide. Moreover, rather than relying on more traditional forms of patronage to create new cultural institutions such as concert halls and art galleries in the city, participants in Austin's progressive country music scene adopted a grassroots approach that built upon the talents of individuals to create a community that benefited everyone.[27]

Yet, just as the participants in Austin's progressive country music scene sought to develop a climate in which creativity and direct interpersonal communication were sacrosanct, they also worked to create an alternative music industry in the city that would rival Nashville, New York, and Los Angeles and encourage continued economic growth in the city. Throughout the 1970s, local entrepreneurs and musicians worked in partnership with major record labels, including Capitol, MCA, and Atlantic, to develop local artists for recording contracts and publishing deals in exchange for outside capital investments in the local scene.[28] Moreover, as the city's reputation spread through word of mouth, nationally and internationally renowned musicians such as rock musician Leon Russell moved to the city, which drew the attention of music journalists, who wrote with increasing frequency about the unique character of both Austin and its progressive country music scene.[29] Such positive publicity encouraged still more people to come to the city to be part of the progressive country music scene and to live in Austin's "liberal oasis." The resulting growth of the scene was so great that, by 1974, many of the musicians who had helped to establish it were becoming quite vocal in their criticism. They openly questioned whether the participants were remaining faithful to the scene's basic principles and, in some instances, even moved away from Austin in disgust.[30]

The participants in Austin's progressive country music scene worked to balance a public rhetoric of resistance to the corporate music industry and unchecked economic growth with its own actions to develop the scene into a vehicle for economic and cultural development. In many ways, Austin's music industry resembled that of most local music scenes, with radio stations, record stores, and concert venues offering a variety of ways for fans to perform their membership in the scene through their consumption of it. Still others worked to create a grassroots music industry that built upon the strengths and talents of the Austin community, sought primarily to serve a local constituency, and attempted to model and market Austin's "laid-back" attitude to musicians and hangers-on who wished to step away from mainstream America. The most successful of these ventures—including the Armadillo World Headquarters, KOKE-FM, and Willie Nelson's Fourth of July Picnics—embodied the duality of Austin's progressive country music scene. They simultaneously attempted to provide local spaces in which audiences could celebrate their communal difference and also to promulgate the progressive country movement's distinctiveness to other communities.

Furthermore, these projects defined Austin as not only a distinctive social, cultural, and economic space but a unique musical space as well. The Austin that was presented through the frames of Austin's entrepreneurial music industry was a musically eclectic city that rejected the perceived homogeneous musical offerings of Nashville, New York, and Los Angeles in favor of musical practices that were shaped by local histories and by the people who resided in the city itself. As such, through its efforts to encourage and sustain local musicians and musical traditions, the local music industry that developed around Austin's progressive country music scene played a central role in defining and articulating "progressive country music" as a genre. Moreover, some figures used their position in the local industry to exert a stronger influence over the construction of progressive country's public image and sound. That is, not only musicians but also disc jockeys, club owners, talent scouts, and journalists had greater authority than the average fan to speak on behalf of the scene. Yet, working against the increasing authority of some members of the scene were those participants—some of whom worked within the industry—who expressed their resistance to the local music industry's hegemony, deliberately complicating the narratives put forth by industry leaders. Although these voices were often squelched, they suggested that local music industries work in dialogue with participants to conduct almost constant boundary work that shaped their experiences and defined the scene for outside observers.

Music scenes are complex organisms that are shaped by individual efforts, shared attitudes and beliefs, local histories, and the transnational music industry. They are also extraordinarily useful structures that allow the participants, as individuals and as a collective body, to articulate a clear sense of identity. This constructed identity often stands in opposition to a perceived hegemonic mainstream and is defined, promulgated, and refined in a variety of public and private venues, ranging from "alternative" music industries such as concert halls, fan publications, and record labels and the display of identity through fashion to the act of listening to and reflecting upon a specific composition in the privacy of one's own home. Yet, while the chorus of competing voices within a music scene might seem to create a cacophonous din, a more focused interrogation of individual contributors suggests that the formation of identity and the definition of a scene's core values is part of a process of commodification that occurs in many music settings, especially those that garner regional, national, or international attention.

Such was the case in Austin, where individuals working within the city's musical community collaborated and competed with other participants to define the city as a free-spited, anticommercial, and musically adventurous metropolis. They also looked for ways to commodify the scene and its projected identity for an audience that sought a distinctly Texan alternative to the American identities put forth by the national mass media. As the following examples demonstrate, musical sounds played an important role in articulating and reinforcing the Texan countercultural identities that were created by leading figures in Austin's progressive country music scene.

Progressive Country Music as Local Music

IN AN AUGUST 1970 article in the *Texas Observer*, journalist Wayne Oakes said of Kenneth Threadgill, a tavern owner and yodeler who had been an active part of Austin's musical community for four decades, that "people from both the rock generation and the country and western milieu know that Threadgill is the real thing. He is of the folk, and his experience includes all those essentials necessary for the making of a bona fide country music artist."[1] The son of a Nazarene minister, Threadgill was the proprietor of Threadgill's, a service station *cum* tavern that had hosted traveling country musicians since 1933.[2] By the time the progressive country music scene began emerging in Austin in the early 1970s, Threadgill was already firmly established as one of the forefathers of the local music scene, in large part due to the role that he had played in supporting the folksinging movement that sprang up in the city during the late 1950s and early 1960s.

The earliest manifestations of a local scene in Austin may be traced to Threadgill's, which began attracting local musicians from the University of Texas to what was then the northern edge of town on North Lamar Boulevard around the year 1960. Threadgill's became an important locus of a growing community of undergraduate and graduate students who were interested in learning about and performing the region's folk musics. It was in that year that several graduate students from the history and English departments at the University of Texas began going to Threadgill's to listen to country music and to enjoy the atmosphere of the city's oldest honky-tonk. Among them were Stan Alexander, a doctoral student in English, who also sang and played guitar, and Bill C. Malone, a doctoral student in history, whose dissertation, inspired in part by the music he encountered at Threadgill's, was later published as *Country Music, U.S.A.*, the first comprehensive history of country music. As Malone recollected:

> I began going out to Threadgill's right at the end of the fifties, or in the early sixties. . . . At that time I was a graduate student in history at the University of Texas, and was singing at parties (sometimes alone, but often with fellow students Stan Alexander, Willie Benson, and Ed Mellon). Willie, I believe, was the person who told me about the picking and singings at Threadgill's. He was a good guitar player, and would often accompany Ken Threadgill (or, Mister Threadgill, as I always called him). Shorty Ziegler played rhythm guitar at the sessions, and was fond of calling out the keys with remarks such as, "This one's in A, as in Aig," or "this is in G, as in Gnat." They were about the only ones who played there before the rest of us started going there. Mr. Threadgill did not play an instrument. Ed Mellon played mandolin, and Stan Alexander and I played guitars. We did mostly old-time country music and bluegrass.[3]

Another regular at Threadgill's in the 1960s was Francis Abernethy, president of the Texas Folklore Society. Alexander and Abernethy soon formed the East Texas String Ensemble, a group that performed traditional folk ballads and old-time country music between 1960 and 1961.[4] These groups usually played on weeknights, traditionally slow nights for bars, but Alexander, Abernethy, Malone, and others who were involved in the early Threadgill's scene were not hoping to make great financial gains through their musical performances. Rather, because of Kenneth Threadgill's personal connections to earlier generations of country singers and old-time country music, these musicians saw in Threadgill's an opportunity to learn early varieties of country music at the feet of the many knowledgeable old-timers who passed through the club.[5] The relationship that was forged between these early folk musicians and the older contingent and Threadgill's was, therefore, beneficial to both groups; the graduate student community could capitalize on the wealth of knowledge there for their own research and entertainment, while the older generation could pass on their legacy to an enthusiastic and caring younger generation.

Concurrent with the development of a burgeoning graduate student folksinging community at Threadgill's was the emergence of an undergraduate folksinging group on the University of Texas campus.

In 1960, the university's English department hired Roger Abrahams, a scholar of African American folkways, and shortly after his arrival in Austin, he established the University of Texas Folk Sing. Meeting at the Chuckwagon in the UT Student Union, the UT Folk Sing primarily comprised Texan undergraduates who, as Shank suggests, sought to affirm identities that stood in opposition both to their conservative Texan upbringings and to the social mainstream of the university.[6] Several of the participants in the UT Folk Sing had even been subjected to great harassment on campus, most notably future rock superstar Janis Joplin.[7] Many of the participants in the UT Folk Sing—including Joplin, John Clay, Powell St. John, Lanny Wiggins, and Tary Owens—also banded together to form not only a musical and an ideological community but a physical one as well, moving off campus into a rundown apartment complex near campus known as "the Ghetto." This move proved useful to the growth of the UT Folk Sing community and to the expansion of the scene in all of Austin. The Ghetto teemed with musical collaboration, resulting in the development of a core group of talented performers and songwriters to sustain the scene in the future. Furthermore, because of its physical marginality from the University of Texas campus, the Ghetto community underscored its difference from the social mainstream of the student body and further marked folksinging as a sign of difference within that broader community.[8]

By 1962, the first generation of folksingers at Threadgill's had graduated from the University of Texas, and some, like Stan Alexander and Bill Malone, left to pursue academic careers, creating space for new members of the Ghetto community to hone their skills and develop their repertoires in front of the knowledgeable audiences at Threadgill's. In 1963, the Hootenanny Hoots were formed, featuring St. John, Wiggins, Owens, Austin songwriter Bill Neely, Shorty Ziegler, and Kenneth Threadgill. With Threadgill as the featured performer, the Hootenanny Hoots was the first folksinging group in Austin to reach out from the local scene and tap into the growing national folk music movement, performing at Minneapolis's Walker Art Center in 1963, where local folk enthusiasts bombarded Threadgill's hotel room with phone calls, asking if he was indeed the Kenneth Threadgill of the "beer joint in Austin."[9] Moreover, in 1968, Threadgill and the Hootenanny Hoots played at the Newport Folk Festival—arguably the most important venue of the folk revival—on the recommendation of Jim Kweskin, leader of the Kweskin Jug Band. As *Rolling Stone* contributor Jon Landau observed of this performance, Threadgill by this time stood in stark contrast to artists such as fellow Newport act and Grand Ole Opry mainstay Roy Acuff, whose polished stage act was the by-product of decades of public performance in the highly competitive commercial country realm. Acuff embodied what audiences perceived to be an authenticity that was based on his life experiences and his down-home image: "[Threadgill offered] a modest but moving performance and when he finished singing I felt that he had reached me with something I hadn't really experienced before. Threadgill's life was the more understandable for his having sung at the Festival. If anyone cared to understand it. Roy Acuff . . . was too corny for most people's taste and I didn't think he sang very well."[10]

The folk music scene that flourished in Austin during the early 1960s was the first direct antecedent of Austin's progressive country music scene of the early 1970s. It represents the first critical mass of musicians who became interested in pursuing a similar musical aesthetic. Rather than acting alone, the core musicians of the overlapping UT Folk Sing and Threadgill's communities collaborated to revive the classic blues and ballads that had formed the basis of early American and Texan folk music and to create an extension of the songwriting scenes of Greenwich Village and, later, Los Angeles. Moreover, while this scene was necessarily based in Austin due to the participants' daily roles as students at the University of Texas, Austin's folksingers were also keenly aware of their position within the larger national folk revival as they interacted with the regional and national touring musicians who performed at the city's other folk music venues, including the 11th Door and the Rubyiat.[11] Furthermore, as the scene in Austin began to gain a regional and national reputation, Austin's folksingers attempted to reach out to communities beyond the city limits. Thus, from the earliest days of Austin's music scene, the musicians working there both enjoyed the communal nature of performing with their peers in the city's venues and sought external validation and financial gain from audiences outside of Austin.

This contradiction shaped the rhetoric and ideology of the progressive country music scene in Austin. On one hand, Austin was perceived to be an inviting alternative site for music making because it was situated far away, geographically and culturally, from the American mainstream. The musicians who worked within the folk music community—as well as in subsequent music scenes in Austin—saw their marginality as a point of pride, often declaring that their musical efforts stood in direct opposition to the mass-mediated sounds of variety shows and format radio. On the other hand, acceptance of their work outside of Austin validated their defiance of the cultural mainstream and provided an impetus for further expansion of the scene both within Austin and around the United States and Canada. In many ways, this contradiction is an essential marker of a music scene's success and plays a role in the remembrance of the setting. That is, music scenes that fail to be recognized beyond their immediate geographic and social milieus are not faced with the dual impetus for preservation and growth. As a result, they are often poorly documented and fail to secure a place in collective memory. Thus, while scene participants who achieve success or recognition beyond a particular setting might be perceived as "selling out" their values and those of the scene as a whole, their engagement with the world beyond the scene is necessary to sustain and renew the scene itself.

Participants in the folk music scene that flourished around Threadgill's during the early 1960s deployed a wide variety of Texan musics, including especially early hillbilly music and the blues, to mark their difference from the cultural mainstream at the University of Texas. Through their performances, these musicians, as well as their counterparts in Dallas, Fort Worth, and Houston, constructed a racially integrated soundscape that challenged the highly segregated environment in which they lived. As a result, they aligned themselves with a more progressive politics than was exhibited by their scornful classmates in the University of Texas's fraternities and sororities, who, as a cruel prank, nominated Janis Joplin for "The Ugliest Man on Campus" award. Yet, at the same time that their performances recast their differences into a force for social good and equality, the folksingers' notable omission of African American voices from the folksings at Threadgill's raises important questions about the racial identity and politics that have shaped the Austin music scene since the 1960s.[12]

Implicit in the student body's marginalization of the folksingers was the belief that, because the singers were not suitable for the university's primary social scene, they were somehow less Texan—and, by implication, less white and less masculine (or, in Joplin's case, less feminine)—than their peers. Thus, while the folksingers' musical avowal of racial equality positioned their work on the side of social "good" and their engagement with the region's vernacular musics allowed them to perform their Texan-ness publicly, they were challenged to demonstrate their Texan *bona fides* through both the explicit demands of their peers and the implicit pressures of their white upbringing in the Lone Star State. Through the constructed histories of the Texan martyrs at the

Alamo and the folklore of the cowboy, these Texan folksingers were encouraged to believe in the presumption of Anglo-Texan dominance. By turning to folk music, therefore, the participants in the UT Folk Sing and the hootenannies at Threadgill's demonstrated a deep awareness of their Texan heritage while exerting the power of Anglo-Texan dominance to create a deracinated and unproblematized "Texan music."

The folksingers' uncritical dominance over Texan culture was exhibited in their attitudes not only toward race but toward the past as well. This process is perhaps best demonstrated in the scene's transformation of Kenneth Threadgill and his musical mentor, Jimmie Rodgers, from vibrant and dynamic personalities into representations of "authentic" Texan expression, a transformation that extended throughout the decade and shaped key beliefs and attitudes in the progressive country music scene of the 1970s.

As early as 1964, Threadgill was publicly celebrated as a living relic of a distant and seemingly simpler Texas past. A piece in the *Daily Texan*, the University of Texas's student newspaper, in December 1964 remarked that, "on North Lamar, out past the cluster of [the] usual Forty Acres places, is an old gas station. Passing by, you probably would not stop. Inside, white-haired, pudgy Ken Threadgill brings back the sounds of the late twenties."[13] Specifically, "the sounds of the late twenties" that Threadgill evoked were derived from the repertoire of Jimmie Rodgers, one of the first stars of the nascent hillbilly genre in the late 1920s and early 1930s. Following a move to the Hill Country town of Kerrville in 1929, Rodgers had become widely accepted as an honorary Texan musician.[14] As country music scholar Jocelyn Neal has suggested, Rodgers's music was an important touchstone of the folk revival and was recorded by many of the leading figures of the movement, including Bob Dylan and Odetta.[15] However, for participants of the University of Texas Folk Sing and the gatherings at Threadgill's, Rodgers's music as embodied in Threadgill's performances did not just evoke vague notions of folk authenticity grounded in the recovery of an apparently transcendent and neglected vernacular music. It also situated their own music making in an essentially unbroken tradition stretching back in time from themselves through Threadgill to Rodgers himself. Greg Olds, writing for the *Austin American-Statesman*, remarked of Threadgill's music making:

> The songs of Kenneth Threadgill are out of the nation's recent past, a time of relative social stability, boundless optimism. He sings, among other numbers, "Silver-Haired Daddy of Mine," "There's a

Star-spangled Banner Waving Somewhere," "Waiting for a Train," "Down in the Old Cherry Orchard," "T for Texas, T for Tennessee," "Just Because," and "It Is No Secret What God Can Do." Patriotism, religion, heritage, the simple and good life. And somehow, even in these times of lost innocence, the songs as performed by Threadgill and the Hoots ring true.[16]

As such, the adulation of Threadgill and Rodgers differentiated the folk revivalism in Austin from the national movement by grounding their activities in the history and sounds of the region.

Threadgill's connection to Rodgers was, by any estimate, a rather tenuous one. But Rodgers exerted a lasting influence on Threadgill's conception of music and of the qualities necessary for a successful performance, as he did for numerous other musicians who fell under his spell. As he recounted in 1975, Threadgill "got acquainted with Jimmie in 1928. . . . I was working at Loew's State Theatre in Houston as a ticket taker. When Jimmie was playing there, he'd arrive early. Anybody could get acquainted with him, so I did. . . . [For his concert, h]e walked out in the middle of that stage, set that straw-bottomed chair up, tuned his guitar and started singing 'My Little Ol' Home Down in New Orleans.' It just fascinated me. He did that one. 'Frankie and Johnnie' and 'Waiting for a Train.'"[17] This brief encounter formed the basis of Threadgill's conception of his musical self, as he repeated it frequently in his onstage banter and in the numerous interviews conducted with him throughout the 1970s and 1980s.[18] Landau, for instance, remarked that Threadgill "told the [Newport audience] how in 1928 he had been working as an usher [sic] in a theatre in Austin, Texas, where he still lives. There he saw Rodgers and from that moment on he had been 'baptized.' He freely admitted to being obsessed with the music of the greatest white country blues singer of them all."[19] Similarly, Bill Neely, a Rodgers-influenced singer-songwriter who frequently performed at Threadgill's, claimed a similar experience at a jockey ground near Dallas, as he recounted in his autobiographical song, "Blackland Farm": "He handed me a guitar, a flattop Martin; he learned me a C chord that I never have forgotten."[20]

Although Threadgill regularly remarked on the differences between his interpretations and those of Rodgers, participants in Austin's folk revival and progressive country music scenes considered his music as the closest thing to hearing Rodgers directly, in large part as a consequence of Threadgill's age and his musical pedigree. As folklorist Nicholas

Spitzer, then a graduate student at the University of Texas, noted in his report on an August 1975 Jimmie Rodgers Night celebration at the Split Rail, Threadgill and collaborators Neely and Hubert Fowler "played and sang in the style of Jimmie Rodgers. . . . [T]hey are what folklorists call 'recreators.' They perform as closely as possible to Rodgers' style."[21] Threadgill was often surprised that the young participants in the progressive country music scene continued to show such an interest in his musical style and in the history of Texas music. To interviewer John Lash, he remarked in 1972, "We do stuff that's so old and goes so far back that the kids down at the university call it folk music. And some of it, I guess would be folk music. . . . Everywhere I go I think 'the popularity will drop out, and they'll want something else.' But they keep wanting me to sing it. And my voice has never changed—I'll be 63 next month. So that's the secret."[22] Yet interest in Rodgers's music had grown exponentially among the participants in the progressive country music scene and other young musicians from across the American South. Citing recent allusions to and covers of Rodgers by groups such as southern rockers Lynyrd Skynyrd, Rodgers's grandson Jimmie Dale Court remarked in 1975 that he "think[s] that a lot of my Granddad's music is coming back. . . . Granddad was really progressive country for his day, he did it all."[23]

For Court and the participants in the progressive country music scene, the appeal of Rodgers's music—and of Threadgill's interpretations of it—rested on its connection to an idyllic and imagined Texan past that, unlike the apparently fragmented, self-interested, and self-serving modern world, valued the communal enjoyment of music, which was reflective of lived experiences.[24] That Rodgers's music was four decades old by the dawn of the progressive country movement in Austin and that its primary practitioners could have been the cosmic cowboys' grandfathers situated Threadgill and Neely's impersonations of Rodgers within the context of this utopian past. Moreover, the environment that Threadgill cultivated both in his own establishment and in performances throughout Austin and beyond broke down the barriers between the musicians and the audience, as well as divisions within the local society. In a 1972 article in the *Daily Texan*, for instance, Threadgill remarked that "music is the biggest common denominator—it brings goat ropers and college students all together just to have a good time." A 1973 feature article remarked that Threadgill's was the kind of place where college students could bring their parents to enjoy an uplifting night on the town.[25] Similarly, Oakes remarked in 1970 that "one finds every type of person at 'Threadgill's,' all enjoying the music and each other. Such an improbable mixture of people never gathered at the tavern next door, nor for that matter at any of the pubs around the University of Texas. Threadgill's personal respect for people, as well as his music, make this social harmony possible, for he is an epitome of tolerance."[26] In addition, Greg Olds observed that "each performance of Threadgill and his Hootenanny Hoots—whether they are playing the Split Rail Inn on South Lamar or Threadgill's old gas station on North Lamar—draw[s] such varied sorts of cedar choppers, hippies, fraternity and sorority types, goat ropers, rednecks, and just plain students and townspeople."[27] For Threadgill, this environment was simply an extension of the social music making in which he had always participated, and the omnipresence of his singing at his North Lamar tavern created a hospitable environment for social discourse and music making. As Malone recalled, "Mr. Threadgill was a kind and genial person. He sold beer during the evenings while we sat around the big round tables and sang. When he got up, he would come over to the table, still in his apron, and sing and yodel while we played. He . . . was a warm friend and good listener."[28]

Threadgill's hospitality and congeniality also extended to his support of younger musicians, many of whom he encouraged to apprentice with him as a member of the Hootenanny Hoots or any of several other configurations of his band. Numerous musicians who were active in Austin's progressive country music scene pointed to Threadgill as an important mentor, but most of them cannot recall him having done any direct teaching. Rather, Threadgill expected his acolytes to learn while on the job, thereby providing them not only with valuable educational experiences but with opportunities for financial remuneration as well. Bobby Earl Smith, who was perhaps best known in Austin as the founder of the honky-tonk band Freda and the Firedogs, played frequently with Threadgill. He recalled showing Threadgill his very first composition, a "bluesy, country, traditional country sounding tune called 'How Long Have I Been Missing You' " at a performance at the Short Horn in Austin, after which

> [Threadgill] put his hand on the mic, and he said, folks, this boy up here—I was always a boy—he said, this boy up here's written a new song, and he played it for me, and I want him to play it for you, and I want you to listen to it. And he asked me to play that same song three times that night. It was the only song I'd written. And I'll never forget it, but I'll always . . . I realize how much that encouragement meant to me. It meant the world to me. And so, personally, he was a huge part of

my musical life. But I'm not the only one. I mean, everybody that ever came into contact with Kenneth Threadgill feels the same way. He encouraged everybody that he played with or that played with him or that came in contact with him. He was an amazing man.[29]

Like Rodgers, whose willingness to share a guitar chord or a yodeling lesson with an interested young musician was the catalyst for innumerable musical careers, Threadgill recognized that, simply by encouraging musicians to present their work before a public audience, he could guarantee the survival not only of the repertoire that he so loved but also of the congenial spirit that he nurtured at Threadgill's and in his frequent out-of-town performances.

Kenneth Threadgill personified the ideals of the progressive country music scene in Austin. By creating a safe space for the city's emerging counterculture in the early 1960s, Threadgill served as the patriarch of its music scene, a role that was underscored by the common knowledge that the recently deceased Janis Joplin had referred to him as "daddy."[30] Moreover, through his public performances and his willingness to mentor younger musicians, Threadgill worked diligently to ensure that the hillbilly and gospel music of his youth was transmitted to progressive country music fans who were hungry for what they believed to be authentically Texan music and culture. Furthermore, as an acolyte of adopted Texan Jimmie Rodgers, Threadgill stood as a direct connection to the presumably unmediated golden age of Texan music. As such, Threadgill—and, by extension, his establishment on North Lamar Boulevard—became important touchstones for the participants in Austin's progressive country music scene and for subsequent generations of Austin musicians. At the same time, the efforts of many musicians and audiences to reshape Threadgill into a symbol of an idealized Texan past reveal the complex process by which the participants in the Austin music scene throughout the 1960s and 1970s positioned themselves as heirs of a distinctly Texan musical heritage. Also, perhaps more important, it was through this process that they also came to understand how the progressive country music scene could allow them to both express identities that were contrary to the American cultural mainstream and to salvage an Anglo-Texan culture that was thought to be in grave danger.

These notions become even clearer in the work of the staff of Austin radio station, KOKE-FM, to develop and market a new "progressive country" radio format in the early 1970s. In 1972, KOKE-FM adopted a new programming format that replaced its long-standing block programming approach, which featured shows dedicated to jazz, Top 40, classical, and rock styles with a more streamlined and consistent sound. Local promoter and KOKE-FM disc jockey Joe Gracey recalled that this new progressive country format was an attempt to "emphasize home-grown artists and their music, reflect a growing sense of Texanness after years of trying to play it down, and act as a counterweight to the pop fluff coming out of Nashville, which had nothing to do with Texas by then, or at least very little."[31] The new format veered sharply away from the comparatively limited and restrictive mainstream country format that had emerged in the late 1950s, presenting a hodgepodge of hardcore country music by Ernest Tubb and Hank Williams, the latest country-rock from groups such as the New Riders of the Purple Sage and the Band, the Austin-based sounds of Doug Sahm and Jerry Jeff Walker, Texas blues by Mance Lipscomb and T-Bone Walker, the western swing of Bob Wills, the contemporary "outlaw" music of Willie Nelson and Waylon Jennings, and the latest rock hits by the Rolling Stones and other questionably "country" groups.[32] As journalist Jan Reid, who covered the progressive country scene for the magazine *Texas Monthly*, observed, "If anything remotely country could be discerned in a recording, it qualified [for airplay on KOKE-FM]. George Harrison was sometimes accompanied by a bottleneck guitar, which sounded almost like a steel [guitar], and even Paul Simon's 'Duncan,' a song about a youth and his first piece of ass, was fair game."[33]

KOKE-FM's progressive country format embodied the grassroots country music activism that country music historian, Diane Pecknold, has suggested characterized many reactions to mainstream country radio and the overt commodification of country fans during the 1960s and 1970s by the Nashville-based Country Music Association, a trade organization consisting of Music Row insiders.[34] The format challenged the dominance of mainstream country and Nashville's increasing hegemony by creating a broadcast format that reflected local, not national, tastes and musical practices. Contemplating the format thirty-five years later, Gracey remarked that progressive country was part of his "personal mission to try to salvage Texas culture before it was overwhelmed by TV and magazines and blandness from popular culture." Along the way, he invoked gendered rhetoric that implied that mass-mediated culture, especially format radio, threatened to emasculate Texan culture, recalling that "we were all tired of the Nashville formula and cornball and the Chet Atkins attempt to market it [country music] to women and city kids and wanted something more earthy that reflected Texas culture."[35] Implicit in this commentary is the belief that Texas music—which emerged organically from "home-grown artists"—was more masculine than the "pop fluff" marketed by the Country Music Association and played on mainstream country radio stations. Moreover, taking this rhetoric into account, these innovators recast themselves as masculine heroes who were using grassroots entrepreneurship to rescue Texan culture from Nashville's attempt to commodify and therefore to emasculate it.[36]

In addition to the gendered rhetoric that Gracey used to defend "authentic" Texan music, the innovators of the progressive country format also implicitly built upon a legacy of Anglo-Texan colonial dominance that allowed the predominantly white middle-class participants in the progressive country scene to transform the vibrant vernacular musics of the Lone Star State—and its equally diverse ethnic, racial, and geographic tapestry—into a unified and fairly homogenous "Texas music" and to recast the practitioners of these musics as "Texans." While there is little doubt that there has always been extensive musical exchange between the many peoples who have settled in or been brought to Texas, the social settings for Texan musics were largely segregated throughout much of the 1970s.[37] Yet the format that Gracey, Nelson, and Wilson devised desegregated these musics, bringing Tejano conjunto music together with urban blues and honky-tonk. As country music historian Bill C. Malone has proposed, the progressive country format—and the scene, more generally—promoted a "myth of Texas music" that itself helped Austin's entrepreneurs to commodify it.[38] But, even more importantly, this process of redefining the diverse musical practices as a more unified Texas music Anglicized all Texas musics, effectively drawing all Texans, regardless of race or ethnicity, into an Anglo-Texan nationalist project that sought to defend Texan culture against the outside infiltration. Thus, the authenticity of the progressive country radio format and, by extension, of all progressive country music was located in three Texas nationalist ideals: masculinity, colonization and ownership of indigenous peoples, and a rhetoric of Texan exceptionalism.[39]

Careful examination of KOKE-FM's programming philosophy and its ambivalent attitudes about commercialism and the commodification of Texas music reveals that the station was both a flagship for and a microcosm of the attitudes and musical approaches expressed by participants in Austin's progressive country music scene.[40] At once, inclusive of a wide variety of musical practices and exclusive of Nashville's version of country music, anticommercial and profit-seeking, local and translocal, KOKE-FM was the sonic embodiment of the progressive country

PROGRESSIVE COUNTRY STEREO 95

AUSTIN, TEXAS

FIGURE 1.1. KOKE-FM's "goat-roper" logo, which adorned T-shirts, bumper stickers, and other of the station's advertisements. Used by permission of Ken Moyer.

movement's idealism while simultaneously betraying the fragility of its ideals. As such, the story of KOKE-FM and the progressive country format lays bare the complex and often controversial process by which Austin's progressive country music scene found its voice.

In the late 1960s and early 1970s, FM radio was one of the principal outlets for the public expression of countercultural ideologies and aesthetics. During the preceding two decades, AM radio, the dominant radio broadcast medium, had focused primarily on the development of the tight Top-40 format, attracting significant attention from younger (teenaged) listeners and, as a result, advertisers. In addition, AM radio was the home of the country radio format, which was refined by the Country Music Association during the 1960s. On the other hand, FM radio had been used primarily for the broadcast of "good music" or "beautiful music"—predominantly classical music and jazz, both of which benefited musically from the increased fidelity (and, later, stereo capabilities) of the FM technology. Because of the specialized audiophile niche that FM catered to, as well as the relative unavailability of FM receivers, the FM format did not offer the pecuniary rewards of AM radio and was, therefore, largely ignored by broadcasters (except for those who wanted to use its subcarrier to transmit background music to supermarkets and office buildings) and resulted in relatively low licensing costs.[41]

All of these factors coalesced in the mid- to late 1960s to make FM radio a vibrant force for the counterculture. Radio historians Christopher H. Sterling and Michael C. Keith have suggested that many FM programmers developed "contrarian approach[es] to programming" with names such as "progressive, alternative, free-form, psychedelic, and even the 'anti-format format.'" These were a response to the growing dissatisfaction felt by many countercultural men and women in their twenties and thirties with the overt commercialism of AM radio, the commodification of audiences through the rise of the Top 40 and (later) country radio formats, and the apparent lack of locality in radio broadcasting as record charts and national broadcasting protocols such as the Drake Method eliminated or greatly reduced the role of the disc jockey in selecting music that suited local tastes.[42] Moreover, the rise of independent, alternative, and progressive FM in the mid-1960s embodied contemporary media studies scholar Marshall McLuhan's suggestion that "the medium is the message."[43] That is, FM innovators created programming that made use of the specific characteristics of FM radio—high-fidelity sound reproduction, a paucity of commercial breaks, and freedom from the restrictive formats that drove commercial AM radio—to create broadcasts that served important cultural functions in local communities. Such was the case in Austin, where FM station KOKE played a central role in defining progressive country music as a genre and in articulating a distinctly Texan response to the hegemony of the country radio format.

Austin had been served by a free-form and locally inflected FM radio station since 1964, when KAZZ-FM switched from a "good music" format to a more progressive block scheduling approach, which made room for Top 40, classical, jazz, and rock music.[44] Led by station manager Bill Josie Sr. and his son Bill Josie Jr. (who, as the station's principal disc jockey, went by the on-air name Rim Kelley), the station's staff undertook an ambitious effort to disseminate the vitality and variety of Austin's live music scene beyond the walls of the city's clubs.[45] As Josie Sr. recalled, the KAZZ-FM live broadcasts served a wide variety of artists, venues, and musical styles:

> We did remote broadcasts in those days from some of the local clubs—the Garacen Club, the Caravan Club, the Seville, the New Orleans Club, the Latin Quarter, the Eleventh Door and many of the so-called folk houses.
>
> We broadcasted Janis Joplin then, who was at that time a folk singer at the Eleventh Door, playing acoustic guitar and singing. We also did

Townes Van Zandt, Jerry Jeff Walker, Don Sanders and a host of other folk singers, including [future progressive country standout] Michael Murphey.[46]

Josie Sr. also used his connections with the Austin club scene to provide artists for his label, Sonobeat Records, which he founded in early 1967. Sonobeat served all of the local band scene, recording fraternity bands like the Sweetarts (who primarily played in the Top-40 vein of the "British Invasion" bands), jazz acts such as the Lee Arlano Trio (which played at the Club Seville in the Austin Sheraton Inn), as well as more progressive rock bands such as the interracial band the Conqueroo, the blues-rock of Johnny Winter, and the Lavender Hill Express, which was led by future progressive country star Rusty Wier. Using the local clubs and the KAZZ-FM facilities as recording studios, Josie sought to capture the energy and sound of the bands' live acts, much as he had done in his live broadcasts over KAZZ-FM.[47] Since KAZZ-FM and Sonobeat Records were the only media outlets available to most local artists, they were instrumental in helping many of them promote their alternative, decidedly anticommercial musical aesthetics, developing local musical talent, and documenting the otherwise ephemeral activities of the local music scene.[48]

The KAZZ-FM experiment with progressive block programming came to an end in the fall of 1967 when station owner Monroe Lopez decided to sell the station to KOKE-AM, the city's top country station. After a brief shutdown in the first weeks of 1968, KOKE-FM made its first broadcasts, simulcasting the KOKE-AM signal.[49] A progressive FM alternative did not reemerge in Austin until 1972, when KOKE-FM switched to the progressive country format. Although the term *progressive country* was coined by KOKE-FM program director Rusty Bell, the notion of a radio format that presented country-rock, Nashville country music, and the music of local artists seems to have emerged from a variety of sources. Ken Moyer, a former KOKE-AM disc jockey who served as the general manager of KOKE-FM from 1969 until 1977, remembered that, sometime in 1971 or 1972, he was approached by a group of people from local rock station KRMH-FM with a proposal to take the station over and develop a format similar to what would become "progressive country." Wishing to maintain control of the station, Moyer refused their offer. However, in 1972, Moyer recalled, Bell approached him with a similar format but proposed that the station's operational structures remain the same, so Moyer agreed, and Bell became KOKE-FM's program director.[50] Gracey, on the other hand, recollected that he, country singer Willie Nelson, and Armadillo World Headquarters co-owner Eddie Wilson introduced the progressive country format to Moyer, who then offered the idea to program director Rusty Bell, who gave the format its "'progressive country' moniker."[51] Regardless of its origins, though, listener interest in the station was almost immediate. In an April 1975 feature article in the regional music newspaper *Pickin' Up the Tempo*, for instance, journalist Nelson Allen noted that, although Moyer "was the first to become interested in programming the new longhair country music . . . [he] admittedly knew little about it. He mentioned this in an interview for a local rock magazine and within days he was bombarded with people eager to work with such a format."[52]

This eagerness to participate is much the same as what helped drive the development and expansion of the Armadillo World Headquarters. Following the Vulcan Gas Company's closure in the summer of 1970, Austin's musicians had no large venue in which to perform and listen to the city's latest sounds. However, Capitol Records offered the members of Austin-based rock band Shiva's Head Band, the most popular act at the Vulcan Gas Company, an advance on a recording contract and suggested that the band audition local talent for the label. As a result, a coalition that comprised lawyer Mike Tolleson, Shiva's Head Band manager, Eddie Wilson, and artist Jim Franklin concocted a plan to spend $4,000 of the advance given to Shiva's bandleader, Spencer Perskin, to lease an old National Guard armory on Barton Springs Road in downtown Austin.[53] In July 1970, the Armadillo World Headquarters opened its doors to the former Vulcan crowd; as Wilson reflected in 1974, "We inherited the legacy of the Vulcan Gas Company."[54] The vast spaces of the armory were divided into several smaller sections, including a seating area on the floor immediately in front of the stage, a dance floor in the rear, a bar area, and even an outdoor beer garden. The variety of spaces contained within the Armadillo provide an indication that Wilson, Tolleson, and Franklin were in tune with the various ways in which the fans in Austin hoped to experience music and the equally numerous reasons that people are attracted to clubs and dance halls. By combining the best aspects of the dance hall and the concert hall, the Armadillo was poised to take the Austin music scene by storm.

The Armadillo could not have been transformed from an armory to a music venue so quickly, however, without the assistance of numerous volunteers from the scene who wished to expedite the process. As Jan Reid observed, "The staff hammered and nailed a stage together, dragged in some carpet scraps, offered some apple juice and pumpkin bread for refreshments, and opened with three top local bands, but the odds seemed against them."[55] Moreover, a dozen bartenders, members of the kitchen staff, and sound technicians lived together at the home of Eddie and Genie Wilson in the early days of the Armadillo.[56] Local legend even has it that most of the volunteers in the early days of the Armadillo were paid a small amount of cash and all of the marijuana they could smoke for their services; because payroll records from this period of the Armadillo's history are nonexistent, such an arrangement cannot be verified.[57] According to Eddie Wilson, though, the Wilsons were drawing a weekly net salary of only $51.29 in 1974, four years after the Armadillo opened its doors.[58] It is clear, however, that because of the skills of these volunteers, the Armadillo quickly expanded from a little-known, Texas-sized concert hall into a world-class audio and video production center, a venue capable of attracting national touring acts of all varieties, and a beer garden and restaurant that served the local community.[59]

This sense of community and local activism was integral to the survival of the Armadillo's communal business model and was equally important in keeping the audiences and owners alike out of trouble with law enforcement. A primary reason that the Armadillo World

FIGURE 1.2. Artist Jim Franklin's poster advertising the grand opening of the Armadillo World Headquarters, August 7–8, 1970. Dolph Briscoe Center for American History, University of Texas at Austin. Used by permission of Jim Franklin.

Headquarters was so successful was the passage of two pieces of legislation in 1973, one that lowered the legal drinking age from twenty-one to eighteen and the other that reduced the penalty for marijuana possession from a felony to a misdemeanor. The loosening of state laws would not, however, be enough to prevent the arrest of intoxicated or troublemaking customers. Rather, stringent self-policing and the complicity of local law enforcement were integral components in keeping the Armadillo out of legal trouble. As Wilson noted, "What we had was a place that was damn near too big to bust, and there was not anything going on that was malicious or vicious or really dangerous to anyone. And I can't say too much for the general attitude of the Austin Police Department. . . . [The cops on the beat] work with us real, real hard."[60] Without the shared talents of the Armadillo's employees and founders, an interest in local and national music, and the communal ideology of the hippie movement, therefore, Austin's live music scene would very likely have faded into a distant memory following the closure of the Vulcan. However, because the scene participants pooled their financial, creative, and physical resources to build a significant venue for live music, the effects of the Vulcan's closure were only short term, permitting the scene to grow exponentially both in Austin and in the perception of the national audience throughout the 1970s.[61]

Much as the Armadillo World Headquarters regularly featured local artists and acknowledged the valuable contributions of Austin's scene participants to the success of the venue, KOKE-FM worked to create a distinctly local radio voice that reflected the progressive country music scene's principle values. The staff of KOKE-FM fostered a similar sense of community by taking up KAZZ-FM's practice of broadcasting live concerts from the city's clubs and actively seeking participation from the city's musicians. In 1973, Bell hired Gracey to do the midday shift (10 AM–2 PM), and, almost immediately, he began to broadcast live concerts from the Armadillo World Headquarters and other clubs. Gracey recalled: "We had a permanent line to [the] Armadillo, and I would go down there live, and we would put them on the air live from the stage. Many of them. We made that a habit."[62] Gracey's passion for live music shaped nearly all of his engagements with the scene and his attempts to promote it. He wrote a music column for the *Austin American-Statesman* newspaper, in which he promoted the scene, produced shows at the Armadillo, and broadcast over KOKE-FM, creating what he has described as "a corner on the market."[63] Gracey used this bully pulpit to advocate not only for local musicians but also for a revival of interest in the traditions of Texas music among Austin's educated, middle-class young adults.[64] As such, KOKE-FM was one part of a broad-based project to create a Texas music revival that built upon the folk music revival of the 1950s and 1960s (as exemplified by the UT Folk Sing and the gatherings at Threadgill's) while also commodifying this music in order to provide continued economic support for the local scene.[65]

Despite the Austin-centered gaze of the progressive country format, the members of the KOKE-FM staff also saw the potential to use the media to transmit the sound and atmosphere of the Austin scene throughout Texas and, ideally, across the United States, further amplifying the colonial ambitions of the progressive country format. The earliest evidence of such attempts can be traced to 1972, when Dallas public television station KERA Channel 13 taped a broadcast featuring several Austin bands, including Greezy Wheels, Freda and the Firedogs, and Balcones Fault. Gracey, who was then working primarily for the *Austin American-Statesman*, challenged Austin's media industry to claim ownership of the city's music scene and to take control of the scene's mediated image. In a "Rock Beat" column, Gracey inquired, "Why didn't Austin's own public station do it first? Austin is rumbling with excitement, talent, and bands, and is about to inject some of its burgeoning culture into the national awareness. . . . The local media should be first, not last, to hear the news."[66] Gracey's observations here bring the motivations of the progressive country movement into relief. Rather than allowing non-Austinites to control the discourse about progressive country music, many of the scene's boosters believed that, to be effective, these grassroots efforts needed to be located in Austin. Much as Gracey and others expressed a distrust of Nashville, so, too, did they exhibit a distrust of many non-Austinites.

Gracey's suggestions, combined with the publication of Jan Reid's foundational book, *The Improbable Rise of Redneck Rock*, prompted Bill Arhos, program director at Austin's public television station KLRN Channel 9, to begin exploring ways to create a nationally viable program featuring Austin's bands to distribute via the recently instituted Station Program Cooperative, which provided an opportunity for stations in smaller markets to produce nationally syndicated programming. After taping a pilot in 1974 featuring Willie Nelson, the show *Austin City Limits* went national in 1976 on 115 of 153 PBS stations. The program showcased a broad cross-section of Austin's music scene and the recently minted "Texas music," which was not unlike the one presented on KOKE-FM. In the first season, for instance, it featured, among others, Willie Nelson, the Amazing Rhythm Aces, the Earl Scruggs Revue, Rusty Wier, Jimmy Buffett, Delbert McClinton, Gatemouth Brown, Steve Fromholz, Guy Clark, Larry Gatlin, and Willis Alan Ramsey.[67]

Billboard lent further momentum to the Texas music format by awarding KOKE-FM the Trendsetter Award in 1974. In addition to validating Bell's, Gracey's, and Moyer's efforts to create and sustain a Texas music format, the award reinforced the notion that one could create an alternative to the Nashville format and further galvanized local support for the music scene. Within months, disc jockeys on competing Austin station KRMH-FM (pronounced "karma" on-air) were also claiming ownership of progressive country music by inviting local music luminaries for on-air interviews. These conversations demonstrate that KOKE-FM's participatory model and Gracey's local boosterism were, in fact, successful in promoting the idea that Texas music was distinct and somehow more authentic than the sounds emerging from the Nashville format. For instance, Art Young, KRMH-FM morning disc jockey, regularly invoked anti-Nashville rhetoric in these interviews even when the musicians themselves maintained close relationships with the Nashville scene. In a January 1977 interview with singer-songwriter Guy Clark, Young seized on a passing remark that Clark made about Nashville's studio musicians and tried to get him to turn that into an indictment of the Nashville system. However, Clark, who had a close relationship with Nashville through both publishing and recording, quickly qualified his observation:

> CLARK: Oh, and the pickers [in Nashville], too, you know, are just incredible. I can't believe how good they are.
>
> YOUNG: Yeah.
>
> CLARK: And some of 'em get stale; some of 'em stay fresh. So—
>
> YOUNG: Uh-huh. Well, that's the thing we always hear, but—I say "we." That's the thing a lot of people hear about, but those people have been in there for a lot of—a lot of staff musicians have been in there for a hundred years . . . and they just pick the notes . . . and it's just a formula. And Chet Atkins comes in and said, It's good.
>
> CLARK: Yeah. Well, it's true to a certain extent, but also you gotta remember that they didn't get to be those staff musicians and—or continue to be—by not being able to play good and not being creative. I mean, I'm sure that they do get stale. I know. I mean, I see 'em. But they can still play *real* good. . . . And there's new ones all the time. So it just—it

depends on whether or not what you're doing in the studio turns 'em on, whether they really want to play it, or whether it's just another hundred bucks.[68]

Exchanges such as these are particularly instructive as they demonstrate the power that the broadcast media had to shape the rhetoric of the progressive country movement. On the other hand, they also suggest that, regardless of the opposition that was perceived by many in the movement, many of the musicians who were affiliated with the Austin scene had much more complicated musical, social, and economic relationships with the national music industry. Austin's progressive country music scene was, regardless of its rhetoric, inextricably linked to the very institution it opposed. In fact, it required these oppositional relationships to Nashville, commercialism, and the older generation of Austinites to motivate others to participate. Whereas many local music scenes use informal media such as the underground and alternative press and word of mouth to circulate knowledge about the scene, the progressive country scene exploited what was rapidly becoming a commercial broadcast medium to create a distinct sense of place. By using the FM radio medium, the scene transcended the clubs, record stores, and underground newspapers—all of which were, in a sense, directed toward people who were already participating in the scene—to reach a still broader audience and to expand the scene across the city and beyond.

The sense of collective ownership that was fostered through FM broadcasts became especially apparent when Rusty Bell began to work toward the establishment of a national progressive country radio network. On June 1, 1976, Bell left KOKE-FM, the progressive country movement's flagship station, which broadcasted the music twenty-four hours per day, to host an overnight show (midnight to 4:30 AM) on fifty-thousand-watt, clear-channel AM station WOAI in San Antonio.[69] While the time slot and block programming at WOAI ghettoized progressive country music in comparison to the situation at KOKE-FM, Bell saw the potential of the clear-channel signal—which prevented interference from other stations—as a way to evangelize for progressive country music nationwide. As he remarked in an interview for the southwestern music magazine *Nashville West*:

[Progressive country] is going to get bigger. . . . How big it gets really depends on a lot of things . . . but the main thing it depends on is the fans. It's got to grow . . . it's got to grow nationwide. It's a Texas thing right now. It's got to get out of Texas, which it is to a certain extent. I'm

not saying that I'm going to WOAI to raise Progressive Country. . . .
I can help it, maybe. But it's gonna take a lot more. It's gonna' [sic] take
a lot of smaller radio stations.[70]

Rick Gilzow, the journalist who covered the transitions at KOKE-FM for
Nashville West, suggested that, while Bell's attempts to spread the message
of progressive country music could benefit people who were in search of
a more authentic and personal form of musical communication, he must
always remember the people and place from which this music sprang:

> The repercussions are obvious. Progressive Country music, which at
> present remains basically a Texas-popular art form, is now available
> [through recordings and *Austin City Limits*, as well as the clear-channel
> AM signal of WOAI] to the housewife in Idaho, the student in New
> York, the blue-collar worker in Montana, the transplanted Texan in
> Colorado and the businessman in Missouri. Rusty Bell has the chance
> to reach millions with OUR music. It's a great opportunity for Bell . . .
> but with that opportunity comes a vital responsibility as the represen-
> tative of Texas country music.[71]

Bell's successful efforts to share progressive country music with the
nation demonstrated Austin's successful resistance to the Nashville
format. Yet, while many Austinites believed that the mainstream country
format had come to neglect its core audience as it gained widespread
national acceptance, the same fears loomed as an expanded, non-Texan
take on progressive country seemed likely. While this explanation surely
fit the colonial goals of the progressive country format and of Austin's
music-related entrepreneurship, such growth also threatened to recast
progressive country radio not as a manifestation of local, grassroots
musical activity but as overtly commercialized music supported by
corporations and mediated by the national culture industry.[72]

When Bell moved to San Antonio, Joe Gracey took over as program
director at KOKE-FM, and, in contrast to Bell's national ambitions, he
began almost immediately to use KOKE-FM to reinforce the locality
and Texanness of progressive country radio. Gracey outlined a plan to
recast the station as an organic outgrowth of the Austin scene by producing more interviews with progressive country artists, recording and
broadcasting live concerts, and allowing disc jockeys to select their own
playlists with few suggestions from the management. He remarked that

> [Bell's] format told you what kind of music to play by category, in other
> words "old," "new," "Country," and "Progressive Country," during
> every minute of the hour. In other words, your whole hour was planned

out for you by this list. It didn't tell you what songs to play, but it did tell you what type of music to play. It wasn't so bad, but I felt it was unnecessarily strict, considering this radio station and the people who work here. The format I've got up there now simply tells 'em to play a Progressive Country oldie out of the news at the top of the hour, which is just a good thing to do, and other than that, all I said was you have to play a well-balanced mix of Progressive Country Music. You've got to cover all of the territory. You've got to play an even amount of cuts, singles and oldies . . . a good balance. I['m] concerned with the over-all sound of the radio station, and I hope that by communicating with each other they will understand what I mean and I'll be able to convince them that this is what they've gotta do. I'd rather talk it over than just have a nursemaid up on the wall. You're in there to entertain and play good records, not to worry about "where I am on the list." So I loosened things up without really loosening anything up.[73]

Gracey's programming philosophy challenged everyone at KOKE-FM to suppress their inclinations to sound explicitly professional in order to allow the unique voices of the individuals of the progressive country movement to shine through even if that meant that mistakes were made on the air. As he explained to Gilzow:

I want the station to sound professional. . . . Now what I mean by professional is entertaining. . . . I can hire any 95-dollar a week jerk to come in and tell me the time and temperature, and so can anybody else, and that's the way it's been for about the last ten years. That ain't where it's at. What you do, is hire a bunch of strong personalities that know what's going on . . . that stay in touch with the scene . . . that get out every night and honky tonk around. I'd rather have a guy that's wasted half the time than a guy that comes in and just says . . . "well, Mr. Gracey, what temperature is it now?" I don't even care if the guy's got a good voice.[74]

In redefining professionalism as "entertaining" rather than a standard of perfection, Gracey echoed his condemnation of Nashville's country music as too slick, too polished, and too far removed from the aesthetic and social values that many younger Austinites sought in their country music. Rather than using the commonly accepted Drake style of broadcasting, which instructed on-air talent to intrude as little as possible in order to foreground the music and, more important, the commercials, Gracey insisted that the voices of KOKE-FM be heard clearly through their on-air discussion of the scene, their personalized musical selections, and, quite literally, the sounds of their predominantly untrained voices.[75] Moreover, Gracey reinforced the local nature of KOKE-FM and, by extension, progressive country music by requiring that all of his broadcasters be imbricated within the scene. Rather than promoting progressive country as universal, the resultant programming and broadcast aesthetics grounded KOKE-FM and progressive country music as distinctly Austin-based phenomena. Mistakes and individual personalities were professional by Austin standards, and Gracey's KOKE-FM sold the image that everyone there cared about the important things: direct communication and shared experience through music.

At the same time that he worked to reinforce the distinctly Austinite nature of the station, however, Gracey was also planning to expand the reach of progressive country music beyond the Lone Star capital. In addition to *Austin City Limits*, which began national syndication just a few months before he took over as KOKE-FM's program director, Gracey envisioned a sort of progressive country radio network that would stretch along the I-35 corridor from Austin to Dallas. However, rather than using commercial recordings for this network (as Bell was doing on WOAI-AM in San Antonio), Gracey's vision brought the sounds of live musical performance into homes, offices, and automobiles by transforming some of the station's office space into a soundstage where bands could perform directly to the radio audience.[76] Gracey had already been doing something similar using direct lines from the Armadillo World Headquarters and, later, the Texas Opry House, and KOKE-FM's predecessor, KAZZ-FM, had pioneered the practice more than a decade earlier. As such, Gracey was sure that such an approach would be successful.[77] While many of the commercial recordings of progressive country music did, in fact, communicate the laid-back, participatory atmosphere of the scene (see chapter 3), live broadcast performances promised to infuse the broadcasts with a fresh energy by making them still more personal, speaking directly to the listeners and creating unique musical events.[78]

Gracey's localized and personalized sound was further reinforced by inviting several of the key musicians, entrepreneurs, and scene participants into the studio to contribute unique programming to KOKE-FM. While any radio station with a strong record library could theoretically broadcast progressive country music, Gracey and KOKE-FM's intimacy with the scene granted it deeper access to Willie Nelson, Townes Van Zandt, and others and, as a result, further allowed the station to distinguish itself as *the* progressive country flagship. When Gracey took over as program director, he developed several types of guest programming, including taped interviews with local figures and guest disc jockey appearances with artists such as Kris Kristofferson, Waylon Jennings, and Nelson.[79] These appearances likely had several effects on the definition of progressive country music. First, although the appearance of prominent musicians and others on the air benefited the artists through mass-mediated promotion, they also served to validate the efforts of everyone in the progressive country scene by showing that nationally recognized musicians such as Charlie Daniels and Roger McGuinn were aware of the scene. Just as projects such as Bell's clear-channel AM broadcasts and *Austin City Limits* demonstrated that non-Austinites were interested in Austin's music, so, too, did such guest broadcasts by highly influential local and national musicians reinforce the idea that progressive country music had artistic integrity. Second, because these musicians brought such cultural capital to these broadcasts, they also exerted a strong influence on the definition of progressive country music as a genre, stretching the generic boundaries of the music just as the nongeneric booking practices of the Armadillo World Headquarters had challenged the country focus of the Austin scene.

The case of KOKE-FM demonstrates that the entrepreneurial spirit that dominated the progressive country movement in Austin informed the approach that many in the movement took to resist the perceived hegemony of the Nashville country music industry and of country format radio. In contrast to the "do-it-yourself" ideal that has shaped much of the academic and popular understanding of local music scenes, this entrepreneurial approach made explicit use of existing industrial infrastructure (the FM broadcast medium) and marketing strategies (the branding of playlists as formats directed toward a target demographic) to create the sense that progressive country music was culturally, socially, musically, and economically distinct from the sounds generated by Nashville's country music industry. Gracey, Bell, and Moyer did not wish to transform KOKE-FM into an anticommercial station; rather, they wished to create a distinct format that rivaled others in terms of popularity and, as a result, economic viability. The success of these strategies can be measured in the longevity of the station. From 1972 until 1978, when the entire progressive country scene itself began to show signs of fatigue, KOKE-FM defined and maintained the progressive country format. As the flagship station of the progressive country movement, therefore, KOKE-FM played a formative role in defining the movement and in sustaining its energy on a daily basis, an energy that was recharged at annual progressive country music festivals.

As the examples provided here demonstrate, the participants in Austin's progressive country music scene resisted the increasing modernization of Texas and the national music industry's commodification of musical expression by creating an alternative realm in which they could celebrate what they believed to be a more authentic, grassroots expression of Anglo-Texan identity that manifested itself in everything from business models to musical tastes. Just as Texas was experiencing seismic shifts in the cultural and physical landscapes caused by the civil rights and women's liberation movements, the upward economic and social mobility of postwar baby boomers, and the rapid construction of highways, skyscrapers, and suburban housing in the Lone Star State's cities, adherents of the progressive country ideal clung to an idealized Texan past that authenticated their own Anglo-Texan experiences in a time when the status quo of Anglo-Texan dominance was being challenged on a daily basis.[80] As Ken Moyer recalled, progressive country was not a single, unified musical style. Rather, it was an approach to programming that effectively destroyed the artificial walls that the national music industry had built around specific musical practices and, by extension, audiences.[81] Similarly, the progressive country music scene in Austin represented an opportunity for participants to use the rhetoric of Anglo-Texan colonialism and the pastoral image of the cowboy to break down the perceived barriers between the predominantly white youth counterculture and their older, more conservative counterparts to create a unified white resistance to ever-encroaching modernity.

"I Just Wanna Be a Cosmic Cowboy"

Pastoral Imagery and Progressive Country Music

IN AUGUST 1972, Dallas-born singer-songwriter Michael Murphey composed "Cosmic Cowboy" on a hotel roof in New York, where he and his band were scheduled to perform at the Bitter End, a folk venue in Greenwich Village. A student of former Threadgill's folksinger Stan Alexander at North Texas State University and a participant in the far-flung Texas folk revivalist scene since the 1960s, Murphey was a music industry veteran who had recently relocated to Austin after spending several years as a studio songwriter in Los Angeles.[1] The song describes a long-haired hippie with an affinity for country music and cowboy attire who hopes to escape to the hinterlands of Texas. Initially intended to be a jab at bassist Bob Livingston, whom Murphey had taken to calling "Cosmic Bob," the contradictions of the "cosmic cowboy" character were immediately apparent to Murphey's pedal steel guitarist, Herb Steiner, and lead guitarist, Craig Hillis.[2] Murphey's sidemen felt great kinship with the fictional character but also believed that the resulting fusion of the "cosmic" drug culture and the more conservative Texan "cowboy" was an uncomfortable one.[3] The term was used, as folklorist Archie Green has suggested, "to mark [the] contemporary social collision and convergence" of young, middle-class, liberal Texans and older, working-class, conservative Texans.[4] These young people, the majority of whom congregated in and around Austin, often wore their hair long and smoked marijuana like "hippies" but dressed in the faded blue jeans, work shirts, cowboy hats, and boots of the rural cowboy. This Texan conflation of the hippie lifestyle and redneck imagery also found parallels in the national counterculture as many hippies left America's urban centers in search of what historian Michael Allen has described as "a near-Jeffersonian vision of an agrarian republic" in rural and small-town America.[5] The cosmic cowboy sprang forth, therefore, from a bundle of cultural conflicts, including not only those resulting from the merger of the drug culture and cowboy symbolism but also from the intersection of communal music making and the national music industry, the ongoing debate about civil rights, and the invocation of rural romanticism in an American metropolis. As such, Murphey's "Cosmic Cowboy" was one of the most important songs to shape the pastoral visions of progressive country music as it offered a constellation of images that scene participants could adopt as part of their personal identities while also taking a stand against the mainstream music industry that Austin's musical entrepreneurs were challenging.

Noting the intense competition in the mainstream music industry of a place like Los Angeles, the cosmic cowboy proposed that Texas offered an alternative space in which competition was not an issue and where people could be as creative as they wished. He observed that "Lone Star sippin' and skinny-dippin' and steel guitars and stars/Are just as good as Hollywood and them boogie-woogie bars." These images offer stark contrasts between the relaxed atmosphere of Austin and the fast pace of Hollywood, but Murphey does not achieve these contrasts simply through the use of stock "western" imagery. Rather, he evokes Austin by pointing to specific elements of Austin's local culture: Lone Star Beer's largest account was at the Armadillo World Headquarters;[6] the local hippies regularly bathed at Lake Travis's "Hippie Hollow";[7] and steel guitars evoked the country music for which Austin was becoming famous in part because of the work of Murphey himself. Thus, for Murphey's cosmic cowboy, the American West (and Austin as its de facto capital) was constructed as a place of refuge from the stifling urban atmosphere. In contrast to the city, the romanticized spaces of rural Texas offered a place in which the cosmic cowboy could "ride and rope and hoot."

The sense of communality and acceptance described in "Cosmic Cowboy" is further amplified by the sonic characteristics of Murphey's 1973 studio recording.[8] Murphey's cosmic cowboy observes that, unlike musicians in Austin, "Them city slicker pickers, they got a lot of slicker licks than you and me." The line implies that the preferred musical aesthetic of Austin's singer-songwriters was less polished than the sounds generated in the professional recording studios of Los Angeles, New York, and Nashville. This implication is reinforced by the background vocals in the chorus of "Cosmic Cowboy," which were recorded and mixed so as to distinguish each individual's contribution to the final product. The singers do not attempt to blend their voices to create a homogeneous vocal timbre but instead allow each individual voice to add its own unique coloration. Nor do they sing each pitch or articulate each syllable precisely. The vocalists sing, to varying degrees, ahead of or behind the beat, bend pitches, and offer their own personal pronunciation of the words. Murphey was not the first artist to employ this type of vocal arrangement, nor was he the last: This imprecise vocal style was an important signifier of communality in rock music in the late 1960s and early 1970s. However, in the hands of Murphey and other contemporaneous progressive country songwriters, this vocal style underscored the cosmic cowboy's idealism. Appearing when the speaker begins to dream of a rural utopia, the background vocals symbolize the cosmic cowboy's retreat from the city. Moreover, the emphasis that this vocal arrangement places on individual contributions to the overall sound seems to underscore the communality of the hippie lifestyle and its perceived presence on the Texas range.

Not only did Murphey's "Cosmic Cowboy" posit that Texas, as a physical space, permitted residents to do as they please, but it also proposed that this liberating space was home to a community of individuals who were interested in supporting the cosmic cowboy's freedom, much as Austin's entrepreneurs were. As the cosmic cowboy observes in the second verse, the Texas plains are populated by communities that were unsullied by the competition and selfishness of metropolitan West Coast culture. Rather, the region's residents were depicted as displaying genuine concern for the physical and spiritual health of the Texan community: "When they come to town, they're gonna gather 'round and marvel at my little baby's health." Unlike the residents of the city, therefore, the rural community into which the cosmic cowboy wishes to escape is seen as exhibiting genuine concern for its neighbors and, through the symbol of the baby, the perpetuation of rural cultural values.

Murphey's cosmic cowboy may have sought to escape into an idealized preindustrial Western landscape, but the language he uses to describe it demonstrates that those rural spaces were actually influenced by the interaction of preindustrial, industrial, and postindustrial cultures. Modernity intrudes in the first lines of the song, juxtaposing "burial grounds and merry-go-rounds." Particularly striking here is Murphey's reference to Native American burial grounds, which stand as symbols of the ravages of Anglo-Texan colonialism, a theme Murphey had explored in the title track of his 1972 debut album, *Geronimo's Cadillac*.[9] Yet at the same time, the song's second line indicates that the cosmic cowboy, himself a colonial figure, has the power to liberate residents of the West. Moreover, in order to escape the West Coast scene for Texas, the cosmic cowboy is forced to "keep [his] little pony in overdrive," juxtaposing a symbol of the unity of man and beast in the riding cowboy and one of the most widespread manifestations of modern industrialism in the automobile or motorcycle. As such, the cosmic cowboy himself is also a symbol of the modern world's invasion of a romanticized American West. In other words, as an interloper from the industrialized world, the cosmic cowboy acts as an agent of cultural change, bringing modernity to his hosts at the same time that he draws strength from their hospitality.

The ease with which Murphey mixes symbols of the unspoiled frontier and modernity in "Cosmic Cowboy" is, in some ways, reflective of his middle-class Texan upbringing and the ease with which Anglo-Texan romantic regionalist myths and modern urbanization coexisted. Whereas historian Arnoldo De Léon has observed that the mythology of romantic regionalism requires the erasure or ignorance of cultural diversity, it seems that Murphey's cosmic cowboy is aware of the West's cultural complexity.[10] At the same time, though, the cosmic cowboy regrets the increased intrusion of modernity on the range, expressing nostalgia for a fictional West while never considering his own modernizing role. Murphey proposed that the mythic West was in danger in the third verse of his 1973 studio recording, where the cosmic cowboy observes that a "home on the range where the antelope play is very hard to find." This statement may be read both as both a confirmation of the Texas range as a simulacrum of liberation and a commentary on civilization's— and especially industry's—incursion into this idealized space.

By the middle of 1974, however, Murphey had revised the song to critique the changing physical and cultural landscape of Austin and the surrounding Hill Country more overtly, challenging local planners to rethink their plans to revitalize the city. In a 1974 performance of the song at Willie Nelson's Fourth of July Picnic, held at Texas World Speedway in Bryan, Texas, Murphey was joined onstage by many of the most prominent musicians of Austin's progressive country music scene: Willie Nelson, Waylon Jennings, Leon Russell, B. W. Stevenson, David Allan Coe, and Jerry Jeff Walker and the Lost Gonzo Band.

Murphey altered the final verse of "Cosmic Cowboy" to state a less ambiguous position on urban development: "Now don't let them bring no bulldozer, no bulldozer across your land/'Cause a home on the range where the antelope play is where I'm gonna take my stand."[11] Here, Murphey's cosmic cowboy entreats his audience to rise up in physical protest against corporate intrusion into the neighborhoods of Austin and the idealized rural spaces of Texas. Yet, while the cosmic cowboy articulates a strong political statement about industry's role in the erasure of the American West, he does not examine the impact of his own interactions with the same landscape. Rather, the cosmic cowboy is constructed as an honest and forthright individual, mirroring the heroic tropes of Anglo-Texan nationalism and romantic regionalism that had shaped Texan mythology.

Murphey's "Cosmic Cowboy" brings together several of the most important aspects of the Anglo-Texan romantic regionalism that were prevalent in Austin's progressive country music scene. First, the generic "city" was a powerful symbol in part because of its multivalence: It stood for the failure of the modern American Dream, for the corruption and greed of industry, and for the distance between humanity and nature, while the rural landscape existed as a more problematic and semiologically slippery symbol of humanity's promise. Austin itself embodied this conflict between urban and rural, the burgeoning city playing host to a community of country musicians. Second, the cosmic cowboys felt the need to escape both to a new region, even if within their home state of Texas, and to a different time: either an idealized, preindustrial past or a utopian, postindustrial future.[12] Finally, the restrictions that the cosmic cowboy generation wished to escape were those put in place by middle- and upper-class whites: competition for employment, social class structures, and the cash-based economy. Rather than working like the perceived majority of society, therefore, Murphey's cosmic cowboy and his followers often expressed the belief that they could simply arrive in a new place with no money and settle on rural land without consequence, just as their pioneer forebears had done as they enacted the Doctrine of Manifest Destiny. These aspects of the cosmic cowboy's philosophy, as expressed by Murphey, may be seen as a manifestation of the privilege bestowed upon the generation of cosmic cowboys through their position as heirs to the same white, middle-class capitalism that had made their parents' generation successful. Murphey and the many songwriters who embraced the same idealistic themes were soon faced with the very real challenge of coexisting peacefully with the same people they venerated in song.

Murphey's "Cosmic Cowboy" was one of the most significant songs of Austin's progressive country scene because it offered a unifying name for the scene participants and because it was the first progressive country song to be exported from Austin. It was not, however, the first song to articulate a desire to escape from a stifling urban environment into the wide open spaces of the West, nor was Murphey the first song-writer to leave the Los Angeles music industry for the more relaxed atmosphere of Texas. Rather, "Cosmic Cowboy" was part of a larger family of songs that depicted the city as an oppressive space and the rural American West as a liberating one.

If Murphey's "Cosmic Cowboy" portrayed a man who was looking for a place "to ride and rope and hoot," Guy Clark's 1971 song "L.A. Freeway" presented a character who felt compelled to escape the city for a rural hideaway: a character that remarkably resembled Clark himself. Because "L.A. Freeway," Clark's first national success as a songwriter, was written on the heels of his relocation from Los Angeles to Nashville in 1971, it may be read as an almost autobiographical treatment of the topic. The lyrics depict a couple in the midst of the final preparations to leave Los Angeles and to go "back to the land" in an undisclosed rural location, invoking the same idealized pastoral tropes as Murphey would two years later in "Cosmic Cowboy." The song opens *in media res* as the speaker requests the help of an unnamed second-person character to pack the kitchen and to dispose of stacks of old Los Angeles newspapers, a reminder of the discomfort of urban life.[13] The speaker appears to be in quite a hurry to leave Los Angeles, leaving the house key in the front door rather than vacating the property in an orderly fashion with the landlord's approval, which could delay their retreat to the country. Even more instructive here is the tone of voice used to convey these requests: Both Clark and Jerry Jeff Walker (in his 1972 cover) perform the song in an affable tone, indicating perhaps that, although the completion of these tasks would be beneficial, it is not necessary. Rather, the most important task facing the speaker is to say *"adios* to all this concrete," leaving the urban world to its own devices.

This release into the rural American West is underscored by the striking musical contrast between the verses and chorus of "L.A. Freeway." The song begins with Clark's finger-picked acoustic guitar, which plays the first half of the verse melody before being joined by a fiddle. The first two phrases of the melody begin on the fifth scale degree of the underlying chord, and Clark takes advantage of this in his voicing of the guitar part, choosing an open voicing that empha-sizes the interval of a perfect fifth and creates a sense of musical and physical space. When Clark's vocals begin, the finger-picked guitar doubles the vocal melody, accompanied by high-hat cymbals sounding on the offbeats and a very quiet electric piano playing sustained chords. The rather sparse texture of the first verse is paralleled in the remaining verses as a plaintive harmonica responds to Clark's vocals in the second verse, and the fiddle takes over in the third verse. This arrangement is especially appropriate for the verses because it creates a sense of emptiness and solitude as the speaker reflects upon his time in Los Angeles as he packs his belongings. Moreover, the fatigue that the speaker feels is amplified as the harmonica's and fiddle's fills are softly articulated and seem to fade into the distance.

The sparse textures of the verses, Clark's lackadaisical vocal delivery, and the downward trajectory of the verse's melody underscore the exhaustion and somberness articulated in the lyrics. In the chorus of "L.A. Freeway," however, the speaker's thoughts turn to his upcoming release into more rural spaces, and the accompaniment here echoes that sentiment. The finger-picked guitar of the verses gives way to a rapidly strummed acoustic guitar playing chords in close voicing in contrast to the open voicings of the verses. The texture thickens as the strummed guitar is joined by a steel guitar descant, and the drummer becomes more active as well, adding the snare drum, tom-toms, and kick drum in addition to the lone high-hat cymbal heard in the verses. Furthermore, Clark intones the first line of the chorus on the highest pitch heard to that point. However, the most dramatic contrast between the verses and the chorus is found, as in Murphey's "Cosmic Cowboy," in the use of exuberant background singers to underscore the song's emotional climax in which the speaker expresses his desire to escape from Los Angeles before the city drives him mad. The female background vocalists disappear when the speaker begins to think about the physical journey away from Los Angeles, but they return at the end of the verse, when Clark thrice repeats the word "bought." The background singers in "L.A. Freeway" create musical contrast and mark the speaker's release into the idealized rural environment of which he dreamed while also implying that this place is also home to a welcoming and supportive community.

Considering the urgency of the imperative mood of the verses of "L.A. Freeway," the relative calm of the second verse feels strikingly out of place. Here the speaker addresses Dennis Sanchez, a friend of Clark's who frequently played bass with him. "Old skinny Dennis" is the only person in Los Angeles that he might miss, suggesting that the only friendships the speaker has developed in the city were forged in musical performance.

The speaker hears Sanchez's "singing" bass playing as a touch of humanity in an otherwise cold and unforgiving urban environment, an honest and sincere conversation experienced through communal music-making.

Such a glorification of music as a way to remain compassionate in a cold, corrupt, and corrupting urban environment is not a surprising element in Clark's work, given his biography. A native of the West Texas oil town of Monahans, Clark set out for California in the late 1960s, first to San Francisco and then to Los Angeles, with the hope of transforming his regional songwriting achievements in the flourishing Houston folk scene into a national success and because "it was the only place where [he] knew anybody."[14] However, by the time Clark wrote "L.A. Freeway," his initial hopes for songwriting success in Southern California had faded. He found himself working as a luthier for the famous Dopyera Brothers, inventors of the Dobro resonator guitar, to pay the bills. While he found this opportunity to apprentice with one of the nation's finest luthiers to be a rewarding one, he still longed to be a professional songwriter, but the competition in Los Angeles was intense as hundreds of aspiring musicians had also migrated there in search of the same dream. Finding the Southern California club scene to have "no real sense of community" and to be "real cliquish," Clark and his wife, Susanna, decided in late 1971 that they had tried their luck in California long enough and set out for Nashville, leaving the concrete jungle to join a burgeoning community of Texan songwriters—including Townes Van Zandt, Kris Kristofferson, and Mickey Newbury—that existed on the margins of Music Row.[15] Moreover, he maintained a part-time residence in Austin, eschewing the common practice of country musicians residing in Middle Tennessee to have ready access to the industry and becoming, as a consequence, an important spokesperson for Austin's singer-songwriters.

"L.A. Freeway" was immediately recognized as representative of the escapist desires of Austin's progressive country musicians and the sense of community that the scene participants were constructing in the city, as demonstrated by its first recorded appearance, which occurred on Jerry Jeff Walker's eponymous 1972 MCA Records release.[16] The sense of community that Clark found in the Nashville counterculture and in Austin is underscored on the back of the jacket of Walker's release, where Walker observes:

> Both L.A. Freeway and Old Time Feelin' [sic] were written by Guy Clark. Townes Van Zandt, Guy Clark, Gary White and myself go way back, seven or eight years to Houston, Texas. Guy was making guitars

then. I lived for a while on Guy & Gary's couch on Fannin Street. Recently, I had the chance to do so again in Nashville, where Guy is trying to get people to hear his songs. He told me once, "You know, I used to hear you & Townes play a new song every couple of days, but it never dawned on me that I could just write one of my own." O.K., Sleepy John, it never dawned on me to build my own guitar either.[17]

As Walker's sleeve notes indicate, many musicians in Austin and Nashville maintained close-knit local communities and exchanged ideas and songs, contradicting the common depiction of Nashville as an impersonal and stagnating city. By informing his listeners of the close personal and musical relationship between Clark and himself, Walker effectively validates his performance of "L.A. Freeway," implying that, because of his friendship with Clark, his reading is a more accurate one. At the same time, Walker's sleeve notes complicate this narrative by reminding readers that Austin's musicians regularly sought to extend their influence beyond Austin by traveling to music industry centers such as Nashville to make recordings, sell songs, and perform concerts.

Walker's inclusion of this brief narrative on the jacket of his 1972 album situated progressive country music in a world partially defined by an overt, conscious, and frequently touted allegiance to the handmade *objet d'art* and to the craftsperson, while playing down progressive country artists' necessary economic reliance on the national music industry. This message is also articulated in the closing scene of James Szalapski's 1975 documentary film, *Heartworn Highways*, which presented the work of "the originals of country music's new wave," including Clark, Townes Van Zandt, David Allan Coe, Rodney Crowell, Steve Young, and Charlie Daniels.[18] The scene documents a sing-along following a Christmas dinner at Guy and Susanna Clark's Mt. Juliet, Tennessee home. Amid the half-eaten plates of food, the empty beer cans filled with cigarette butts, and the oil lamps, the Clarks, Steve Young, Steve Earle, Rodney Crowell, and others are seen gathered around the dining room table with guitars in hand to sing "Silent Night." The smiling faces in this impromptu assembly are prominently displayed, demonstrating the pleasure that these musicians derive from performing with their friends and colleagues. Moreover, as the song continues, the singers forget the words to the later verses, compose new ones to some hilarity, and create new (and often musically questionable) countermelodies. As the conclusion to a documentary film that follows the young singer-songwriters around the country and portrays them onstage and in more domestic settings, this is a powerful scene, drawing attention to the idea that progressive country music was the result of a collaborative experience, not a commercial directive.

While Murphey's "Cosmic Cowboy" and Clark's "L.A. Freeway" captured and encouraged the rural utopianism of Austin's progressive country movement and the broader back-to-the-land movement, neither of the songs overtly situated Austin as a rural hideaway. In fact, given the city's exponential population growth and physical expansion during the 1960s and 1970s, such a conceit would have been difficult to maintain. Yet, because Austin was the seat of the progressive country music movement and, as a university city, played host to tens of thousands of idealistic youths, the city became the closest approximation of the rural spaces of Texas in the minds of many of the scene participants.

Murphey's "Alleys of Austin," which appeared on the *Cosmic Cowboy Souvenir* album immediately after "Cosmic Cowboy," makes this connection explicit. It was one the most idealistic songs to treat the rural utopianism of Austin's progressive country movement. Cast in three verses, it first explores "the alleys of Austin," then "the alleys of Heaven," and finally the similarities between the alleys of both places. In both Austin and heaven, music is omnipresent: In Austin, "there's a song on the side of a wall," while in heaven "there's a funky-feeling angel strumming chords." In the third verse, the speaker observes that, in both Austin and heaven, "the song they're playing is the same," implying that Austin is a sort of earthly manifestation of paradise in part because of musical performance.[19] Furthermore, after this connection between Austin and heaven is articulated in the third verse, the preachers and Jesus Christ of the second verse may be interpreted as synecdoches for the songwriters and fans of Austin's progressive country scene. By equating Austin and heaven, Murphey seems to propose that the progressive country music scene is a sacred space and that participation in it is a religious experience. Yet, this comparison also leaves open a more ironic interpretation of "Alleys of Austin" that transforms the second verse into a biting criticism of progressive country, chastising Austin's youths for what many progressive country detractors often perceived as their ersatz sincerity. Yet, regardless of Murphey's intent, the comparison of Austin and heaven is indicative of the romanticism and idealism that pervaded the progressive country scene, on the one hand lauding Austin's youths for their progressive values and, on the other hand, criticizing them for believing in themselves too much.

"Alleys of Austin" does not contrast city and country like "Cosmic Cowboy" and "L.A. Freeway." The song's narrative does not demand the same type of dramatic musical and lyrical release found in the latter songs' choruses, and Murphey therefore chose a strophic form in which to make this comparison. Yet, "Alleys of Austin" does suggest musically that Austin is a liberating space by interpolating a wordless verse between the second and third narrative verses. Here, a choir of male and female singers, led by Murphey himself, performs a wordless version of the song's melody, using only the syllable "la." Like the bridges of "Cosmic Cowboy" and "L.A. Freeway," this section exploits the choir's imprecise articulations and pitch to add emotional weight to the speaker's release from the grips of the city. The vocalise thus functions both as an emotional release—a kind of ecstatic state that transcends words—and as a musical depiction of the participatory nature of Austin's music scene. The textures of the surrounding verses are particularly sparse, featuring only a finger-picked acoustic guitar, bass guitar, and light drums and making the density of the added vocalists sound almost overpowering. This interlude is also repeated at the conclusion of the recording, fading into the sonic distance and, like "L.A. Freeway" and "Cosmic Cowboy," further evoking the unlimited space and liberating power of the American West.

Songs such as "Alleys of Austin," "Cosmic Cowboy," and "L.A. Freeway" musicalized the anti-industrial and decidedly pastoral attitudes that shaped much countercultural thought in the 1960s and 1970s by offering compact, repeatable, first-person testimonies of the glories that awaited those free-thinking individuals who might want to relocate to the Texan capital. For the speakers in these songs, the city of Austin, the Lone Star State, and the American West stood as the antithesis of what they viewed as the impersonal and inauthentic state of the modern world. Perhaps more important, though, these voices did not simply offer a back-to-the-land rhetoric. Rather, they couched their rhetoric within the context of catchy hooks that encouraged listeners to sing along—whether at concerts or while listening to the songs on their record players—and, like the background singers that characterize many of these recordings, to express their collective support for the ideals of the progressive country movement and their acceptance of the cosmic cowboy image.

Yet, just as these compositions galvanized support for the progressive country music scene and its alternative visions of country music composition and distribution, they also drew the attention of numerous detractors who challenged the cosmic cowboy's primacy in Austin and throughout Texas. Within months of the release of Murphey's "Cosmic Cowboy," the song and the cosmic cowboy image had become ubiquitous in Austin, not only forming the basis of numerous new musical compositions and the fashion and rhetoric of progressive country fans but also appearing in a wide variety of advertisements for everything from progressive country radio station KOKE-FM to Lone Star Beer, which invoked a line from Murphey's song and pastoral images of skinny-dipping in Austin's Hippie Hollow to sell beer to progressive country fans. In the cosmic cowboy, the entrepreneurs who were attempting to transform Austin into a major music industry center found a trademark that would allow them to market progressive country music and the Austin lifestyle to musicians and audiences alike. Yet, for many observers on the margins of the progressive country music scene, this commodification of the cosmic cowboy image and its concomitant popularity represented the downfall of the countercultural movements of the 1960s. These commentators, many of whom were active members of the Austin counterculture of the previous decade, publicly decried the cosmic cowboy and the progressive country music scene for what they viewed as a misguided—and, in some cases, completely rudderless—idealism that was motivated by selfish desires and the culture industry rather than grassroots efforts to address the troubling racial, gender, and socioeconomic issues that Texas and the United States faced in the 1970s. Perhaps more important, these commentaries engaged directly with the idyllic representations of rural Texas and the progressive country music scene that were put forth in the work of Michael Murphey, Guy Clark, and other singer-songwriters, resulting in a backlash that was informed musically, as well as socially.

One of the earliest critiques of the cosmic cowboy can be found in an interview with Austin folk musician John Clay, which appeared in *The Rag* on September 4, 1973. The interview is little more than a biographical sketch of Clay, who, after moving from Stamford, Texas, to Austin in 1960, was part of the first generation of Austin folk musicians that resided in the neighborhood known as "the Ghetto." Clay had a long history of public resistance to the changing tides of the Austin music scene, as a June 13, 1968, interview in *The Rag* suggests. When asked, "Why haven't you joined an electric rock group" like the then popular Austin groups The Conqueroo, Shiva's Head Band, and the 13th Floor Elevators, Clay responded simply, "I believe in banjo."[20] By 1973, Clay was a symbol of Austin's idealized musical past with deep personal ties to the city of Austin and to the wide variety of Texan musical traditions. As such, he was positioned to serve as the conscience of the Austin music scene, both actively and symbolically reminding participants of the core values that had come to define authentic musical expression there. In the introduction to the 1973 interview in *The Rag*, the author remarked that, although the progressive country music scene in Austin was flourishing, many of its most prominent participants were only superficially connected to it, lived elsewhere, and were, as a result, ignorant of even the city's most recent musical past (which Clay embodied):

> With all the Michael Murphy's [*sic*], Marc Benno's [*sic*], Leon Russell's [*sic*], various recording studios, etc., etc., zeroing in on Austin (as the entire state of New York moves to Texas), we must recognize and remember the music that was already here. So we decided to get in touch with John Clay at his South Austin home. When we pulled up John was busy repairing his VW. He was quite amicable [*sic*] to our interruption.[21]

Furthermore, the anonymous author heard Clay's music as "a refreshing respite from the usual boogie-woogie scene. There's not a bit of slickness in his approach, he is totally hisself [*sic*]. What he lacks in hype is made up [for] in his original songs and blue stories."[22]

These framing paragraphs demonstrate that, for many musicians and scene participants of Clay's generation, progressive country may have been perceived as either another passing fad or a substantial threat to the sanctity and purity of local culture. The latter sentiment is made especially clear in the powerful rhetoric employed by the interviewer/editor of the article, who described non-Austinite musicians as "zeroing in on Austin" and characterized the influx of nonnatives as a postbellum Yankee invasion as "the entire state of New York moves to Texas." Moreover, the author's references to the "slickness" of progressive country music—an adjective that Murphey would have avoided when describing his music—may be read as a criticism of the perceived lack of authenticity of both the music and the musicians who performed it, as the rough edges that tied it to the folk music tradition were sanded off in favor of a more commercially viable musical style.

Appended to the interview is Clay's song "Drifting through the Seventies," a rambling ballad that recasts the cosmic cowboy's idealism as naïveté and challenges the participants in Austin's progressive country music scene to reject the mass-mediated image of the cosmic cowboy and to seek instead deeper interpersonal relationships.[23] The version published in *The Rag* is a strophic ballad whose fourteen stanzas are divided roughly into three sections: an expository passage that introduces the cosmic cowboy (stanzas 1–2), a meditation on the failures of the psychedelic generation (stanzas 3–7), and a critique of the cosmic cowboy image that predicts the ultimate failure of the scene and its lofty goals (stanzas 8–14).

From the outset of "Drifting through the Seventies," Clay argues that one cannot make a positive contribution to the community simply by attending the university there and participating in the local music scene. Rather, he remarks that such commitment was fleeting, as the vast majority of the students would eventually graduate and move away, whereas the long-term residents of Austin (like Clay) would stay behind to improve the city. However, perhaps more important, Clay posits that the progressive country music scene allowed its participants to be even more detached from the surrounding community because it created an alternative, touristic space—complete with a soundtrack and drug culture—to shape the participants' University of Texas experience.[24] Furthermore, the scene participants are cast as children of privilege who were simply playing a role and were buying into a mass-mediated counterculture that focused on image and not on the improvement of the local community, unlike the musicians of Clay's generation, who had aligned their folksinging activities in Austin with pro–civil rights organizations such as the Student Nonviolent Coordinating Committee (SNCC) and Students for a Democratic Society (SDS).[25]

In the second section of "Drifting through the Seventies," Clay draws parallels between the psychedelic rock movement, which swept Austin in the late 1960s, and the progressive country music scene of the 1970s, suggesting that both were little more than passing phases with little significance beyond the immediate gratification of the scene participants. As the third stanza indicates, many young people in late 1960s' Austin believed that psychedelic music and drugs had the power to affect positive change in the world by facilitating personal exploration and creating strong social relationships. Yet, as Clay asks, "And where has Psychedelic America gone?" By Clay's estimation, the scene ultimately failed to achieve its goals because its participants destroyed their minds with drugs and were too eager to participate in the consumer counterculture. Pointing out that the posters and records that signified consumer participation in the psychedelic movement had disappeared from the marketplace, Clay suggests in the fourth and fifth stanzas that participants in Austin's psychedelic scene were, like the cosmic cowboys, too busy chasing mass-mediated images of the counterculture to make a positive difference in their community. By 1973, these symbols had been sold for quick cash to support the drug habits that the psychedelic generation had developed in the late 1960s. "That bright new day we thought was almost due," Clay observes in the sixth stanza, never arrived because "the lightshows all burned out." The middle stanzas of "Drifting through the Seventies," therefore, stood as a cynical warning to the participants in the progressive country music scene that, no matter how much positive energy might surround a local music scene, its importance will inevitably diminish as the core participants age, mature, and move on to other entertainment outlets.

After presenting a particularly bleak outlook on the power of local music scenes to enact social change in the second section of "Drifting through the Seventies," the final six stanzas unleash a direct attack on the cosmic cowboy's idealism and authenticity. In the eighth stanza, Clay's speaker exclaims that he wants to be a "plastic plowboy," punning the name of the cosmic cowboy and drawing attention to his artificiality. This criticism could have been, and often was, leveled on nearly all aspects of the cosmic cowboy, ranging from the commercial origins of his preferred types of music to the strange combination of hippie and cowboy imagery he drew upon in his attire and attitudes. Furthermore, as the ninth stanza indicates, part of the cosmic cowboy's perceived artificiality was the result of his own socioeconomic status: "The city's not my home, it's the suburbs that I'm from/But the country's where I wanna spend my time." For Clay, therefore, the cosmic cowboy/plastic plowboy's social standing allowed him to colonize rural spaces without concern for the consequences. That is, whereas the full-time rural dwellers he emulated often led lives that were less glamorous than his pastoral language might suggest, the cosmic cowboy/plastic plowboy could always afford to move home. As the speaker observes in an offhand comment that concludes the song, he needs only to "be a plastic plowboy/Till something better comes around."

The plastic plowboy's half-hearted commitment to the pastoral experience and his naïveté begin to come into clearer focus in the tenth and eleventh stanzas of "Drifting through the Seventies." Unlike Murphey's character, Clay's plastic plowboy is quickly confronted with a number of almost insurmountable challenges, posing a more realistic alternative to the idealized rural landscape described in "Cosmic Cowboy."[26] Although he moves to the country with hopes of having a barnyard full of animals, his tenacity and idealism are soon challenged as conditions worsen in the winter, food becomes scarce, and he is forced to eat all their pets to survive. These challenges turn out to be much too difficult for Clay's plastic plowboy, who grows weary of the hard work needed to cultivate a crop, the instability of food supplies, and the absence of a regular source of marijuana. In fact, as the speaker realizes the possibility that the goat could eat his stash of marijuana, he contemplates aloud, "How can you live out in the country/If you always have to see it when you're down?" While Clay's portrait may appear to be overly cynical, many people who, like the cosmic cowboy/plastic plowboy, left middle-class suburban neighborhoods for the country, found the daily challenges of rural life to be too difficult and eventually returned to their suburban environments. They had decided that "if things get too hard, I will know it's gone too far/And I'll be a plastic plowboy back in town."[27]

"Drifting through the Seventies" was written and published at precisely the moment that the participants in Austin's progressive country music scene were the most optimistic: The first progressive country recordings were being made, the scene was starting to garner national attention, and outside investments were helping to provide much-needed capital for the scene's ambitious growth. Clay's critique of the cosmic cowboy occurred, therefore, when the scene's idealism was most pronounced, and, as a consequence, Clay and the editors of *The Rag* likely saw the piece's polemical tone as a much-needed corrective to the overzealousness of the cosmic cowboys. "Drifting through the Seventies" is a particularly instructive song, therefore, as it provides insight into the ways that authenticity is constructed within music scenes. As a long-time resident of Austin and a founding member of the city's earliest countercultural musical community, Clay was profoundly invested in the scene and clearly felt compelled to speak on behalf of the city's older musicians and audiences. While songs such as "Drifting through the Seventies" can be interpreted as sage advice for the city's perpetually young population, they also betray a power struggle between the folk music practitioners who flourished in Austin during the early 1960s and the participants in the progressive country music scene. The song implies that Clay felt marginalized by the latter setting. He, therefore, struck a defensive pose against the perceived inauthenticity of the progressive country music scene and its participants in order to secure his position as a paragon of authenticity and honesty. Moreover, progressive country's economic success made it an easy target for musicians who, like Clay, wished to dismiss the latest musical trend as a mass-mediated product of the culture industry. Yet, as the rhetoric of the progressive country movement demonstrates, the scene participants were interested in many of the same things that Clay was, including more direct interpersonal communication, musical experiences that exhibited clear ties to Texan traditions, and ways to be socially and politically active through music. Furthermore, Clay's own musical experiences in Austin were built upon a similar idealism and were equally mediated by the commercial music industry. His invective is all the more interesting, therefore, when this common ground is taken into consideration, as it clearly demonstrates that his perspective on the authenticity of the progressive country music scene was informed by his own changing position within it and reflects the dynamics of change within the Austin music scene.

Clay was not alone in his critique of the image of the cosmic cowboy and the idealism of progressive country music. Rather, the themes that he outlined in "Drifting through the Seventies" were regularly invoked to challenge both the dominance of the city's progressive country music scene and the authenticity of its participants. One such example was a speech titled "The New Hicks: Mellow, Righteous, Sincere," written by University of Texas English professor Joe Kruppa and delivered at the campus's student union sometime in the early 1970s.[28] The undated typescript comprises one hundred numbered sentences offering not a laundry list of charges against the New Hicks but a fairly unified and cohesive invective that sought to explain why the participants in the progressive country music scene were "full of crap."[29] Kruppa offered three examples to support his contention: (1) the nostalgia and anachronism of the cosmic cowboy image, (2) the contradictions inherent in a largely middle-class youth population adopting a working-class musical style as their anthem, and (3) the pseudoreligious aspects of cosmic cowboy gatherings. Kruppa suggested, therefore, that the progressive country music scene was merely a simulation of more authentic and less mediated musical and cultural experiences. As such, he searched for reasons that the scene participants might want to contribute to something that had, by his estimation, so little value.

Like Clay, Kruppa proposed that progressive country fans adopted western and countercultural imagery without reflecting upon the consequences or responsibilities that accompanied them. He argued that the progressive country music scene was little more than "an exercise in nostalgia," as demonstrated by the cosmic cowboy's rhetoric and imagery. First, the cosmic cowboy's adoption of mass-mediated cowboy imagery, which derived from late nineteenth-century cowboy ballads, dime novels, and mid-twentieth-century movie cowboys, seemed to situate the scene participants' activities in the same idealized but unrealistic western spaces that Gene Autry and Roy Rogers inhabited.[30] By embracing rural modes of dress and espousing an appreciation of rural musical styles, these New Hicks appeared to Kruppa to be unaware of—or perhaps worse yet, to be ignoring—the complex racial, socioeconomic, and gender issues that accompanied the adoption of such imagery. Kruppa argued that the privileged New Hicks could adopt the imagery of rural Texas to articulate a countercultural perspective, while the rural working-class population from which they borrowed was born into that culture and often had little opportunity to escape it. Kruppa also worried that the participants in the progressive country music scene were fetishizing rural life without acknowledging the racism, misogyny, and xenophobia that had characterized many rural reactions to the ongoing civil rights struggles in Texas and the bitter debate over the Vietnam War. As such, Kruppa challenged the cosmic cowboys to be more reflective and to think critically about the implications of their imagery and rhetoric, which their privileged positions allowed them to do. As he observed, "New Hicks should not be confused with Rednecks who don't know any better. New Hicks would *like* to be Rednecks who don't know any better, but they're having a hard time pulling it off."[31]

More disturbing to Kruppa than the cosmic cowboys' uncritical adoption of rural imagery was what he saw as their nostalgia for the countercultural idealism of the previous decade. Kruppa, who, like Clay, was himself a product of the cultural revolutions of the late 1960s, remarked that "The New Hicks have nothing to do with the Counter-Culture, which is a nostalgic relic anyway."[32] Later Kruppa posed several rhetorical questions about the counterculture's ability to create positive change in the world, opining that, just as the previous generation of Austin's musicians had failed to create a music-centered utopia, so, too, would the progressive country music scene fall short: "What is the likely outcome of a state of mind like that of the New Hicks? What are its possible social and political consequences? What does it suggest about the *American Experience*?"[33] Mocking the sincerity and zeal of many of the scene participants, Kruppa presented a satirical response, complete with pseudoscholarly citations, that suggested that the progressive country music scene was little more than an excuse for socioeconomically privileged young people to enjoy themselves under what he believed was the guise of countercultural change: "'The New Hicks represent a revolt against a mechanized, technological society and a return to values in the American Experience. . . . They are questing for a new genuineness in human relationships, a new simplicity and sincerity in forms of expression, a mellow and righteous mode of living' (from *The New Hicks*, ed. by Corn & Bull)."[34]

Kruppa found evidence of the superficiality of the progressive country music scene in what he interpreted as religious rhetoric, vocabulary, and attitudes exhibited by the scene participants in their daily lives. He compared the scene's live music venues to temples where "the New Hicks gather together in little clumps for ceremonial observances. These observances are often punctuated with utterances like 'far out,' 'down home,' 'mellow,' and 'righteous.'" Kruppa demonstrated particular concern about the New Hicks' use of the word "righteous," which under normal circumstances describes something that is morally correct. In the common parlance of Austin, however, "righteous" was used to describe anything that was deemed to be outstanding, regardless of its moral standing. Yet Kruppa, a professor of English, believed that the cosmic cowboys' regular use of the term had great significance. He interpreted it as a sign that the participants in the progressive country scene were trying to justify the efforts morally and to insist that their activities had social significance beyond the fleeting enjoyment of live music, beer, and marijuana. Kruppa asked: "Do today's New Hicks still *need* righteousness? Obviously. Otherwise what would they be doing repeating that word over and over again?"[35]

Kruppa found the ultimate proof of the progressive country music scene's ignorance and irrelevance in their musical choices. Progressive country music brought together two elements that were equally suspect among the Texan counterculture of the 1960s: country music, which embodied conservative (and, by implication, racist) values, and commercialized popular music, which was to be distrusted because of its ties to industry. In the longest section devoted to any one line of reasoning (twelve sentences), he observed:

> The New Hicks have managed to create a new musical genre: Marijuana Muzak. This Muzak is usually created by "solo" artists who have broken away from groups in order to realize their "creative potential." Any number of ex-Byrds and ex-[Flying] Burritos have created splendid examples of the New Muzak. Austin is trembling on the verge of becoming a center for the New Muzak. Country and Western Music lends itself beautifully to the creation of the New Muzak. The New Hicks have even made a creative breakthrough: *Progressive* Country Music. Poco. Maybe they'll soon discover Third-Stream Country Music! Classical Country Music! Jazz Country! I'm only kidding, of course. Just kidding.[36]

Yet again, Kruppa proves to have been an astute observer of the progressive country music movement in Austin, noting the influence of

Californian country-rock music on local music and the anti-industrial rhetoric of many of Austin's singer-songwriters, who, by their own estimation, came to Austin in search of a space in which they could explore their own identities and enjoy greater creative freedom. Moreover, Kruppa implied that, no matter how much Austin's concertgoers and record buyers might wish otherwise, country music could never be "progressive" because of its status as a signifier of the conservative and reactionary opposition to the counterculture. By positing further developments in Austin's country music almost to the point of absurdity ("Third-Stream," "Classical," and "Jazz" country), Kruppa also hinted at his own disrespect for country music and the redneck culture that created it by suggesting that, because of its origins in a "regressive" culture, country music could never be "progressive."

By April 1974, Michael Murphey was beginning to agree with the criticisms levied by Clay and Kruppa, shocking many participants in the scene by disavowing the idealism and romanticism that so many listeners had heard in "Cosmic Cowboy" and "Alleys of Austin." Seven months after the publication of "Drifting through the Seventies," Murphey, in an interview with *Rolling Stone*'s Chet Flippo, noted that he was disappointed with the results of his work and observed that "Cosmic Cowboy" was "meant . . . as satire. People here [in Austin] took it seriously[,] and now we've got a bunch of long-haired rednecks running around."[37] Similarly, in a second interview with Flippo for *Texas Parade*, Murphey remarked that he had "never intended that it ["Cosmic Cowboy"] be taken seriously. . . . Somehow that phrase caught on and people said, yeah, that's what we are and they started wearing boots and huge cowboy hats. It went too far."[38] By Murphey's estimation, therefore, progressive country fans had fundamentally misinterpreted the message of "Cosmic Cowboy," hearing the song not as a satire of the emerging "back to the land" movement but instead as a literal celebration of Austin, Texas, and the American West.

Less than a year after "Cosmic Cowboy" premiered before an enthusiastic Armadillo crowd, the ironic distance Murphey had placed between himself and the primary interpretation of his local hit may have seemed suspicious to many fans and musicians in Austin. Yet his proposed ironic intentions with "Cosmic Cowboy" and his attempts to distance himself from the flourishing cosmic cowboy generation make little sense when his contemporaneous local political activities are taken into account. In early 1974, Murphey was on a whirlwind publicity tour to establish distance between himself and his most popular song, positing that the influx of newcomers to Austin had misinterpreted the romanticized portraits of unspoiled Texan spaces in "Cosmic Cowboy." For instance, Murphey's 1974 performance of "Cosmic Cowboy" at Willie Nelson's 4th of July Picnic in College Station, Texas, stands out as a vocal criticism of the increased rate of development that was taking place in Austin, as well as in Dallas, Fort Worth, San Antonio, and Houston. Furthermore, he commented in a March 22, 1974, article in *The Daily Texan* that the local residents needed to fight the city of Austin's attempts to implement the "Austin Tomorrow" initiative, a citywide rezoning project that was intended to alleviate the pressures of new growth in the city: "I get the feeling right now that Austin is like a small town that's about two years away from becoming a city. I admit I shared in starting up the mystique, so now when I go around the country[,] I don't play up the scene. . . . I'd like to get people to work together to change the zoning ordinances in Austin so realtors cannot subdivide the land around Lake Travis into lots and destroy the woods for apartment complexes."[39] Murphey's desire to prevent widespread development in Austin was likely motivated by his concern for the sanctity of his own privacy; he resided near Lake Travis. Coupled with the introduction of cocaine to the scene around that time, these developments troubled Murphey, who continued to seek ways to effect positive change in his community.[40] Sensing an imminent collapse of the city and the local music scene, Murphey moved to Colorado in 1974 to avoid competition with other musicians and to establish a ranch for special-needs children with his girlfriend.[41] Thus, just like the plastic plowboy of John Clay's "Drifting through the Seventies," Murphey left Austin when the pressures of daily existence as one of the figureheads of the city's music scene grew to be too much to handle. Ironically, Murphey's idyllic depiction of Austin played a central role in exacerbating the destruction of the city's tranquility and led him to flee from the very place to which he had initially escaped.

At the core of these critiques is the issue of preservation. The participants in the countercultural movements of the 1960s, who arguably paved the way for the rise of the progressive country music scene in the 1970s, wished to preserve both the memory of their efforts and the antiestablishment, grassroots nature of their musical and social activism. For them, the cosmic cowboy represented an ersatz counterculture that was built around fashion, not values. They called upon the scene participants, therefore, to use their collective cultural capital to effect positive social change rather than to enjoy themselves self-indulgently. On the other hand, the musicians who returned to Texas in order to escape the competition of Los Angeles, New York, and Nashville in the early years of the progressive country movement found that their own creation encouraged too many people to come to Austin, changing it from a laid-back small town into a booming metropolis with national influence. These transformations threatened the close-knit communities that many musicians had formed upon arriving in Austin as competition for work and cultural capital became more intense. All of these commentaries about the cosmic cowboy point to a specific moment in the history of Austin that represented the same idyllic space that the cosmic cowboy dreamed of, one in which everyone worked together for the common good in the privacy of a small community. As the critiques here demonstrate, many observers felt that space was threatened by mass mediation, the commodification of the counterculture, and the influx of socioeconomically privileged scene participants. For many of the participants in the progressive country music scene, however, this space was endangered not by their activities but by the very people who would "gather 'round/and marvel at [his] . . . little baby's health."

"Up against the Wall, Redneck Mother"

Cosmic Cowboys and Cultural Conflict in Rural Texas

WHILE MUCH OF the external criticism of the progressive country music scene averred that the cosmic cowboy image encouraged people to adopt a self-indulgent, mass-mediated, and fashionable lifestyle that would ultimately fail to achieve its lofty goal of creating a creative, egalitarian, and socially conscious community, criticism of the cosmic cowboy's idealism also arose from within the scene itself. However, unlike those observers who looked at the progressive country music scene from the margins, insiders questioned the feasibility of escaping to a rural idyll when the people who inhabited them—predominantly conservative, white, working-class Texans—were inhospitable and even violent toward the long-haired young men that composed the core of progressive country music fans. Although commentators such as journalist Jan Reid publicly celebrated the scene's ability to bring hippies and rednecks together, such claims could be made only of Austin itself, not the surrounding rural communities or, in fact, many working-class country dance halls in Austin.[1] The cosmic cowboys may have created social spaces that encouraged cross-cultural interactions in places like the Armadillo World Headquarters, but once they ventured into the rural areas around Austin, they encountered people who were highly suspicious of their attire, drug use, and liberal political attitudes. These white working-class Texans generally viewed the cosmic cowboy's image and attitude as anathema in the wake of the countercultural upheavals of the late 1960s. The cosmic cowboys faced public ridicule, harassment, and even physical violence in these encounters, much as hippies had since the 1960s.[2] As a result, many of the scene participants harbored their own distrust and fears of rural, working-class, white Texans even as they celebrated their musical culture in Austin. Several songwriters associated with the progressive country music scene responded to these anxieties by caricaturing—and, consequently, dehumanizing and disarming—their rural detractors in song. Building upon the model of the jingoistic, hippie-hating speaker in Merle Haggard and Roy Edward Burris's 1969 hit, "Okie from Muskogee," these musicalized "rednecks," "cedar choppers," "goat ropers," and "cowboys" were characterized as brutish, ignorant, and racist, acting as a foil for the cosmic cowboy generation's naïveté, which critiqued the progressive country movement while also challenging the values of its detractors.

Since its release, fans and critics of country music alike have debated Haggard's intentions in writing "Okie from Muskogee."[3] The son of working-class Dust Bowl migrants who settled in Bakersfield, California, Haggard honed his musical skills in the region's many large dance halls, playing bass for Wynn Stewart, Buck Owens, and others. After signing with Capitol Records in 1965, Haggard established a link to the legacy of fellow Dust Bowl migrant Woody Guthrie, becoming immensely popular among some pockets of folk music enthusiasts with songs such as "Mama Tried," which chronicles a convict's criminal path and the unceasing love of his mother, and "Sing Me Back Home," which recalls the last request of a condemned convict.[4] However, Haggard's cultural capital among the liberal, folksinging crowd was spent following the release of "Okie from Muskogee," a song that depicts a conservative, middle-American man's perspective on the wrongdoings of late 1960s' counterculture. Adherents to the all-white populist political movements of the Silent Majority and high-ranking officials in the Republican Party alike rapidly embraced the song, propelling it to the number one position on the *Billboard* country charts.[5] Although Haggard has often claimed in interviews that "Okie from Muskogee" was intended as a satire of conservative America that was tossed off as a bit of comic relief, the song's message encapsulated working-class attitudes toward the hippie counterculture's liberal politics and galvanized mainstream American opposition to the counterculture of the late 1960s.[6] Like Murphey's "Cosmic Cowboy," therefore, the reception of "Okie from Muskogee" left little room for irony, accepting instead a literal interpretation of the song.

Regardless of the intended meaning of "Okie from Muskogee," the song's speaker suggests that mainstream Americans and the hippie counterculture were polar opposites.[7] The Okie speaker obliquely criticizes the counterculture by describing the residents of Muskogee as its antithesis. In the first verse, for instance, the speaker explains that drugs and rebellion are not acceptable in Muskogee. Haggard's Okie is particularly critical of what he perceives to be the self-indulgence of the hippie counterculture: Hippies consumed drugs, partook of free love, and, through their public resistance to selective service, refused to fight for the safety and security of their country. Conversely, the Okie proclaims in the chorus that he is proud of his heritage and enjoys simple pleasures such as drinking moonshine and "pitchin' woo," which, when done in moderation, satisfy his entertainment needs.[8]

While Haggard's juxtaposition of urban and small-town values in "Okie from Muskogee" appealed to his conservative listeners (as evidenced by its four weeks at the top of the *Billboard* country charts) and the dozens of cover versions released in the years immediately following its release, liberal commentators, including academics, journalists, and musicians like those in Austin, were much less receptive. The most common critical response to "Okie" was informed by the ongoing politics of the civil rights conflicts in the American South and West. In the late 1960s and early 1970s, Nashville's country music establishment allied itself with the Republican Party and with ardent segregationist George Wallace,[9] while the descendents of Okie migrants developed a grassroots conservative revolution that effectively segregated Southern California.[10] Sociologist Jens Lund observed in 1972, for instance, that songs like "Okie from Muskogee" underscored the tensions between the cultures associated with mainstream country music and the counterculture: "The efforts of the peace marchers must have inflamed the ire of a number of country songwriters, because many of the Vietnam War songs refer to the demonstrators, and in such terms as 'cowards,' 'bums,' 'beatniks,' 'traitors,' and 'scum.' "[11] Lund concluded that these stereotypes extended throughout the entire corpus of country music because the people who created and consumed it were low-class, uneducated racists:

> In the United States, the rural and lower classes have traditionally been hotbeds of conservatism and reaction. Their music, both folk and

commercial, has consistently reflected such themes. When not overtly expressed . . . these traits have been manifested in the vocal and instrumental styles of their musical performance. Indeed, country music's distinctive "sound" reflects its conservative and discriminatory make-up, even when a given song has no overt political or religious message.[12]

Furthermore, sociologists Paul DiMaggio, Richard A. Peterson, and Jack Esco Jr. contended that, while such an interpretation of country music required a dismissal of more socially progressive songs by some of the same artists, songs such as "Okie from Muskogee" wreaked untold havoc on country music by leading "popular commentators to see all country music as right-wing know-nothingness."[13]

Perceptions of country music drawn from outside observation, therefore, denied country artists a satirical voice and resulted in the widespread caricature of rural dwellers, conservatives, and Southerners in progressive country music. The caricature of the conservative, reactionary Southerner proved to be a perfect foil for Austin's cosmic cowboys as they ventured into the real rural spaces of Texas to realize their romanticized visions of preindustrial society. The cosmic cowboys' idealistic imaginings were often free of social conflict and focused on personal liberation, but when they occasionally ventured outside of Austin to hear country music in rural dance halls, they encountered people who more closely resembled the Okie than the cosmic cowboy. Many rural Texans were, like Haggard's Okie, distrustful of the cosmic cowboys for a number of reasons, not the least of which were their shaggy appearance, their liberal political views, and their middle-class upbringing. While most encounters between the real "cedar choppers" or "rednecks" and Austin's youths resulted in nothing more than mere social discomfort, other occasions proved violent as native rural dwellers challenged the legitimacy of the cosmic cowboys' presence in the rural social space of the honky-tonk. Many of the participants in Austin's progressive country scene, in their search for authentic rural experiences and country music, thus encountered firsthand the stereotypes defined in "Okie from Muskogee" and "The Fighting Side of Me."

In 1972, Ray Wylie Hubbard, a Dallas native and long-time participant in the Austin music scene, penned the first antiredneck song, "Up against the Wall, Redneck Mother." He purportedly wrote the song in response to an incident that occurred when he purchased beer at the D-Bar-D Bar in Red River, New Mexico, in which an older woman sitting at the bar criticized Hubbard's long hair and challenged his patriotism. Upon returning to his home, which he shared with bassist Bob Livingston, he composed the first verse of "Up against the Wall, Redneck Mother" and a rousing acrostic of the word "mother," which concludes the song, in response to the "redneck mother" at the bar. The song's second verse, Hubbard claims, was composed over the telephone during a break in the recording session for Jerry Jeff Walker's ¡Viva Terlingua! for which Livingston was the bassist.[14]

The song's two verses caricature the redneck by building on the imagery of Haggard's "Okie." Hubbard's redneck "was born in Oklahoma," invoking Haggard's model directly in the very first line of the song. His decision to grant this line such structural significance represents a very clear attempt to tie the redneck to the Okie. Moreover, Hubbard grants the redneck the same type of sensitivity that the Okie grants "the hippies out in San Francisco," describing only the most superficial aspects of his character. His wife has an absurdly long name ("Betty Lou Thelma Liz"), and he drinks cheap beer and cheap liquor, drives a fifteen-year-old pickup truck (probably out of necessity, not choice), and is a self-described "goat roper" who spends his free time in a honky-tonk. Hubbard's use of stereotypes functions to reduce the redneck's humanity and to underscore the cultural distance between the outside observer and the threatening monster who is "kickin' hippies' asses and raisin' hell." As such, "Up against the Wall, Redneck Mother" in some ways represents the confrontation of stereotypes that must have characterized many initial meetings between cosmic cowboys and rural Texans.

This cultural distance is further accentuated in the chorus, in which it is clear that the speaker is not in the immediate presence of the redneck but is instead recounting his encounter to someone else in the safety of his own community.[15] This physical distance allows the speaker to exaggerate the redneck stereotype and to perform a critique of the redneck that would have been dangerous to perform in person. Because of the physical and cultural distance between the speaker and his subject, performances of the song took on an almost carnivalesque character as the cosmic cowboys challenged the redneck's hegemony from a safe space. In most performances of "Up against the Wall, Redneck Mother," including Jerry Jeff Walker's initial 1973 recording and live performances by Willie Nelson guitarist Jody Payne, the chorus becomes a participatory free-for-all, in which the audience and sidemen alike taunt the redneck and the redneck's mother.[16] At the end of the chorus's second line, which comments sarcastically that the mothers have "raised their sons so well," everyone repeats "so well" at least three times in order to drive the criticism home; Willie Nelson's band often traded the final "so well" for "so what?," alluding to the futility of any efforts the mother might have made to groom her son into a well-mannered young man. Furthermore, some live performances also added a participatory response to the chorus's first line, adding the words "mean motherfucker" to suggest that the mother—like the one that Hubbard encountered at the D-Bar-D Bar—is just as ignorant and mean spirited as her son.[17] It would have been imprudent for someone like Hubbard or any of his cosmic cowboy contemporaries to express such sentiments in a rural honky-tonk as it would have most certainly led to a physical altercation. Rather, as cultural critic Barbara Ching has theorized, such commentaries typically indicate the physical and cultural distance between the speaker and the object of his critique.[18]

The song's narrative climax occurs in its conclusion, an acrostic of the word "mother" that satirizes the sentiments of innumerable Mother's Day greeting cards and parodies Theodore F. Morse and Howard Johnson's 1915 sentimental composition, "M-O-T-H-E-R (A Word That Means the World to Me)."[19] Performed by most interpreters with a marked hillbilly accent, replete with excessively imprecise pitch and overly exaggerated pronunciations, the acrostic originated as an improvisatory component of the song, as Hubbard has recalled, as each performance yielded a different set of items.[20] In Walker's recording, the items signified by each letter of the word "mother" are limited to clear symbols of redneck stereotypes—mud flaps, oil for his hair, and Merle Haggard—but this performance is a much tamer and more marketable take on the acrostic than is found in other performances. In Payne's performances, references to the mud flaps, oil, and Haggard remained, but the letter "e" was often replaced with "enema," perhaps implying something that the redneck was perceived as needing. The acrostic represents, therefore, an extension of the taunting and torment of the redneck character that first emerged in the chorus, mocking the redneck's love for his mother by lampooning sentimental emotions. Thus, Hubbard's "Up against the Wall, Redneck Mother" may be read as resistant to the dominance of rural Texan and southwestern culture while still acknowledging the cosmic cowboy's marginality within that culture.

Hubbard and nearly all of the artists who performed "Up against the Wall, Redneck Mother" further underscored the song's caricature of the redneck by turning the sounds of the Texas honky-tonk against him. The honky-tonk style of Hank Williams, Ernest Tubb, Webb Pierce, and other similar artists from the 1940s and 1950s is characterized by a two-beat metric pulse and twanging, naturalized vocal deliveries. In performances of "Up against the Wall, Redneck Mother," these sounds are also caricatured as the bass and drums articulate a plodding two-beat pulse, the guitarists bend and slide into pitches, and the vocalists exaggerate the twang almost to a point of absurdity. Whereas the participatory vocals and instrumental arrangements of Murphey's and Clark's songs reflect the idealism of the cosmic cowboy, the exaggerated performances of Hubbard's song make the cultural division between hippies and rednecks abundantly clear. Furthermore, the song was often paired with "Okie from Muskogee" in live performances by progressive country musicians such as Willie Nelson, who featured bassist Dan Spears as the voice of the Okie, further amplifying the antipathy between the redneck and the cosmic cowboy.[21]

Whereas Hubbard's "Up against the Wall, Redneck Mother" pokes fun at the Okie stereotype from a distance, Kinky Friedman's 1975 composition "They Ain't Makin' Jews like Jesus Anymore" engages with him directly. Friedman, the only son of one of Austin's most prominent Jewish couples and leader of the band The Texas Jewboys, first broke into the progressive country scene with his 1973 Vanguard release *Sold American*, which introduced his sardonic wit in songs like his anti–women's liberation rant "Get Your Biscuits in the Oven and Your Buns in the Bed" and his light-hearted retelling of Charles Whitman's 1966 shooting spree from the University of Texas bell tower in "The Ballad of Charles Whitman."[22] Reviews of his debut album and the subsequent supporting tour often remarked on Friedman's tendency to exaggerate stereotypes to the point of absurdity. A *Variety* review of a 1973 performance at Max's Kansas City in New York City exclaimed, for instance, that, while his "delivery is tongue-in-cheek," Friedman "carries C&W images to illogical extremes."[23] As a Texan Jew living in a predominantly Anglo-Texan world, Friedman had been reared in an environment in which his worldview was always marginalized. By adopting the role of a country musician, however, he could critique Anglo-Texan hegemony from the inside, at once demonstrating reverence for the traditions of country music and ridiculing them. Moreover, Friedman's adopted identity (and that of his band, whose name was a pun of Bob Wills and the Texas Playboys) also created a distance between himself and middle-class Jewish culture that gave him the freedom to exact a relentless attack on the cultural and social politics he had experienced at home.[24]

As he explained in a 1973 interview with Chet Flippo, one of the primary reasons he felt compelled to challenge these cultures was his deep-seated discomfort with his own identity as a Texan Jew: "Texas Jews are nerds, basically. Texas people have an attachment to Texas, Jews have an attachment to Jewish shit, and both are as repellant as they can be to everyone else. I don't dig country folks, don't like hanging around the truck stop, but I don't feel at home with the Jews either."[25] Friedman observed further that a similar discomfort with his Jewish identity led many executives within the Nashville music industry to grant him expressive liberties that were not always afforded all emerging country artists: "What's funny is that the people in Nashville are taking us extremely seriously. You know, like a Charlie Pride thing: Jewish kid trying to break through. Southern people just don't know Jews; all they know is niggers. They regard Jews like Chinese: Give 'em enough rope and they'll start a rope factory."[26] Despite the freedom that the Nashville establishment granted Friedman, he observed in April 1975, on the eve of his eponymous ABC Records release, that Nashville's culture was no more comfortable for him than was Texan or Jewish culture: "I phased out of Nashville. . . . I realized *why* the other night watching the Country Music Association awards. I saw Johnny Rodriguez, the spic, Charlie Pride, the coon, so there was a place for me, a white Jew. But I didn't want to be their pet Jew, basically. I might have had a safe shot there but it would have been bad because it's not me, man, those aren't my people."[27] As a result, Friedman's marginality became a position of strength that permitted him to expose and satirize the prevailing stereotypes and sacred icons of Texan, Jewish, and hippie cultures alike while also claiming a home in each of these cultural spaces.

Such is the case in "They Ain't Makin' Jews like Jesus Anymore," a narrative in which the speaker (presumably Friedman himself) engages in a heated encounter with the Okie-redneck stereotype that, as in Hubbard's "Up against the Wall, Redneck Mother," ends in a fight in which the speaker prevails. However, whereas Hubbard uses the verses of "Up against the Wall" to recount the speaker's own biased perceptions of the redneck, Friedman permits the redneck to speak for himself, utilizing the verses to convey the dialogue that took place. The redneck conforms to much of the imagery already laid out in "Up against the Wall"; the speaker confronts "a redneck nerd in a bowlin' shirt/a'guzzlin' Lone Star Beer." When this redneck is permitted an opportunity to speak, though, his exaggerated ignorance and racism are made very clear. He instigates an argument with the protagonist (who is presumably Friedman himself): "They oughta send you back to Russia [pronounced "rue-sha"], boy, or New York City, one./You just wanna doodle a Christian girl, and you killed God's only son!" Unlike Hubbard's speaker, Friedman's does not slink away to criticize the redneck from a distance. Instead, he replies to the redneck's charges by inverting the redneck's anti-Semitism: "We Jews believe it was Santa Claus that killed Jesus Christ!" Shocked at the outsider's brazenness, the redneck inflicts what he believes to be the greatest insult, comparing the Jewish speaker to an African American: "'You know, you don't look Jewish,' he said, 'near as I can figure/I had you lamped for a slightly anemic, well-dressed country nigger.' "[28]

Within the context of a rural, all-white honky-tonk, therefore, the Jewish protagonist of "They Ain't Makin' Jews like Jesus Anymore" is not able to pass as Anglo-Texan and, as a result, is immediately marked as racially "other." Perhaps more important, he is situated with blacks at the bottom of the racial economy of central Texas. Thus, despite his attempts to assimilate into Anglo-Texan culture by taking on cowboy imagery and expressing an affinity for country music, the speaker is prevented from fully assimilating as a citizen of the Lone Star State. Moreover, the racial insults lead the protagonist to respond to the redneck in a manner characteristic of many working-class Anglo-Texan men, throwing fists and hurling the "ethnocentric racist" to the floor, demonstrating that Jews "don't turn the other cheek the way they done before" and that he can compete with the redneck on the redneck's own terms. As "that honky . . . hit the hardwood floor" of the honky-tonk, therefore, the speaker proved that, in spite of his middle-class Jewish background, he had indeed assimilated. By extension, the physical and intellectual triumph of the racial "other" successfully challenged the redneck's own Anglo-Texan superiority by rendering him impotent.

At the same time that he diffuses the redneck's power, Friedman also implicitly criticizes the cosmic cowboys for their naïve desire to enter the rural honky-tonk in the first place. By describing an actual verbal exchange between the redneck and the outsider, he suggests that, unlike the speaker in Hubbard's song, the outsider had transgressed significant social and physical boundaries. This reported speech represents what ethnomusicologist Aaron A. Fox has described as the tendency for country songs to utilize "direct discourse," which involves the representation of not only the syntax but also the timbre, accent, pitch, and rhythm of the original dialogue in order to capture the voice of the culture itself.[29] Direct discourse permitted Friedman to capture the immediacy of the conflict, something lacking in the romanticized songs of Murphey and Clark and in the resistant songs of Clay, Hubbard, and others. Perhaps more important, though, is the way that

Friedman's caricature of the redneck's speech facilitates the type of intensely personal criticism to which he was most attracted. In reporting the dialogue in a voice that exaggerates the timbre, rhythm, and accent of the redneck's voice, Friedman could attack the redneck's words and expose his contempt for everything the "ethnocentric racist" represented.

Friedman's "They Ain't Makin' Jews like Jesus Anymore" and Hubbard's "Up against the Wall, Redneck Mother" illustrate the conflict between rural Texans and cosmic cowboys by lyrically and musically lampooning the Okie character and Haggard's song. Gary P. Nunn's "London Homesick Blues" (1973), on the other hand, avoids caricature and presents a more sensitive analysis of the impact that the cultural conflict had on Texan culture. Nunn, the keyboardist for Walker's Lost Gonzo Band and formerly a member of Murphey's band, posits that the cosmic cowboy's progressive ideals were often misunderstood or ignored altogether because of his rural image. Furthermore, he suggests that the adoption of rural fashion and music might lead liberal non-Texan observers to accidentally mistake the cosmic cowboys for Okies.[30] Written in March 1973 while Nunn was on a trip to London with Michael Murphey, "London Homesick Blues" takes the form of a letter home to Austin, written by a young Texan tourist in London who is surprised by British inhospitability.[31] In the first verse, he observes that the people he encounters in London lack two integral cowboy traits: charity toward one's neighbor and a colorful sense of humor. Londoners immediately fail to meet the standards of the cowboy code of ethics, which demands that, among other things, every man be socially responsible and able to demonstrate his masculinity through the exchange of bawdy jokes and the telling of tall tales. It is noteworthy, therefore, that the Texan speaker is ready to leave London by the end of the first verse to return home to a more congenial and humane setting "just as fast as [he] can."

In the last verse of "London Homesick Blues," the speaker becomes aware that his discomfort is not solely the result of his distaste for British culture and his homesickness. Rather, it is compounded by British misunderstanding of his Southern heritage. He relates that he has encountered people who comment: "You're from down South, and when you open your mouth, you always seem to put your foot there." While the meaning of this statement is obvious, Nunn highlights its condescending tone by referring directly to Haggard's "Okie from Muskogee." In the line preceding the British condemnation of his apparent rural background, the speaker relates that "[them] Limey

eyes, they were eyin' the prize some people call 'manly footwear.'"
This passage invokes the third verse of Haggard's song, in which the
speaker slyly criticizes hippie fashion by noting that, in Muskogee,
Oklahoma, "leather boots are still in style for manly footwear./Beads
and Roman sandals won't be seen." To his British counterparts, Nunn's
speaker is not a member of the countercultural vanguard. He is rather
the living embodiment of the Okie himself. He soon realizes, however,
that in "tak[ing the] chance" of donning his cowboy hat during a
sight-seeing trip, he immediately becomes an object of ridicule for
conservative values that he does not hold. Because the British see his
leather cowboy boots only as Haggard's "manly footwear," they believe
that the speaker is equally conservative and provincial. When he "opens
his mouth," therefore, he is destined "to put [his] foot there" because
he appears to be ignorant of or opposed to progressive social values.
The Londoners in Nunn's "London Homesick Blues" seem to have interpreted Haggard's Okie as a literal representation of conservative rural
and small-town values, and they use that exaggerated stereotype against
the Texan traveler. Additionally, they ignore subtle geographical dis-
tinctions that actually set the speaker apart from the Okie. The speaker
in Haggard's song is from Oklahoma, not Texas, and certainly not the
South, but the Londoners believe they are all the same. The speaker
senses this hostility and wishes to "go home [to] the Armadillo," the
home of Austin's cosmic cowboy, where both his Texanness and his
countercultural aspirations can be valued equally.

As Jeff Nightbyrd's 1975 essay in the *Austin Sun* warned, the
Londoners' conflation of cowboy boots and the Okie's attitudes was
a common one even among the scene participants. Titled "Cosmo
Cowboys: Too Much Cowboy and Not Enough Cosmic," Nightbyrd
commented upon the ease with which many participants in the
progressive country music scene displayed the attitudes and behav-
iors of their redneck counterparts. Like Clay and Kruppa, he
remarked that, because the cosmic cowboy was little more than an
image that could be obtained by "spend[ing] a couple hundred bucks
in mod shops," the scene participants who hailed from rural,
working-class Texan communities were not called upon to change
their attitudes:

> Any young dude can come in from Amarillo, grow moderately long
> hair under his cowboy hat, smoke a little grass, maybe wear a little
> simulated Indian jewelry and be a cosmic cowboy. It doesn't take much.
> Particularly it doesn't require any changes in attitude like being a hippie

in the sixties did. You don't have to know anything about the war, give a damn about race, tussle with psychedelics, or worry about male chauvinism.[32]

Even the well-intentioned scene participants were at risk of acting like rednecks because, as Nightbyrd asserted, all whites from rural and small-town Texas carried the biases of their conservative upbringing with them, and "being hip in Austin requires too many changes" in their attitudes.[33] In fact, Nightbyrd remarked, the cosmic cowboys often behaved worse than their redneck counterparts, especially in their relationships with women. He observed that, while women were central to the culture of "the rodeo crowd," women in the progressive country music scene were "relegated to spectators or hangers on. They can buy records or hang out with their cool dude. But what is their position? Basically on their back. That's what they're good for, and maybe a little cooking."[34] Playing the part of a cowboy, it seems, created an ironic stance toward the redneck that allowed and even encouraged the largely middle-class participants in Austin's progressive country music scene to behave like the redneck caricatures depicted in Friedman's and Hubbard's songs and, as a consequence, to act in ways that ran counter to the stated social and political goals of the leaders of the scene.

At the center of these staged conflicts between cosmic cowboys and their redneck counterparts was a dispute over the ownership of the cowboy as a symbol and the right to define the image and its meaning. In a 1974 interview, for instance, Armadillo World Headquarters co-owner Eddie Wilson remarked that the participants in Austin's progressive country music scene had transformed the functional hats, boots, and denim of their rural Texan forebears into a fashion that reclaimed their Texan heritage and that commented upon the modernity of their contemporary Texan challengers: "What we've got in Austin now is a bunch of young, longhaired [shit]kickers that look a whole lot more like our grandfathers than the kickers of the last generation ever thought."[35] However, as Archie Green has astutely observed, "From our national beginning, 'cowboy' has functioned to span polar meaning," and, during the 1970s, the term signified "redneck audience and isolated artist, straight and freak, hunter and hunted."[36] Songs such as "They Ain't Makin' Jews like Jesus Anymore" demonstrate and lay bare the dangerous effects of this polarity by depicting real situations in which the prejudices of the redneck and the cosmic cowboy were revealed publicly and privately. While the principle target of these songs was clearly the rural, working-class white Texans in the songs' foregrounds, these compositions also subtly criticized the naïveté of many progressive country music fans who performed their socioeconomic privilege by attempting to colonize the working-class sanctuaries of the honky-tonk and the dance hall. As the scene participants claimed the right to be in these spaces, their redneck counterparts felt the need to defend them. Thus, much as John Clay attacked the cosmic cowboy's agricultural goals as unrealistic, so, too, did Friedman, Hubbard, and Nunn observe that unifying rhetoric does not, on its own, result in a unified community.

The dialogue that took place around the image of the cosmic cowboy demonstrates that musical compositions—and especially texted music—often play a key role in both responding to and acting as a catalyst for the public debate of important issues within music scenes. While fashion, visual art, and rhetoric all work in conjunction with music to shape the imagery and values expressed by the scene as a whole, music may in fact be the most important site for such discussions. First, the ease with which musical compositions can be repeated in live performances, radio broadcasts, and the private consumption of recordings allows for the nearly constant replication of the ideas expressed therein. Such is the case even when the musicians working in a scene attempt to distance themselves from their creations, as Michael Murphey's later repudiation of the cosmic cowboy indicates. Second, when music making occurs within the context of regional, national, or global production and distribution networks, the potential power of individual compositions is increased exponentially. The vast majority of Austin's progressive country music musicians, especially those who promulgated the cosmic cowboy's image and escapist rhetoric, remained tied to national and international record labels. These labels used the industrial infrastructure to promote their roster of artists in advertisements, radio interviews, and support for radio stations and to shape the public image of Austin's music community. The resultant imbalance of power within the scene prompted those people who felt marginalized by the music industry to respond critically and vociferously to the hegemony of the emergent scene. Unlike rhetoric, fashion, and visual art, which often remain situated at the grassroots level, mass-mediated musical compositions can, therefore, exert a stronger influence on the overall dynamics of a music scene.

As the foregoing analysis demonstrates, perhaps the greatest power of individual musical compositions lies in their musicalization of the terms of debate. The harmonies, melodies, textures, timbres, rhythms, and performance practices employed in individual compositions are purposely and consciously brought to the piece because of their existing musical associations. As such, the musical meanings that are created must be examined within the contexts of both the music scene and the broader soundscape in order to reach a culturally informed understanding of the significance of musical sound.

¡Viva Terlingua!

Live Recordings and the Authenticity
of Progressive Country Music

ETWEEN 1972 AND 1974, several prominent Texas musicians who had moved to Los Angeles and San Francisco during the 1960s began flocking to Austin, where they believed they could escape the structured regimen of the mainstream recording industry and rediscover creative voices as songwriters and performers that they thought had been stifled by the demands of the industry. As Dallas-born singer-songwriter B. W. Stevenson explained in a 1974 interview in *The Gar*, the music industry required artists to create a saleable product on a consistent basis, an expectation that stifled the creativity of some musicians who resisted the industry work ethic and compelled many to relocate to Austin:

> If I'm in L.A. . . . . I'm always workin', even when I'm off. Before, it was having time to record. The first three albums were done in two weeks—two-week periods—and that's just not enough time. I like to have time off. . . . There's a lot of times I can't seem to get through to somebody, you know, that I want some time off. . . . I have to have time to write . . . or I'm just not happy. I gotta have time to myself.[1]

Although several of Austin's progressive country musicians traveled to Nashville, Los Angeles, Chicago, and New York to make studio recordings throughout the 1970s, they returned often to Austin because they believed that the city's club scene could offer them a greater sense of creative freedom and a stronger support system made up of friends, collaborators, and audiences who better understood their sense of regional culture.[2] As journalist Pete Axthelm observed in a 1976 *Newsweek* piece, "Austin was a refreshing place to be. . . . [I]t was bracing to wander through honky-tonks like the Soap Creek Saloon and Armadillo World Headquarters, where down-to-earth musicians swilled beer in longneck bottles and shared their songs and dreams."[3] The spontaneity and artist-audience interaction that were characteristic of live performance in Austin's progressive country venues were essential, therefore, to the musical aesthetics of progressive country music, which privileged the imperfections and idiosyncrasies of individual musicians over the precise playing and overt technological mediation heard in much of Nashville's country music. For many artists and fans alike, the shared belief that progressive country music was independent of the mediating forces of the national music industry helped to convince them that this homegrown musical genre was more artistically "pure" and more capable of serving as a legitimate means of communicating authentic local culture. Comparing the Austin scene to that of New York City, Jeff Nightbyrd, writing for the national music magazine *Crawdaddy*, argued in March 1973 that Austin musicians and audiences valued music as a form of expression, not as a commodity: "In New York you spend two-fifty to get into a joint where it doesn't take very long to figure out they're using music to sell alcohol. In Austin you pay a buck to get in and get off."[4] Despite such praise for the perceived authenticity of the progressive country music scene, though, some critics also pointed out the difficulty inherent in trying to capture on record the dynamic interplay between performers and fans at a live venue. For instance, Ed Ward remarked in an August 1975 *Rolling Stone* review of the Lost Gonzo Band's eponymous MCA Records album that "Most of the bands [in Austin] play drinkin'-and-dancin' music of the sort that doesn't easily transfer its excitement to vinyl."[5] Of course, the difficulty of recording live performances without compromising either sound quality or the experience of having actually been present was nothing new. Even the most successful efforts at capturing the essence of a live show on record fall short because they simply cannot duplicate the full sensory experience of being in an audience.

Perhaps the most important element of live performance that is missing from most studio recordings is the spontaneity enjoyed by the artists. During a typical recording session, musicians perform songs or parts of songs several times until they have the "best" version possible.

This often involves hours of arranging, performing, mixing, and mastering in order to correct the irregularities in tone, pitch, and execution that are common in live performances. Furthermore, studio albums usually require artists to minimize the kind of musical improvisations that are an important element of many live performances. Finally and perhaps the most problematic with regard to the improvisational spirit of the progressive country movement, studio recordings transform the spontaneity of a live performance into a fixed musical object, which can be repeated over and over ad infinitum.[6] Live albums, on the other hand, create a simulation of the concert event that allows consumers to feel as if they are part of an unmediated musical experience.[7] These recordings often preserve the artists' stage banter between songs, reveal musical mistakes that might be removed in a studio recording, and situate the sounds of the audience in the mix alongside the featured artists.[8] In addition to these sonic markers of "liveness," the packaging of live albums often encourages vicarious participation in the concert experience by including images from the performance, such as candid onstage photographs of the musicians and the audience, along with copies of concert advertisements, tickets, or other memorabilia.

Although live albums may allow listeners to perceive a direct connection with a spontaneous concert experience, this perception is, of course, encouraged by the musicians, producers, and engineers who construct the live aesthetic. Live albums, like all others, are highly mediated cultural products shaped by the marketing strategies of record companies, the postproduction manipulation of producers and engineers, and the musical choices of the artists. For members of Austin's progressive country music movement of the 1970s, live recordings provided an opportunity to reinforce local notions of musical authenticity—the value of musical collaboration, the importance of direct communication between musicians and their audiences, and, above all, the joy of the musical experience—while also commodifying the scene and distributing it for profit to a wider audience. Live albums offered the most passionate fans and the least committed audiences alike an opportunity to partake in the communal exchange that characterized Austin's live club scene, while also allowing the musicians to showcase their creativity, spontaneity, and prowess as performers. At the same time, the resulting emphasis on a homegrown or natural aesthetic allowed the scene participants to dismiss types of music that did not conform to this ideal. Consequently, the wide-ranging acceptance of the live aesthetic exerted a hegemonic force that marginalized many other forms of musical expression that coexisted with the progressive country scene (including disco, arena rock, and Nashville country music) and squelched competing voices. The resulting musical expressions of this aesthetic mapped the carefully constructed "natural" sounds of Austin's live music scene onto the pastoral visions described in songs like Murphey's "Cosmic Cowboy," in which the Anglo-Texan masculine hero could reclaim his culture and protect it from emasculation by an ever-encroaching modernity.[9]

Despite concerns that the essence of a live performance would be lost in the studio recording process, records did provide artists the potential for additional income and greater regional and national exposure. As a result, many Austin musicians did, in fact, attempt to capture the excitement of their live performances on record for local and national labels such as MCA, Capitol, ABC Probe, and Atlantic. In order to accommodate the limitations of the recording medium and to convey the excitement of the city's music scene, several progressive country musicians recorded "live" albums in Austin venues. Still others who hailed from outside of Texas, such as Commander Cody and His Lost Planet Airmen, Frank Zappa and Captain Beefheart, and Phil Woods, came to the city to record concert performances for national distribution.

One of the first Austin-based musicians to achieve substantial critical and commercial success using this model was Jerry Jeff Walker, a singer-songwriter from Oneonta, New York, who gained national popularity in late 1968 with the AM radio single "Mr. Bojangles."[10] Walker had always balked at the process of making records in professional studios, stating in a 1974 *Rolling Stone* interview that studios cause musicians to "lose all sense of time and space. Because no matter what time you go in there and close the door, it's twelve o'clock midnight. It always was. You don't know if you're making a rally or dying. It drives me fucking nuts. I don't like to play music in a dead space. I'm always saying, 'Okay, can I be excused now? Can I go out in the street and be with real people?' You have to play music over and over too much. It loses all spontaneity."[11] For Walker, the recording studio was a sterile space that eradicated his creative spark, and he was not the only musician who felt that way. He found that the process of recording an album can be an alienating experience as well, inasmuch as the environment of the recording studio typically eliminates the audience, physically separates musicians into individual sound booths to prevent signal bleed, and reduces the spontaneity of the performance in order to make the recording process more efficient and less expensive. In addition to these concerns, recording in a studio can be stressful because label executives often pressure artists to create a polished, radio-ready product while adhering to a strict budget that limits the amount of time one has to work in the studio. Rather than providing the immediate gratification of performing before a live audience, studio recording places a tremendous demand on the artist to produce a record whose primary purpose is to ensure commercial viability, not artistic creativity.[12]

Walker tried to cope with these challenges in the same way in which the Beatles, Brian Wilson, Jimi Hendrix, and others had in the second half of the 1960s. These artists viewed the recording studio not simply as a place to create the most polished and marketable music possible but also as a space within which they could experiment with new sounds and document their creative process. For Walker, the ability to record with familiar musicians in a less structured setting made the entire process more artistically rewarding. Because Walker intended to document the creative process and provide the engineer with enough material for an album, he believed he was able to reclaim the studio as a workspace by displacing the ultimate responsibility for the final product from himself to the creative minds employed by the studio.

Jerry Jeff Walker came to Austin principally to escape the pressures of major-label recording studios. He had been a fixture in Austin during the 1960s, when he toured throughout Texas, but he did not settle there permanently until the early 1970s. In 1971, Walker rented a cabin in Red River, New Mexico, a resort town in the Sangre de Cristo Mountains, which had become home to many young expatriate Texas songwriters. Walker came to Red River intending to write new material for his debut album with MCA Records. Shortly after arriving, he met bassist Bob Livingston, who had just left Michael Murphey's band to join Texas Fever, a Red River–based group featuring songwriter Ray Wylie Hubbard. The three musicians quickly became friends, and Walker shared several of his new compositions with them, including "Hill Country Rain," "Charlie Dunn," and "Old Beat-up Guitar." By 1972, Livingston had rejoined Murphey in Austin, and soon afterward Walker also moved to Austin and began searching for a band to accompany him on his upcoming MCA sessions. As Livingston recalled, "Jerry Jeff shows up in Austin . . . so I called him up, and I said, 'Jerry Jeff, you need to come and hang out with us. We're rehearsing with Murphey.' And he goes, 'Really?' So he shows up, and when he sticks his head in the door, it's like an instant band."[13] Livingston's recollections are complicated by the observations of Jan Reid, who remarks in *The Improbable Rise of Redneck Rock* that:

> the best band in town was known to work for the perfectionist Michael Murphey. Walker didn't steal the band; he just happened to be in the right place at the right time. At a rehearsal Murphey blew up over their general lack of discipline and with harsh words stormed out—just as Walker was coming in. In the course of an evening he gained the Lost Gonzo Band.[14]

Murphey, on the other hand, recalled to Jack Bernhardt in 1993 that the band left him following a surgical procedure to remove nodes from his vocal cords in 1972, a procedure that rendered his voice useless for more than six months and led to an extended period of depression.[15] However, the credits in the liner notes to Walker's first Austin album suggest a much more congenial split, noting Murphey's contributions on acoustic guitar.

Regardless, Walker recruited Murphey's band, which included pianist Gary P. Nunn, pedal steel guitarist Herb Steiner, fiddler Mary Egan, and guitarist Craig Hillis. Walker then contacted Michael Brovsky, his manager and producer in New York, to arrange a session at Odyssey Sound, the only recording studio in Austin capable of producing a record for a major label. Although it proved to be adequate, Odyssey Sound was not comparable to the high-tech commercial studios of Nashville, Los Angeles, or New York. As Walker later recounted in the album's liner notes, "We found a tape machine in the old Rapp Cleaner Building (Steve and Jay's Odyssey Sound), and anyone who wanted to contribute came by and picked or just listened."[16] Livingston recalls that the studio was primitive, but the unorthodox setting fostered a more collaborative atmosphere and minimized the pressure on the performers to produce a slick, polished recording:

> We go into this funky studio situation. They didn't even have a board. . . . It was on 6th Street in this old converted dry-cleaning house that was not even converted. All it was was burlap all over the wall, big ceilings, and a sixteen-track tape recorder sitting in the middle of the room. No board. A bunch of microphones. Everybody just plugged into this tape recorder. . . . It was so involved to listen to a playback [that] we never listened to anything back. We just would go in there, and [Jerry Jeff]'d start making sangria in a big tub around 7 o'clock, and everybody'd have several glasses of sangria, and then we'd start

recording at about 8:00 or 8:30. We would go until midnight or 2:00 in the morning and then listen to everything we'd done. It was real ragtag. Really funky.[17]

Mickey Raphael, one of two harmonica players who took part in these sessions, remembered that the musicians were:

set up pretty close together. I mean, pretty tight. It wasn't like every-body was spread out in different rooms with lots of separation. Everybody was set up where they could see each other, and there was, y'know, recording gear, a tape machine somewhere in the room, and we would just . . . It would be like a picking session. That's exactly what transpired. . . . They could've had an audience in there. It would have been great. It was just like sitting up on stage and playing.[18]

Unlike most professional studios, the setting of the Rapp Cleaner Building allowed Walker to believe that, unlike the recordings he had made in major-label studios, this recording project would be an organic outgrowth of the Austin music scene, a genuine reflection of the local music community's creative output, and, most important, an authentic representation of his artistic vision. By plugging directly into a tape recorder and performing "live," Walker and his collaborators were able to produce a record that could minimize the distance between themselves and their audiences.[19]

This album, which would be titled *Jerry Jeff Walker*, would not remain entirely free of the influence of a major studio, however. Walker finished making the record, which included Guy Clark's "L.A. Freeway," with engineer Tom Cacetta at Soundtek Studios in New York. Nevertheless, Walker would later reminisce about the spontaneous and organic nature of the recording process to describe the sessions, again reinforcing the idea that the progressive country music he was creating was more natural and, as a result, musically superior to the overtly mediated products of the commercial music industry. He men-tioned that he was inspired to enter the studio after spending a weekend at a farm near Hudson, New York, casually jamming with folk musi-cians David Bromberg and Larry Packer. Adding to the impromptu nature of the situation, Michael Murphey's band, with whom Walker had recorded at Odyssey Sound, happened to be in New York City playing at the Bitter End in Greenwich Village. The fact that the very same musicians who had been involved in the original "spontaneous" recording sessions in Austin were also able to participate in the New York tapings helped alleviate much of Walker's discomfort over being in the studio and allowed "new songs [to] start . . . flowing."[20]

Just as the genesis narrative that Walker constructed for the *Jerry Jeff Walker* album placed it within the context of an egalitarian jam session, the recordings themselves also provide ample evidence of the loose atmosphere of the recording sessions. The final mix, supervised by Steve Katz at New York's Electric Lady Studios, includes spontaneous banter, hand clapping, laughter, and shouts of approval by the musicians and others present. All of these additional, nonmusical utterances lend the recording a feeling of "liveness" that imbued the recording with a sense of the individual contributors' personalities and implied that the context of music making in Austin was entirely noncompetitive and completely natural. For example, at the beginning of the song "Her Good Lovin' Grace," Walker asks the band for "one of those intros," to which a musician laughingly replies, "One of *those* intros?" The slow, blues-inflected introduction that follows sounds like a false start, as the pianist, guitarist, and bassist struggle to find the downbeats. Likewise, the album's concluding song, "The Continuing Saga of the Classic Bummer, or Is This My Free One-way Bus Ticket to Cleveland?," also begins with a false start that is met with exuberant laughter, and the ensemble struggles to find a consistent tempo throughout the record.

In a typical studio session, the session's producer would work to correct such "mistakes" as those heard in the *Jerry Jeff Walker* album by asking the musicians play as many additional takes as necessary to render a polished final product. However, Walker indicates his distaste for the practice of creating multiple takes in the song's tag by saying, "Thank God you don't have to hear the take after this," suggesting that subsequent attempts would lack the verve and relative precision of the first take. The rather sloppy performance, exuberant and sometimes overmodulated vocals (which result in distortion of the vocal signals), and muddy mix all contribute to Walker's vision of a recording that captures an imperfect, unmediated, and, therefore, more organic musical performance. This reflected Walker's conscious desire to abandon the more polished and "professional" sound typically created in a conventional studio in favor of emphasizing the communal experience of musicians jamming in an informal, spontaneous setting. As a result, the *Jerry Jeff Walker* album helped reinforce the notion that Austin's progressive country music scene welcomed impromptu musical interaction and exchange through unmediated live performance, jam sessions, and creative collaboration.

Walker further explored the concept of "liveness" in his next album, *¡Viva Terlingua!*. The *¡Viva Terlingua!* sessions were held in August 1973 in Luckenbach, a hamlet located just outside of Fredericksburg in the Hill Country of central Texas. Walker had hinted in the liner notes to *Jerry Jeff Walker* that Luckenbach—a town "where they barely have electricity!"—would be the ideal place for his next recording.[21] Much like the 1972 Rapp Cleaner sessions, Walker's decision to record in an unconventional and, in fact, impractical location subverts the standard music industry conception of the recording studio as a "professional" space and redefines it as a social space. In the case of the Luckenbach sessions, this social space involved not only the musicians but also two of the town's unique and most colorful residents—John "Hondo" Crouch and his daughter, Cathy Morgan. Crouch and Morgan purchased the town in 1970 with hopes of transforming it from a ghost town into a hangout where people could come to relax and drink beer. Adopting the motto "Everybody's Somebody in Luckenbach," they transformed Luckenbach into an environment that purported to allow people from all backgrounds to meet, exchange ideas, and make new friends.[22] Walker began traveling to Luckenbach shortly after his arrival in Austin and found in Hondo Crouch a close friend who encouraged his creativity by providing a nurturing atmosphere in which to work. As Bob Livingston observed, Crouch "was like a surrogate father for [Jerry Jeff], and he was kind of a rambler and liar and dancer and guitar player . . . and the grand imagineer of Luckenbach. And Jerry Jeff really took to him."[23] Crouch's almost constant presence and his empathy for Walker's own ceaseless search for freedom was, it seems, a comfort to Walker and created a supportive environment in which he could compose and perform music freely. Moreover, as physical manifestations of a bygone era, both Crouch and Luckenbach represented a very tangible connection to the unique history and culture of Texas and were, as a result, embodiments of the Anglo-Texan masculine and pastoral ideals. As such, Luckenbach represented to Walker a space in which the pastoral visions of the cosmic cowboy and the natural musical aesthetics resulting from live performance could be fully realized.

While Walker's experimentation with unorthodox recording venues had proven to be relatively successful following the *Jerry Jeff Walker* sessions, Michael Maitland, the president of MCA, was understandably worried about the proposed Luckenbach sessions. The financial risks that the company might incur were substantial since it would need to supply a mobile recording unit that cost the label considerably more than a conventional studio. Another logistical and financial concern was that, rather than following the standard studio protocol in which musicians arrive with prearranged and rehearsed compositions in order to minimize costly delays, the material for the Luckenbach sessions was to be created, arranged, and performed for the first time right there on location. What this meant was that Walker and Brovsky were asking MCA not only to underwrite the costs of recording Walker's material but also to pay for the time it took to compose, arrange, and perform, something almost unheard of for an artist with as limited a track record as Walker. Further complicating matters was the fact that Luckenbach offered little in the way of amenities, including its undependable supply of electricity, which created significant technical problems for the recording engineers.[24]

Despite the extensive financial and technical risks inherent in the project, Brovsky managed to convince Maitland to finance the Luckenbach sessions. For nearly two weeks, Walker and the Lost Gonzo Band—Michael Murphey's former group—joined with several of Austin's leading session players to create ¡Viva Terlingua!. Much like his 1972 recording sessions at Odyssey Sound, Walker worked to create a casual environment in which individual musicians could rekindle old friendships, write songs, and contribute their musical talents to the larger project. Mickey Raphael, who had been touring with Willie Nelson and Waylon Jennings, remembered, "It was a good time for everybody to hang out because, if we all had different jobs with different people, we'd be out on the road separately. So, this kind of brought other musicians that were friends that didn't get to play together a lot."[25]

The casual mood of the sessions is reflected in the ¡Viva Terlingua! album cover, which includes a sepia-toned photograph of the musicians relaxing around the woodstove in the Luckenbach post office. Other photographs taken during the sessions and included on the album cover document the personal relationships developed among the participants. They show the smiling faces of Crouch, Walker, and background singer Joanne Vent, along with the conversations, meals, and drinks the musicians shared. The overall visual effect underscores the key themes of Walker's approach to the songwriting and performing process. More specifically, the visual message is that this was a communal effort; the musicians' priority was exercising creative freedom in an informal setting rather than producing a marketable commodity in a sterile studio.[26]

With the exception of Guy Clark's "Desperados Waiting for a Train" and Michael Murphey's "Backslider's Wine," the songs recorded for ¡Viva Terlingua! were fully or at least partially composed at Luckenbach. As such, they serve as musical analogues to the album cover's images, further documenting the sessions' casual atmosphere. The opening cut, "Gettin' By," draws Maitland into the narrative by poking fun at the president of MCA Records' initial resistance to the Luckenbach sessions. In the second verse, Walker comments:

> Last week I was thinking, it's record time again,
> And I could see Mike Maitland pacing his floor.
> Ah Mike, don't you worry, something's bound to come out.
> Besides, I've been down this road once or twice before.

During the instrumental interlude, Walker reassures Maitland that the song will work even though "it's not really a monster track," creating an ironic distance between himself and the visibly mediated album upon which this comment is documented. In addition to "Gettin' By," many of the songs on the album began simply as improvised lyrics or melody lines and were cobbled together on the spot. This rather haphazard approach to composing helped create instrumental and vocal arrangements that reflected the spontaneous nature of the informal picking sessions and the communal process of making the record. "Sangria Wine," for instance, began simply as a recipe for making drinks, along with the refrain "Oh, oh, I love sangria wine." While Walker worked on the lyrics, the band experimented with the accompaniment, trying to match the theme of the song with the ideal groove. As Livingston recalled:

> We would try everything "reggae" at least once. We might take a song like "London Homesick Blues" and try it bluegrass and rock and reggae and every kind of way, just for fun. And so Jerry said, "We ought to do ['Sangria Wine'] reggae." But we didn't know anything about reggae. Michael McGeary, our drummer, said, "Man, it's just kind of this thing. You have to have some guitar parts. Like Craig [Hillis], you should go 'do-do-do-do-dut,' and then Bob, you answer it with the bass 'boom-boom-boom' something."[27]

The informal approach to arranging and recording the album is also evident in the way the Lost Gonzo Band performed background vocals on several of the songs. Their imprecise vocal performance, which includes pitch, control, and timing problems, adds an element of realism and suggests that the band is drinking alcohol while making the record. By highlighting this improvisational technique of composing, arranging, and performing, ¡Viva Terlingua! rejected the more structured, commercially oriented approach to recording contemporaneous country music and instead celebrates an attitude of mutual artistic respect and communal enjoyment symbolized by the entire progressive country music movement.

The Luckenbach sessions concluded with a "live recording concert" held in the town's dance hall on August 18, 1973. Nearly three hundred people paid one dollar each to be part of what turned out to be the only true "live" segment of *¡Viva Terlingua!*. According to some of the musicians, the concert was somewhat of an afterthought. Despite last-minute planning and minimal advertisement, the hall was filled with friends of the band and a few others who found out about the concert at the last minute. Bob Livingston remembered that "people just showed up and said, 'What's going on here?' and the town of Luckenbach was jumping." Raphael observed that "most of [the audience members] were kids from Austin that were into that 'cosmic cowboy,' 'progressive country' scene at the time. . . . It was the same crowd that was going to the Armadillo and Castle Creek."[28]

In many ways, the concert was also a realization of the idealized, collaborative, and free-wheeling recording session that Walker had described on the jacket of his self-titled 1972 album. Instead of isolating the band members from each other in recording booths, the concert setting facilitated musical collaboration and exchange by allowing the musicians to play together exactly as they would have in one of Austin's live music venues.[29] Likewise, the presence of a live audience was an essential element of Walker's informal attitude, which he wanted to communicate to potential record buyers. As such, the live concert allowed the artists to remain within their normal social context of performing onstage, while also presenting an opportunity for Brovsky to capture the energy of the local live music scene in order to market it to a larger national audience.

Perhaps the best example of this type of artist-audience interaction at Walker's Luckenbach concert is Ray Wylie Hubbard's "Up against the Wall, Redneck Mother." During this song, the enthusiastic audience members sing along on the chorus. One particularly exuberant fan yells out his approval at the end of the first and third lines of the beginning verse. Throughout the song, audience members are prominently featured clapping their hands and, in the song's signature chorus, singing loudly in the background. By making the audience an integral part of the recording of "Up against the Wall, Redneck Mother," Walker and Brovsky help convey the exuberance of live performances while also explicitly reinforcing the cosmic cowboys' antipathy to their redneck counterparts. This helped to reinforce the notion that fans are an essential ingredient of the progressive country music phenomenon, and it gave listeners the sense that they were part of an authentic and unmediated concert experience, whether or not they actually were there in person.[30]

While the loose vocal arrangements of *¡Viva Terlingua!* and the direct involvement of an audience reinforce the "live" feel of the record, most of the album was not taken from a live performance. The liner notes mention that the songs are part of a "live recording concert," but, in fact, only "Up against the Wall, Redneck Mother" and Gary P. Nunn's "London Homesick Blues" were drawn from the live show. Everything else on *¡Viva Terlingua!* was recorded prior to the August 18 concert. Furthermore, three songs—"Desperados Waiting for a Train," "Sangria Wine," and "Get It Out"—conclude with a "fadeout," which underscores the fact that the listener is not experiencing an unmediated musical event but rather one in which studio engineers have had a hand in shaping the final product. These fadeouts imply that the improvisations will continue in perpetuity but out of earshot of the listener. The effect of the fadeouts is quite ironic. On one hand, fadeouts highlight the fact that much of *¡Viva Terlingua!* is not actually live since they are the result of technological manipulation and mediation of the recordings. At the same time, however, the fadeouts reinforce the perception that the progressive country music scene is based on a live performance environment in which a wide variety of musicians can join together in unceasing collaboration and experimentation.

Critics praised *¡Viva Terlingua!* as a milestone in the progressive country music movement and commented on how well it captured the organic, spontaneous nature of this new musical genre. Music journalist Chet Flippo, who had remarked earlier in 1973 that "the present crop of Texas musicians are followers, rather than innovators,"[31] observed just one year later in 1974 that *¡Viva Terlingua!* was important because it demonstrated that Austin's relaxed and liberal environment could yield an album of great artistic and commercial merit. According to Flippo:

> The rest of the recording industry has a wary eye trained on Austin . . . Will this noble experiment, wherein writers and singers do things their way . . . work? Heretofore, singers have been treated as wayward, slightly batty infants whose whims must be ignored. If they start a liberation movement, can it be accommodated? No reason why not, argues Jerry Jeff Walker. He is the only prominent singer who refuses to set foot in a recording studio.[32]

Flippo believed that the success of *¡Viva Terlingua!* played a direct role in shaping Austin's progressive country movement by guaranteeing that it could function as a sanctuary for independent-minded artists while also exerting a significant influence on the mainstream music industry. Others also hailed *¡Viva Terlingua!* as an accurate representation of the styles, rhetoric, and image of Austin's live music scene. As Joe Gracey, disc jockey at Austin's KOKE-FM, said in a November 1973 *Austin American-Statesman* article, "They . . . sat down and made the best record that anybody in Texas will ever make. Every cut is tremendous. . . . Some of the cuts are taken from the Saturday night concert, and all of 'em are live, whether there's an audience or not."[33]

The historical importance of Jerry Jeff Walker's Luckenbach sessions became fully apparent in 1977, with Waylon Jennings's recording of Chips Moman and Bobby Emmons's tune "Luckenbach, Texas (Back to the Basics of Love)."[34] The lyrics bemoan the stress and malaise of an urban existence and express a longing for a more peaceful, rural setting and a simpler way of life.[35] The singer asks his partner to trade her expensive jewelry for "boots and faded jeans" and to trade her "high society" and "four-car garage" for a place where they can "get back to the basics of love." In the chorus, that place is revealed to be Luckenbach.[36] The town depicted in the chorus of "Luckenbach, Texas (Back to the Basics of Love)" bears little resemblance to the Luckenbach of Walker's *¡Viva Terlingua!*. The song offers few details about the community's unique characteristics, and the artists named in the song have no direct relationship with Walker's recording session there. The link to Walker himself in "Luckenbach, Texas (Back to the Basics of Love)" is not established until the final chorus, when Willie Nelson joins in and replaces the reference to Mickey Newbury with a line about "Jerry Jeff's train songs," an allusion to Walker's version of Guy Clark's "Desperados Waiting for a Train." Jennings, who had recorded his 1976 album *Waylon: Live* at Austin's Armadillo World Headquarters in 1974 and whose 1976 RCA compilation *Wanted!: The Outlaws* became the first country music album to be certified platinum (reaching sales of one million),[37] remarked that the lack of specific details about Luckenbach was necessary because, neither he nor cowriters Moman and Emmons had been there prior to recording the song. In fact, Jennings said in his 1996 autobiography that much of the song's success, which included reaching number one on the *Billboard* country chart and number twenty-five on the *Billboard* pop chart,[38] was due to the universality of the song's pastoral retreat narrative: "Every state has a Luckenbach; a place to get away from things. That's why it succeeded."[39]

Jerry Jeff Walker's Luckenbach recording session became an important milestone in the evolution of the progressive country music movement and was a powerful expression of the anti-industry attitude exhibited by many of the genre's most prominent musicians. At the same time, *¡Viva Terlingua!* reflected contradictions inherent in the notion of an "independent, non-conformist" approach to artistic creativity since it still relied extensively on the financial backing and marketing expertise of a national label in order to make this "live" album successful. Furthermore, while *¡Viva Terlingua!* offers a broad cross-section of sounds and lyrical themes heard throughout the progressive country genre, this perspective was shaped in large part by the musical tastes and social relationships that each individual musician brought to the session. As a result, the album represents a mediated vision of the progressive music scene despite its aura of unmediated "liveness."

The success of Walker's *¡Viva Terlingua!* allowed him to reinvest in Austin's music technology infrastructure since he and Brovsky used some of the profits from the record to upgrade Odyssey Sound, the site of Walker's first Austin recording. This meant that the rudimentary studio that had contributed to the rough, "live" feel of those early recordings could be transformed into a professional workspace capable of producing high-quality material for regional and national distribution. This made it possible for emerging Austin bands to make first-rate demo records to send to major record labels.[40] Consequently, *¡Viva Terlingua!* stands as a carefully constructed musical manifesto of Austin's emergent progressive country movement by conveying a sense of spontaneity and freedom to potential audiences and musicians with similar ideologies. Yet, the album also was very much a part of the larger commercial music industry infrastructure since it relied on the technology, financing, and marketing that MCA provided. In the end, *¡Viva Terlingua!* represented progressive country's break with mainstream creative limitations, but it also revealed that most artists, no matter how "independent" they envisioned themselves to be, still had to rely on certain industry conventions in order to have successful recording careers. Walker's MCA sessions in Austin and Luckenbach also represent another compromise between the isolation of the professional recording studio and the dynamic interplay of live musical performances. By downplaying the mediating influence of the music industry, highlighting the humanity of the people who helped create the recordings, and situating the albums within specific geographical, social, and temporal contexts, Walker sought to achieve a balance between creative freedom and commercial vitality and, in the process, tapped into the pastoral visions, communality, and anti-industrial stance that characterized the public image of Austin's progressive country music scene.

"Bob Wills is Still the King"

Progressive Country and the Revival of Western Swing

O N DECEMBER 3, 1973, sixty-eight-year-old western swing pioneer Bob Wills entered the Sumet-Burnet Studio in Dallas, Texas, to record an album for the California-based United Artists label. This project was organized by bassist and producer Tommy Allsup as "a homecoming for Bob Wills and his Texas Playboys" and reunited the gravely ill Wills with members of his legendary band, who had participated in western swing's genesis and heyday. Along with former Playboys steel guitarist Leon McAuliffe, pianist Al Stricklin, and drummer "Smokey" Dacus,[1] the members of Asleep at the Wheel, an Austin-based band modeled after Wills's legendary ensemble, were also in attendance at this historic event. Traveling to Dallas at the invitation of United Artists—which was their label as well—the group hoped to meet with Wills, talk with him about his music, and receive his blessing for their own work.[2]

The auspicious occasion of this historic session was unfortunately marred by tragedy. After a long day in the studio, Wills began to feel ill. His wife, Betty, wheeled him past the members of Asleep at the Wheel and returned him to his home in Fort Worth, where, later that night, he suffered a massive stroke that left him in a coma for the last eighteen months of his life.[3] For the gathered Playboys, this recording session marked the end of an era and a fitting tribute to Wills's independence and fortitude. For Benson and Asleep at the Wheel, on the other hand, this session signaled a new beginning. Motivated by a desire, as he recalled more than three decades later, to "rediscover the roots of American music," bandleader Ray Benson and his bandmates returned to Austin with a renewed mission to bring western swing music, postwar rhythm and blues, and honky-tonk music to the city's progressive country audiences.[4]

By the time Asleep at the Wheel made their pilgrimage to Dallas, western swing had already been popular for more than four decades in Texas, Oklahoma, and California. Emerging from the region's string-band and fiddle traditions of the late 1920s, it challenged artificial generic and racial boundaries between "hillbilly" music and jazz by incorporating a wide variety of musical practices and repertories, including traditional Texan fiddle breakdowns, contemporary popular songs, and the improvisatory and rhythmic practices of ragtime and early jazz. Built at once on the performance practices of rural Texan and Oklahoman dance music and the ever-changing sounds of cosmopolitan popular music, western swing was a dance music that was popular in the burgeoning urban centers of Fort Worth and Tulsa, both of which benefited from widespread rural emigration during World War I and the Depression. It was also popular in the many rural communities that dotted the landscape of Depression-era Texas and, by World War II, in the massive dance halls of southern California, where thousands of Oklahomans and Texans lived following the Dust Bowl migrations of the 1930s. However, as a result of the often fickle trends of the national music industry and the changing economic conditions of the postwar economy, western swing underwent more than two decades of retrenchment in the postwar years before the progressive country music scene emerged in Austin. Western swing bandleaders dramatically reduced the size of their bands from the twenty or more musicians one might find in the prewar years to a lineup of six to ten musicians in order to reduce the cost of maintaining the group. Furthermore, after a period of great economic success on the West Coast during World War II, weakening economic conditions there forced many bandleaders to return to Texas and Oklahoma in the 1950s, where they performed for audiences in dance halls throughout the region and cultivated a core audience of working-class white Texans. Remembering the national heyday of western swing and fearing that the music industry was neglecting valuable vernacular musics like western swing, the members of Asleep at the Wheel, as well as Alvin Crow, an Oklahoma-born fiddler who was a favorite in Austin, recast western swing into a musical symbol that distinguished Austin from Nashville and Los Angeles musically and ideologically. At the same time, by directly evoking the sounds of the 1930s and 1940s in their live performances and recordings, these western swing revivalists also provided a way for scene participants to realize the cosmic cowboy's desire to escape into an idealized Texan frontier situated in an idyllic Texan past.

The origins of western swing can be traced directly to the regional fiddle traditions of Texas, Oklahoma, and Arkansas, where proficient fiddlers played dance music for house parties and other social occasions in the rural Southwest. Dances provided a fertile training ground for aspiring young fiddlers by offering opportunities to apprentice with older, more experienced musicians. There they learned specialized techniques to reduce the amount of effort exerted while playing, including outlining the tune's melody and rhythm and playing with a "shuffling" bow technique that limited the bow arm's range of motion. At the same time that frontier dance fiddling proliferated in the American Southwest, a more ornate style of fiddling developed for contests in the region, requiring the fiddler to employ more complicated bowings and nuanced ornamentation. These social events, often held in public venues such as town squares or hotel lobbies, pitted one fiddler against another in a head-to-head competition.[5]

By the late 1920s, the functional dance style and the more ornate contest style had coalesced in western swing, resulting in a music that was heavily influenced by local and regional dance musics (including German and Czech schottisches and waltzes and Mexican norteño music, among others) and featured jazz-influenced improvisations.[6] Although western swing was not considered to be a distinct musical genre in its earliest iterations, retrospective analysis reveals it to be an easily distinguished subgenre of swing music with key defining traits. The typical western swing band featured a rhythm section of bass, drums, piano, and either guitar or banjo and a front line consisting of a combination of fiddles, saxophones, trumpets, and occasionally trombones.[7] Like their national counterparts, western swing bands also featured a diverse musical repertoire, including regionally popular fiddle tunes and blues alongside contemporary popular songs composed by Tin Pan Alley songwriters.[8] Improvisation was also a central component of the western swing aesthetic. The music was influenced by southwestern "contest" fiddling, which required the demonstration of a fiddler's virtuosity, and by ragtime and jazz improvisation, which demanded extraordinary melodic and rhythmic inventiveness. Many western swing bandleaders, therefore, showcased the improvisatory skills of their sidemen through "takeoff" solos.[9] Finally, the underlying rhythm of western swing was characterized by the so-called swing beat, a rhythmic practice in which the first subdivision of the beat is played slightly longer than the second.[10] Western swing music, therefore, was characterized by musical traits drawn from both the southwestern frontier and contemporaneous popular music.

In its heyday in the 1930s and 1940s, western swing was primarily an urban music directed toward the thousands of rural émigrés who moved to Fort Worth, Tulsa, Los Angeles, and other major southwestern cities during the 1920s and 1930s in search of secure employment in the region's burgeoning manufacturing, energy, and service industries. As southwesterners migrated back and forth from the country to the city, western swing reinforced regional identities in the dance halls and honky-tonks where the music was performed by offering a safe space for these migrants to gather.[11] At the same time, its similarities to and interactions with Tin Pan Alley and contemporaneous jazz offered them a connection to more cosmopolitan cities like New York and Chicago. Western swing, therefore, embodied two conflicting cultural processes: the preservation of distinct regional identities and folkways and their assimilation into mainstream American society. As western swing bandleaders increasingly transformed their repertoires, instrumentation, and performance practices to parallel developments in swing music in other parts of the United States, they created music that sharply juxtaposed its rural and urban influences and mirrored the transformation of their fan base from rural emigrants into more cosmopolitan urbanites and suburbanites.[12]

By the early 1970s, however, western swing's wartime visibility was a distant memory, the first generation of western swing musicians was approaching old age, and many hardcore fans believed that the music was endangered. In the 1950s and 1960s, the retrenchment of western swing allowed musicians, journalists, and audiences to redefine it as an organic outgrowth of the people and folkways of the American Southwest. Following World War II, many western swing musicians returned to Texas and Oklahoma, where they reduced the size of their ensembles and made rigorous tours from one rural dance hall to another in order to remain fiscally solvent. At the same time, the major labels—including Columbia, the label for which Wills recorded prior to World War II—began to withdraw their support of western swing, allowing a new group of independent regional labels and lesser major labels to record and distribute the music. Bob Wills and His Texas

Playboys, for instance, recorded for MGM Records, a smaller major label, between 1947 and 1954.[13] Furthermore, as the former sidemen in the pioneering western swing bands left to form their own groups, more opportunities were created for younger musicians to apprentice with the older masters and to develop their musical talents in a professional setting. While most of these second-generation sidemen never started their own ensembles, several of them become leading session musicians in Los Angeles, New York, and Nashville, where they brought a western swing sensibility to mainstream popular music and, more important, commercial country music.

However, seizing upon the retrenchment of western swing bands in the 1950s and 1960s, dozens of musicians in Austin's progressive country music scene undertook a complex program to resurrect western swing and to redefine it as a traditional "folk" music that was rooted in the experiences of rural Texans. Much as Kenneth Threadgill's presence within the progressive country music scene provided a visible connection to the dawn of countercultural music making in Austin and to the roots of hillbilly music, so, too, did this reformulation of western swing create a cultural touchstone that served as a symbolic link to the premodern, pastoral utopia into which the cosmic cowboys wanted to escape. For participants in Austin's progressive country music scene, the definition of western swing as a traditional, rural folk music created an opportunity for them to connect to an imagined rural Texas (which, as the songs discussed in chapter 3 demonstrate, was not necessarily hospitable to them) and to what they perceived to be a more authentic musical culture than the overtly commercialized country music that was being promulgated by the Nashville music industry. Yet, ironically, the revival of western swing by Austin's progressive country musicians was greatly influenced by the efforts of figures working within the national country music industry to validate western swing in the late 1960s.

Although western swing continued to thrive in Texas dance halls during the postwar years, it had nearly vanished from the national consciousness by the late 1960s. Still, between 1968 and 1970, Nashville—which had long shunned western swing—began to embrace it, recasting it as one of the many folk roots of modern country music. First, the Country Music Association (CMA) inducted Bob Wills into the Country Music Hall of Fame (CMHOF) in 1968. A source of great pride for Wills, this honor placed him not in the company of the jazz artists with whom he had been so closely affiliated in the 1940s but in the pantheon of country music pioneers Jimmie Rodgers and the

Carter Family. Moreover, as the CMA and the CMHOF connected the pop-influenced "Nashville Sound" of contemporary country music to regional musical antecedents, western swing's retreat from the national spotlight made Wills a powerful choice for induction. Wills was not lauded as a sophisticated, cosmopolitan bandleader who had worked diligently to make the Texas Playboys and their music accessible to a larger public. Rather, he was celebrated as a folk legend who was thought to be responsible for the creation of a musical style that captured the essence of the region by combining rural musical traditions and the sounds of contemporary popular music that presaged the work of "Nashville Sound" producers Chet Atkins, Don Law, and Owen Bradley.[14]

The construction of western swing as an American folk music was further supported by Merle Haggard, who in April 1970 led a three-day recording session with former members of Wills's Texas Playboys and later that year released *A Tribute to the Best Damn Fiddler Player in the World (or, My Salute to Bob Wills)*. Joining Haggard and his band, The Strangers, were Playboy alumni from the group's earliest recordings to its postwar incarnations, including Johnny Gimble, Joe Holley, Tiny Moore, Eldon Shamblin, and Johnnie Lee Wills, who were invited to the sessions in order to help Haggard "duplicate with some reality the unique sound that was found on each Bob Wills recording." Haggard, who just one year earlier had recorded a tribute album honoring early hillbilly singing star Jimmie Rodgers, clearly envisioned this project as an attempt to salvage the disappearing history of western swing and, as his comments in the album's sleeve notes suggest, to "introduce to a new generation, and bring back to the ones who remember, the great sound of Bob Wills & The Texas Playboys."[15] As such, Haggard treated the album as a history lesson in which, as the self-positioned guardian of the western swing tradition, he presented classic Wills songs such as "Right or Wrong," "Take Me Back to Tulsa," and "San Antonio Rose," along with a laudatory biographical narrative that proclaimed Wills's status as "a legend in his own time." *Tribute to the Best Damn Fiddle Player in the World (Or My Salute to Bob Wills)* reached the number two position on the *Billboard* Country Albums chart in 1971 and served as a catalyst for subsequent attempts to revitalize western swing music. Suggesting that the tradition was facing extinction, the album called for cross-generational dialogue about the importance of western swing to the cultural heritage of people throughout the Southwest. Perhaps most important, *Tribute to the Best Damned Fiddle Player in the World* distilled the rich variety of western swing styles into a relatively stable body of musical signifiers and a core repertory—largely centered on the work of Wills and the Texas Playboys—that would exert a profound influence on the western swing revival of the 1970s.

Despite its continued regional success in Texas and Oklahoma, therefore, western swing was redefined as an endangered folk music in the late 1960s. No longer did audiences view western swing as the commercial popular music it had been during its heyday. Rather, as Asleep at the Wheel founder Ray Benson remarked in an encomium to Wills, western swing was seen as "the West Texas dirt-farmers' blues, the way Bob played them, and the way John, his father, played them," a "Southwestern folk" music that expressed the challenges and joys of a distant and ideal rural past.[16] By the time progressive country music began to develop in Austin during the early 1970s, therefore, western swing had become an unquestionably Texan musical style, one that Austin's young musicians eagerly sought in their attempts to carve their own place in Texan musical history. As Austin journalist and music critic Joe Nick Patoski suggested, the decline of western swing was caused, in large part, by Nashville's neglect, much as it was apparently doing to contemporary country music by failing to support artists who, like Wills, "expanded the boundaries."[17] It was with this notion of western swing as a distinctly Texan "folk music" in mind that Austin's progressive country musicians sought to preserve and resurrect the music for their generation.

The western swing revival in Austin was led by two bands representing both ends of the hippie-redneck spectrum but that, surprisingly, approached the music with extraordinarily similar attitudes and from remarkably similar backgrounds. Alvin Crow, an Oklahoma City–born fiddler and leader of the Pleasant Valley Boys, was celebrated by the Austin press as an authentic redneck who "play[ed] western swing and dance music with all the expressiveness and musical ability of the dance bands that made the music an American tradition 30 years ago" despite his background as a classically trained violinist who claimed to have become a member of the Oklahoma Symphony at age five.[18] Crow's group, the Pleasant Valley Boys, was celebrated in working-class dance halls as "a redneck's dream of what American youth should look like" and "nothing short of down-home country boys."[19] Asleep at the Wheel, on the other hand, was a band of musicians with countercultural ideals who hailed from both the east and west coasts. The group was led by Ray Benson, a native of Philadelphia who navigated a vibrant musical background that included playing dance tunes at a Quaker summer camp, singing in the city's folk clubs, and exploring big band jazz.[20] Yet, regardless of their respective paths to the music and their positions within the cultural milieu of the progressive country music scene in Austin, both groups set out to preserve and to revitalize western swing music by publicly celebrating the people who pioneered the tradition, the sounds of prewar western swing, and the culture that supported its development. In the process, Crow and Benson shed the trappings of their middle-class urban upbringing to recast themselves as organic outgrowths of the Texan white working class.

Although liberal commentators and members of the youth counter-culture often heard country music as the voice of the conservative Silent Majority, progressive country's western swing musicians were convinced that Texan music had the power to transcend the generational divisions between white Texans and, more ambitiously, heal the growing national "generation gap." Benson remembered that, although he could "hear the incredible beauty and craftsmanship and poetry in this music [country music] . . . kids who grew up with their father loving this music couldn't because of the sociological stuff."[21] Jim Haber, who took the stage name Floyd Domino and served as Asleep at the Wheel's pianist from January 1972 until May 1978, also recalled: "What was interesting was that, when we moved to Texas and started playing the festivals around here . . . we constantly had people come up to us and say, 'This is our parents' music, and I never liked it. . . . But I like it when you guys play.' We were bringing it back to them, but for us it was all new."[22] Believing that the music could unlock the mysteries of the American past and unite a nation divided, progressive country's western swing revivalists set out to dedicate their lives to researching and representing country music to Austin's young people and to offering new interpretations of it to its most dedicated (and most conservative) fans. As a result, Domino remembered, many "traditional western swing audiences—that is, those people who had been caricatured in Hubbard's "Up against the Wall, Redneck Mother" and Friedman's "They Ain't Makin' Jews like Jesus Anymore"—showed the band a warm welcome in large part because of the group's enthusiasm for western swing and honky-tonk music.[23]

While the early musical efforts of the Pleasant Valley Boys and Asleep at the Wheel took place primarily in rural and small-town honky-tonks, the groups also worked to develop a younger, more urban fan base for their music as well. Crow, for instance, has recently drawn special attention to the fact that, during the Pleasant Valley

Boys' tours between 1969 and 1973, he "moved in both hippie and redneck circles."[24] While Crow's direct connections to and affinities for the hippie scene have not been substantiated, Asleep at the Wheel's early musical efforts took place squarely within the domains of both communities. While living in Paw Paw, West Virginia (where the band squatted in an apple orchard), Asleep at the Wheel played a regular gig at a white working-class beer joint. Then, in 1971, San Francisco-based hippie leader Wavy Gravy brought a caravan of hippies through Paw Paw on their way to a rock festival in Washington, D.C. Upon hearing Asleep at the Wheel, he asked the group to participate in the festival alongside Hot Tuna, Alice Cooper, and Commander Cody and His Lost Planet Airmen, which provided them one of their first opportunities to play country music before an audience they resembled. Following their successful debut in the nation's capital, Commander Cody, whose affinity for honky-tonk, rockabilly, western swing, and rhythm and blues mirrored Benson's, invited the members of Asleep at the Wheel to relocate to Berkeley, California, where they could become more involved in the counterculture. Encouraged by the offer, the group headed to the West Coast in 1972. While in California, Asleep at the Wheel recorded their first album, *Comin' Right at Ya*, but it did not sell well even among the countercultural crowd they had hoped to reach. Searching for other opportunities, the group found work as the road band for a legion of mainstream country artists, including Stony Edwards and Connie Smith, performing in numerous small towns across the United States.[25]

By 1973, both Alvin Crow and the Pleasant Valley Boys and Asleep at the Wheel had accumulated a great deal of experience playing for hippie audiences and Middle American country fans alike, and Austin seemed to be a favorable site in which to continue their attempts to transgress the boundaries between these two groups. Crow explained that his decision to move to Austin in 1973 was influenced by the cultural exchange he witnessed at the 1972 Dripping Springs Reunion, a three-day country music festival held just a few miles west of Austin that brought together some local country artists and several national stars (see the conclusion to the book). He reported that he saw "Hank Snow, Charley Pride, Loretta Lynn, Roy Acuff, as well as Willie Nelson, Billy Joe Shaver, Waylon Jennings. Kenneth Threadgill was there with Bill Neely, doing 'Coming Back to Texas,' and [they] yodeled in harmony. It bowled me over. I thought, 'If a guy like that can make a living in Austin with that kind of country music, I'm getting my ass back to Austin.' "[26] Similarly, following their stint on the West Coast,

Asleep at the Wheel relocated to Austin in 1974 at the behest of Willie Nelson and Doug Sahm, both of whom were then enjoying significant success at the Armadillo World Headquarters and the Soap Creek Saloon, respectively. Despite the boundary crossing already under way in Austin, Benson has remembered that Asleep at the Wheel was special because, following their experiences with Smith and Edwards, they could convincingly "play the Armadillo and the Soap Creek Saloon—the hippie joints—and then go out and play all the redneck dance halls."[27]

Many of Austin's young Texans must have heard western swing music while growing up in the Lone Star State, and the sight of a group of long-haired young people embracing the western swing tradition was likely a powerful one. In effect, these performances demonstrated to Austin's cosmic cowboys that, although country music may have symbolized the conservative Silent Majority of their parents' and grandparents' generations, the music and the culture from which it emerged belonged to all white Texans. At the same time, just as the cosmic cowboys in the songs of Murphey, Clark, and others often perceived rural Texas as a welcoming environment for idealistic hippies, Benson and Crow appear to have viewed their performances of country music in much the same way. By demonstrating their facility as country musicians, they believed that they could convince honky-tonk patrons in central Texas that the hippies were not fundamentally bad people. Although the violence they faced in rural honky-tonks undermines such romantic visions of country music's power to bridge the generation gap, both Benson and Crow arrived in Austin with the idealistic goal of uniting Texans around their shared musical culture.[28]

Austin's western swing revivalists wished to break down the cultural barriers that divided hippies from Middle America by adopting and adapting the sounds of western swing and honky-tonk music and presenting it to audiences from both groups. At the same time, they also became authorities on the history and stylistic nuances of these musical styles, striving to rekindle interest in these musics before they passed from the nation's and especially the region's collective memory. Through careful study of source recordings, collaboration with the pioneering musicians of western swing and honky-tonk music, and the composition of new songs in the style of the old hits, Crow and Benson brought Texan musical traditions to Austin's progressive country music scene and guaranteed that the music would survive for future generations.

By living and working in central Texas, Austin's western swing revivalists had many opportunities to interact with and to learn directly from the pioneers of western swing, many of whom lived in the area and were in their sixties and seventies when the progressive country movement began to flourish. Although none of Austin's progressive country musicians were able to work with Bob Wills because of his failing health, they interacted regularly with members of the Texas Playboys. Many of the former Playboys performed throughout the region as bandleaders and at Playboys reunions, and Jesse Ashlock, one of the pioneering Playboy fiddlers, relocated to Austin in the early 1970s and became a regular presence in the city's music scene. As both Domino and Benson have recalled, the Playboys acted as mentors and friends to the members of Asleep at the Wheel, offering musical advice, sitting in on sessions, and supporting the musicians as they learned about the inner workings of the music industry.[29] Domino recounted that long-time Playboy pianist Al Stricklin "offered musical lessons. . . . He played, and I would just kind of sponge it up." He also remembered that the Playboys taught the members of Asleep at the Wheel more than chords and idiomatic passages; they helped shape the group's conception of western swing by pointing out that it is "not an orthodoxy. . . . You can listen to everything, and then . . . it's wide open."[30] Similarly, Joe Nick Patoski reported in April 1975 that Crow's enthusiasm for western swing music and his dedication to the history, culture, and performance practices of the genre pleased the genre's elder statesmen, including Dewey Groom, the proprietor of the Longhorn Ballroom in Dallas: "Alvin is on his good side—the first time he walked in uninvited to the Longhorn and sat in with Dewey's band, Groom asked if he's [sic] come to play. Alvin replied, 'No sir, I come to learn,' heartening words to the proprietor of one of Texas's last outposts of western swing."[31]

The access that Austin's western swing revivalists had to the music's pioneers facilitated several public collaborations in concerts, on recordings, and in television broadcasts (table 5.1). As in Asleep at the Wheel's 1973 album, *Comin' Right at Ya*, former Playboys were often invited to be session musicians on the revivalists' albums, augmenting the ensemble for the entire album. In other, less common, instances, former Playboys were showcased on only one or two songs, playing takeoff solos or offering solo vocals on a signature composition and allowing the "host" artists to pay tribute to the pioneers of western swing. Such collaborations offered clear benefits for students and teachers alike. For the students, firsthand contact with former Playboys Jesse Ashlock, Al Stricklin, and Johnny Gimble allowed them to learn new musical techniques,

TABLE 5.1. Collaborations between western swing revivalists and former Texas Playboys (1973–1977).

Artist	Title	Label/Catalog No.	Date	Playboy Collaborators
Asleep at the Wheel	Comin' Right at Ya	United Artists 0598	1973	Johnny Gimble
Asleep at the Wheel	Asleep at the Wheel	Epic KE 33097	1974	Johnny Gimble
Asleep at the Wheel	Texas Gold	Capitol ST-1441	1975	Johnny Gimble
Asleep at the Wheel	Austin City Limits	Episode #101	1975*	Leon McAuliffe Eldon Shamblin unknown others
Alvin Crow and the Pleasant Valley Boys	Alvin Crow and the Pleasant Valley Boys	Long Neck LN-001	1976	Jesse Ashlock
Asleep at the Wheel	Wheelin' and Dealin'	Capitol ST-11546	1976	Johnny Gimble Tiny Moore Eldon Shamblin
Alvin Crow and the Pleasant Valley Boys	High Riding	Polydor PD-1-6102	1977	Al Stricklin

* This episode was first aired in 1976 as Austin City Limits' first syndicated broadcast (Endres, Austin City Limits, 21–23).

to discover details about the history of the music they loved, and to imbue their own performances with a degree of authenticity. The teachers, on the other hand, earned some extra money, guaranteed that future generations would commemorate their role in the development of western swing, and enjoyed the much-deserved celebration of their noteworthy careers. As fans' memory of the older generation of western swing musicians was beginning to dwindle, therefore, Austin's revivalists established relationships that positioned themselves as heirs to this musical tradition and secured their teachers' legacies.

The Playboys' work as session musicians and supporters of the western swing revival in Austin is best exemplified by the recorded relationship of Asleep at the Wheel and former Playboy fiddler and mandolinist Johnny Gimble, who, in 1975, was described by KOKE-FM's Gracey as "the current flag-bearer in the Texas fiddle tradition."[32] Gimble worked with Wills between 1949 and 1951 and spent most of the 1950s and 1960s as a session musician for honky-tonk and western swing sessions in Dallas, Waco, and Springfield, Missouri. He relocated to Nashville in late 1968 to become a session musician on Music Row and quickly became one of the most sought-after session musicians in the city. It was no wonder, then, that he accompanied Asleep at the Wheel on all of their sessions between 1973 and 1976. Legendary producer and former Buddy Holly sideman Tommy Allsup introduced the members of Asleep at the Wheel to Johnny Gimble in Nashville during the recording session for their first album, *Comin' Right at Ya*, and he joined them in sessions for the band's later releases on the United Artists, Epic, and Capitol labels. Gimble did not appear on every cut of these albums, but the fact that he played on more than half of them indicates that his primary purpose on Asleep at the Wheel's albums was to fill a specific studio role.

In addition to drawing upon the wealth of available western swing talent to augment studio recordings, Asleep at the Wheel and Alvin Crow and the Pleasant Valley Boys also featured former Playboys as honored guests in their recordings, much as they might in a concert or dance setting. While these recordings form only a very small part of the groups' recorded output, such occasions created opportunities for listeners to witness firsthand the transmission of a musical culture. Like Jerry Jeff Walker's albums, therefore, these recordings concentrated the ideals of the progressive country music scene into a single, commodified product that reinforced local notions of authenticity. Consequently, these recordings allowed progressive country musicians to assert their superiority over musicians and musical practices that could not claim the same cultural heritage, including most notably those stars of the Nashville system.

In 1976, Alvin Crow and the Pleasant Valley Boys featured former Playboy fiddler Jesse Ashlock on their eponymous album, recorded at the Odyssey Sound studio with engineer Chet Himes.[33] Ashlock, who apprenticed with Milton Brown and the Musical Brownies between 1932 and 1934 before joining Bob Wills in 1935, was greatly influenced by the fiddle style of jazz musician Joe Venuti and, as such, was instrumental in bringing "hot" improvisational techniques into western swing. Moreover, when Ashlock joined the Texas Playboys, Wills was able to incorporate the twin-fiddle style that Ashlock had developed alongside former Brownie Cecil Brower, creating in the process one of the most identifiable signifiers of western swing music.[34] By asking Ashlock, one of the oldest Playboys, to perform on their 1976 sessions, Alvin Crow and the Pleasant Valley Boys earned cultural capital in Austin and in rural Texan dance halls, positioning themselves as engaged culture bearers of western swing and, more broadly, Texan musical traditions. Crow's recorded collaboration with Ashlock is marked by several characteristics that emphasize the importance of his appearance on the record. First, Ashlock is featured on only two compositions: an Ashlock original called "When I Stop Loving You" and Jesse Winchester's song "That's a Touch I Like." These cuts appear on the album's second side as the album's seventh and eighth cuts, respectively. Much like guest appearances in a live performance, therefore, the album first presents the Pleasant Valley Boys as the featured musicians, and, after the group has established a rapport with the audience, the guest artist is introduced to change the pace of the concert. The album then concludes with two more songs featuring the Pleasant Valley Boys, further establishing the group as the featured act. Ashlock's performance on the album, therefore, is constructed almost as a coincidental appearance and as a rare opportunity to witness the collaboration between a local star, which Crow was by 1976, and one of his musical heroes.

In conjunction with the placement of the songs on the album, the two songs that showcase Ashlock as a featured performer are more reflective of his distinctive musical style than the other cuts on the album. "When I Stop Loving You," for instance, is the first of only two songs on the album to feature a twin-fiddle duet, one of the two innovative techniques for which Ashlock was responsible. As is typical of many western swing songs, the recording begins with a legato duet between Crow and Ashlock in which they play the final eight measures of the song's melody and are accompanied by Herb Steiner's pedal steel guitar harmonics and a four-beat shuffle rhythm in the bass and drums. After Crow sings the entire thirty-two-bar song, Ashlock and Crow again play the opening twin-fiddle duet. Crow then sings the bridge and the concluding A section, and the song ends with a four-measure coda that repeats the last four bars of the melody.

The second Ashlock feature number focuses on Ashlock's improvisatory skills. "That's a Touch I Like" is a jump blues number that serves as an excellent vehicle to showcase individual improvisation. After Crow sings the entire song, harmonica player Roger Crabtree is featured in a twelve-bar chorus, followed by a twelve-bar solo by Ashlock. Crow introduces both soloists when each begins to play, shouting "Brother Roger" and "Take it away, Jesse" in much the same way that Bob Wills called on soloists in the Texas Playboys on recordings and in concert. While twelve measures might seem like a fleeting opportunity to solo, especially in the era following the extended psychedelic jams of the late 1960s and the progressive rock epics of the early 1970s, Ashlock would have been prepared to develop a significant solo in this brief span of time. Most early western swing recordings showcase soloists for between eight and twelve measures, in large part because these performances were limited by the time constraints of 78-rpm records, and later recordings continued to adhere to that format even following the advent of the long-playing (LP) record format.[35]

Many people, including the revivalists, their collaborators, and the record label executives, were involved in the decision to invite collaborators into the recording studio with Austin's western swing bands, and an examination of the industrial forces at work in these collaborations sheds light on the nature of these temporary partnerships. For instance, the collaboration between Ashlock and the Pleasant Valley Boys is noteworthy because, unlike the Asleep at the Wheel–Johnny Gimble projects, *Alvin Crow & the Pleasant Valley Boys* was recorded in Austin for a local label. Moreover, Alvin Crow and the Pleasant Valley Boys are listed on the album jacket as the album's producers. One may surmise, therefore, that all of the creative decisions regarding the songs recorded, the arrangements performed, the way the album was recorded, and the design of the physical album were made by the group. As such, the decision to include Jesse Ashlock, an elder statesman of western swing who would die just a few months after these sessions, may be interpreted as an attempt to position themselves securely within the western swing tradition.[36] On the other hand, Asleep at the Wheel was signed to major labels, produced by Tommy Allsup and Nashville songwriter Norro Wilson, and recorded in Nashville. The decision to include musicians such as Johnny Gimble on their sessions was, therefore, likely influenced more by his role as a Nashville session musician than by his Playboy pedigree.[37] While Gimble's performances on Asleep at the Wheel's albums imbue their work as revivalists with a degree of authenticity, they are not positioned to be the strong witnesses to cultural transmission that the Pleasant Valley Boys' collaboration with Jesse Ashlock was.

The inclusion of pioneering western swing musicians on the studio recordings of revivalist groups like Alvin Crow and the Pleasant Valley Boys and Asleep at the Wheel authenticated the efforts of Austin's young musicians during the 1970s. At the same time, the public profile of these groups in Austin was higher than that of the former Playboys, who were no longer touring as a group. The Playboys' contributions to albums by local and regional stars also endowed the older generation of musicians with cultural cachet among Austin's young people.[38] However, as folklorist Robert Cantwell has posited, the greatest beneficiary of this type of exchange is the revivalist who finds validation through the work of the folk.[39] While the former Texas Playboys were, in fact, commercial musicians of great renown in their heyday, the changing dynamics of the folk revival had effectively transformed them into culture bearers whose principal role was to pass the traditions of western swing on to western swing revivalists who, like Benson and Crow, hoped to establish a deeper connection to the Anglo-Texan past through musical performance.

At the same time that Benson's and Crow's groups were collaborating with the pioneering musicians of western swing in the recording studio, they also positioned themselves as heirs to the legacies of western swing and honky-tonk by reconstructing these musical styles. These artists were concerned, to varying degrees, with re-creating the specific details of instrumentation and performance practice exhibited in the recordings of western swing and honky-tonk artists such as Milton Brown and the Musical Brownies, Bob Wills and His Texas Playboys, Ernest Tubb, and Hank Williams. Unlike their collaborations with the musicians who made them, the recordings were, as musicologist Mark Katz has suggested, portable and repeatable, thus allowing the progressive country acolytes an opportunity to study the primary texts of Anglo-Texan dance music.[40] For example, Tommy Goldsmith, a guitarist who performed with Alvin Crow in the mid-1970s, recalled that Crow insisted that his band members study the source recordings carefully in order to comprehend and re-create the rhythmic intricacies and idiosyncrasies of early western swing musicians.[41] Similarly, Marcia Ball and Bobby Earl Smith recall that, when Freda and the Firedogs began performing country music in 1970, they, too, mimicked the source recordings of Loretta Lynn, Tammy Wynette, and other contemporaneous Nashville country artists.[42]

Austin's western swing revivalists found their source recordings in many places. Benson, for instance, fueled his interest in American roots music by collecting 78-rpm recordings, and Domino recalled purchasing 78s at a record store on Lower Broadway in Nashville and at Village Music in Marin County, California. When direct access to 78s was not possible or when it was impractical to play them, Austin's musicians created their own compilations. Goldsmith, for instance, remembered that cassette tapes of old western swing recordings circulated among his bandmates and often provided entertainment when they traveled from one performance to the next.[43] Finally, some record labels began offering LP reissues of old recordings, which allowed cheap and easy access to the labels' back catalogues. One of the more popular LP reissues was the double LP *The Bob Wills Anthology*, released by Columbia Records in 1973.[44] The set featured recordings that the Texas Playboys had made between 1935 and 1946, the height of the band's national popularity, and included western swing standards such as "Take Me Back to Tulsa," "Steel Guitar Rag," "Roly Poly," "That's What I Like about the South," and "New San Antonio Rose."[45] So, too, was Haggard's tribute album an important source of repertoire and performance practices, as Lucky Oceans, steel guitarist with Asleep at the Wheel, recalled:

> When the band got "Greatest Damn Fiddler" [*sic*]—Haggard's Wills tribute, it turned our heads around. This was country music, but with the swing and jazz elements that Ray and I had grown up on. So I copied what Norm Hamlet was playing with Merle, then discovered Bob's lap [steel] players—Leon McAuliffe, Herbie Remington, Shorty Moessner, Noel Boggs . . . and set about copying them. . . . [I]f I heard it on record or radio and it appealed to me, I had to learn how to play it myself.[46]

The influence of early western swing recordings is most evident in the recorded repertoire of Austin's revivalists and in their approaches to the performance of those songs. In addition to original songs composed by talented songwriters such as Benson, Crow, and Asleep at the Wheel guitarist Leroy Preston, both groups also featured numerous cover versions of earlier western swing, honky-tonk, and rhythm-and-blues hits.

In his three progressive country–era albums—*Alvin Crow and the Neon Angels* (1973/1979), *Alvin Crow and the Pleasant Valley Boys* (1976), and *High Riding* (1977)—Crow included several Wills standards from the 1930s and 1940s, including "San Antonio Rose," "Faded Love," and "Maiden's Prayer," all of which were regularly featured in Crow's live performances.[47] Many of the covers on Asleep at the Wheel's albums were also culled from the Wills catalog, but the band also included several songs that are representative of a slightly broader conception of Texas music. Their debut album, *Comin' Right at Ya*, showcased Wills's "Take Me Back to Tulsa," honky-tonk pioneer Ernest Tubb's 1946 composition "Drivin' Nails in My Coffin," Hank Williams's 1952 hit "I'll Never Get Out of This World Alive," and Moon Mullican's 1951 "Cherokee Boogie."[48] On their second album, however, the band broadened their horizons beyond the Anglo-Texan genres to include big-band jazz and rhythm-and-blues recorded music such as Louis Jordan's "Choo Choo Ch'Boogie" and Count Basie's "Jumpin' at the Woodside."[49] In the act of redrawing the boundaries around the western swing tradition, these musicians unconsciously performed the progressive country music scene's ambivalence toward racial integration and equality, at once suggesting that African American musical traditions deserved to be treated with the same care and respect as identifiably white musical traditions and deracinating these musical practices by associating them with a seemingly raceless, but predominantly Anglo, "Texan music."

The racial politics of the western swing revival are also evident in the ways that progressive country audiences engaged with the work of Asleep at the Wheel and Alvin Crow. Although western swing was created primarily to facilitate dancing, the vast majority of the audiences in Austin approached these musical styles as listeners, not dancers. That is, progressive country audiences typically treated the performances of groups such as Asleep at the Wheel as concerts, in effect sacralizing western swing, honky-tonk, rhythm and blues, and other vernacular musics brought under the progressive country umbrella.[50] The western swing revivalists encouraged such attitudes by presenting their efforts as attempts to preserve musical styles that they believed to be of great cultural importance but that were either on the verge of death or already long forgotten. By trying to make this music relevant to Austin's cosmic cowboys, to reconnect their audiences with their heritage, and to ensure the music's long-term preservation, the consumption of western swing was also transformed from a predominantly social act into a primarily political one. To appreciate western swing was to demonstrate one's commitment to the salvation of Anglo-Texan culture, to resist the modernizing effects of the Sun Belt expansion, and, as a corollary, to resolve the progressive country audience's collective ambivalence about the numerous social changes that were afoot in Austin and the rest of Texas.

The progressive country scene's western swing musicians publicly displayed their resistance to modernization and ambivalence toward social change through their approaches to performance practice. As musicologists Richard Taruskin and John Butt have discussed in their respective work on historically informed performance practice, a musician's efforts to re-create the original performance practices of a composition transmit not the composer's intentions but the intellectual and political ideals of the contemporary musician.[51] While mastery of the western swing and honky-tonk canons was essential in demonstrating the cultural authority of Austin's western swing revivalists, the artists added an additional signifier of authenticity through the use of period instrumentation. Benson recalled that, when Asleep at the Wheel went to Mercury Custom Studios in Nashville to record their debut album, *Comin' Right at Ya*, many of the session musicians and recording technicians were surprised that steel guitar player Lucky Oceans chose to perform on both the pedal steel guitar (the preferred steel guitar in Nashville) and the older lap steel guitar. The musicians were not surprised that Oceans was technically proficient on both instruments; in fact, Nashville's studio musicians were also capable of performing on both. Rather, as Benson observed, the Nashville establishment "wanted to forget their hillbilly roots," and the lap steel guitar, which was first electrified by Musical Brownie Bob Dunn around 1935, became a symbol of Asleep at the Wheel's "authenticity."[52] For revivalists like Benson, who harbored the belief that mainstream country music was forsaking its roots, the lap steel stood as a weapon in their battle to preserve western swing and honky-tonk music, and, as such, it validated both the artists and the audiences who paid to see them in person or to obtain their recordings.

In addition to mastering the instruments that gave early western swing and honky-tonk music its distinctive sound, Austin's revivalists borrowed one of Bob Wills's sonic trademarks, his holler. Wills was not a singer, but, as the bandleader and master of ceremonies, he often offered a lilting falsetto holler to signify his approval of a band member's takeoff solo, to comment on the lyrics of a song, or to call on a specific soloist. In the fourth verse of the Texas Playboys' 1941 recording of "Take Me Back to Tulsa," for instance, Tommy Duncan explains, "We always wear a great big smile./We never do act sour," to which Wills replies, "Nah," in a lingering falsetto. Wills's vocalizations also offered the Austin revivalists a clear signifier of western swing tradition through which to connect to Wills. In Asleep at the Wheel's 1973 recording of "Take Me Back to Tulsa," for instance, Benson is featured on a takeoff guitar solo. As the band's emcee, he, like Wills, was responsible for calling out the names of the soloists for the audience's benefit (whether live or on recordings). Unlike Wills's recordings, in which takeoff solos were almost always performed by someone other than Wills, Benson had to call out his own name. To resolve this conflict, Benson turned to comedy, commenting after a few notes of his solo, "That sounds like me. . . . It *is* me!" Similarly, Patoski reported that Crow often seemed to channel Wills's stage presence in his live performances: "Alvin is the Son of Bob Wills, both as fiddle and front man. . . . The hollers, each 'Ahhhh-ha,' the point of the fiddle bow to his pickers on their breaks, even the hazy finger pop and fiddle plucks are more than casually similar to those of the Daddy of modern Texas music."[53] As such, the overt borrowing signifiers from the recordings of Bob Wills and His Texas Playboys indicated to informed and uninformed audiences alike that the Austin revivalists deserved to be recognized as members of the western swing community.

Using western swing signifiers drawn from early recordings was not, however, merely a matter of inserting them liberally throughout a recording. Rather, the decisions they made concerning what elements of a source recording to preserve in their re-creation and which ones to omit reveal important details about the relationship between Austin's revivalists and early western swing and honky-tonk recordings. For these musicians, the recordings were not considered fixed representations of a performance that should be faithfully reproduced in subsequent performances. Rather, source recordings served as a compendium of musical resources from which Austin's revivalists could freely borrow. In other words, the revivalists were engaged in a dialogue with the source recording that allowed them to interpret the standard repertoire of western swing and honky-tonk music in an idiomatic manner. As Floyd Domino recounted, for instance, the solos that Asleep at the Wheel played on their early recordings were often "copped" from other sources, leading some of the band members to think that the recordings did not convey the excitement of their live performances: "On 'Cherokee Boogie,' I think I copped a Fats Domino lick. . . . I fitted it in there, but at the time, I remember thinking, 'Oh, it's all canned. It's all rehearsed.' "[54] Like jazz musicians who base their solos on the improvisations of earlier artists and "early music" specialists who look to performance practice treatises to learn how to embellish a baroque sonata, Austin's revivalists borrowed freely from the recordings of Bob Wills, Milton Brown, Ernest Tubb, and Hank Williams while infusing their own performances with their personal musical aesthetic.[55]

Alvin Crow and the Neon Angels' 1973 recording of "Roly Poly," Bob Wills's postwar ode to his infant son, James Robert Wills II, offers an interesting example of this process at work.[56] Wills's recording, made with the Texas Playboys in Hollywood on January 26, 1945, comprises two verses, each of which is in standard AABA song form, that describe to the point of hyperbole the energy and resulting appetite of his young son.[57] Throughout Crow's recording, the group draws upon and manipulates key melodic gestures from the original Wills recording and uses them as the basis for their own improvisations.

Both recordings begin with an eight-bar introduction that spins out a melodic sequence. In the Wills recording, this motive is performed twice by one guitarist and is then repeated twice more as a duet between the two lead guitarists, Cameron Hill and Jimmy Wyble (figure 5.1). The introduction to Crow's performance, however, is arranged and executed with much less precision than the Wills recording, with Crow simply repeating the figure three times using a very loose bow, making the performance sound more like the older contest-fiddling styles of Eck Robertson and other pre-Wills fiddlers than the fiddle styles of Ashlock, Gimble, and other Wills sidemen (figure 5.2). Moreover, in both recordings, the lead guitarist takes a sixteen-measure solo following the completion of the first verse. Rick Crow bases his takeoff solo on the opening notes of the guitar solo from Wills's 1945 recording, which was performed by either Cameron Hill or Jimmy

FIGURE 5.1. "Roly Poly" introductory motive.

FIGURE 5.2. Comparison of "Roly Poly" introductions.

Wyble.[58] After playing this brief fragment, his solo diverges from the original source. Whereas the soloist in Wills's recording plays a descending melodic sequence in thirds on the B and upper E strings of the guitar, Crow offers a less active descending lick built around a glissando on the B string.

Within the western swing tradition, the changes that Crow and the Neon Angels made would not be noteworthy. In fact, as a living musical tradition in the dance halls of Texas and Oklahoma, western swing musicians were expected to transform compositions to feature their individual musical talents and to cater to the tastes and demands of local dancers. Yet the similarities between Crow's recording and the 1945 Wills recording indicate that Austin's revivalists were responsible for a standardization of the western swing repertoire and performance practice. While musicians such as Wills often demanded that their sidemen "never copy anyone" and improvise new and innovative solos with each performance, Austin's revivalists clearly reproduced elements of the source recordings both as a way to gain competence as western swing and honky-tonk musicians and to demonstrate the depth and breadth of their immersion in the music. Like folk revivalists in a variety of musical traditions, Alvin Crow, Ray Benson, and their bandmates meticulously studied western swing source recordings, from which they learned both the nuances of the style and its key solos as a way of becoming competent to perform in the idiom. Furthermore, such study helped make their music relevant to both the cosmic cowboy audience and the patrons of rural dance halls. Their mimicry educated the cosmic cowboys by transmitting previously unknown solos to a new generation. At the same time, by demonstrating idiomatic mastery, Austin's revivalists could placate the patrons of the rural Texan dance halls he frequented by demonstrating that, despite their long hair and residence in Austin, they were performing western swing with a clear understanding of its musical and cultural heritage.

Such careful study of the primary sources of western swing and honky-tonk music and collaboration with the musicians who made the original recordings also facilitated creative decisions that would not have been possible without the depth of knowledge that Benson, Crow, and others gleaned from recordings and their collaborations with older musicians. As the previous examples illustrate, source recordings served as a launching pad for creative decisions that allowed the revivalists to demonstrate their cultural authority, their musical *bona fides*, and their interpretive prowess. Moreover, because these musicians worked diligently to learn and to promote western swing and honky-tonk music, they positioned themselves as heirs to the legacies of earlier Texan musicians and in the process established themselves as "Texan."

The rhetoric of preservation put forth by Austin's western swing revivalists certainly appealed to some segments of the progressive country music scene in Austin. As folklorist Archie Green has explained, for instance, many of the young people who relocated to Austin during the 1970s either to begin their academic careers or to become part of the city's growing local music scene were ambivalent about their Texan heritage, at once wishing to distance themselves from the Texanness of their parents while searching for roots in more "authentic" representations of Texan identity.[59] By attending live performances by Austin's revivalist bands, Austin's youth could eschew the Texas of their parents' generation by associating themselves directly with the music and imagery of their grandparents' generation. Moreover, western swing emerged in Texas and Oklahoma in the 1930s as the region's rural farmers began to migrate to cities like Fort Worth, Dallas, Tulsa, and Oklahoma City in search of upward socioeconomic mobility. As a result, it was connected musically and socially to both rural and urban Texas, drawing on pioneer fiddling practices and contemporary popular music. As many of Austin's youth sought a sort of downward mobility, therefore, their affinity with western swing and honky-tonk music also permitted them to bridge the gap between their primarily middle-class upbringing and their desire to get "back to the land." The western swing revivalists who were active in Austin's progressive country movement, like the cosmic cowboy songwriters with whom they coexisted, therefore offered an alternative definition of Texanness to a population that actively sought exactly that. By building upon the musical foundations of modern Texas, the western swing revivalists offered a more historically informed Texan identity. Through their attempts to reconstruct and resurrect a musical culture that had flourished more than three decades before progressive country, the revivalists proposed that the performance of western swing and honky-tonk music could bridge the generation gap between young Austinites and older generations of Texans while also providing an expressive medium through which the progressive country audience could temporarily resolve its own ambivalence about mounting social change.

Conclusion
"A Gathering of the Tribes":
Music Festivals and Confluence in Austin

O<small>N INDEPENDENCE DAY</small>, 1973, Willie Nelson hosted his first Fourth of July Picnic on a Hays County, Texas, ranch, initiating an event that would become an annual Texan institution that continues to the present day. This one-day event featured musicians representing every part of Austin's progressive country movement, including singer-songwriter Michael Murphey; rock musician, session musician, and impresario Leon Russell; yodeler and folk music pedagogue Kenneth Threadgill; and Nashville-based "Outlaw" Waylon Jennings. The picnic drew a critical mass of Austin's music fans to witness a showcase of the emerging progressive country movement. However, while this initial gathering in the Hill Country of central Texas and its subsequent iterations throughout the state provided a literal stage on which to promote Austin's musical community, Willie Nelson's Picnics also served as a public forum in which to negotiate the political, ideological, personal, and musical conflicts that shaped the progressive country scene through live performance. Furthermore, Nelson's Picnics were the capstone of a long-standing tradition of music festivals in Austin. Since the mid-1960s, the music festival had proven to be an effective means of displaying the city's latest musical innovations and of articulating the scene's collective identity. At the same time, these festivals permitted a few motivated businesspersons to generate much-needed revenue for the local musical community by showcasing the most popular local and regional bands and occasionally a few national touring artists. Austin's music festivals, therefore, blended the idealism of communal music making and the opportunism of grass-roots entrepreneurship, creating in the process an identifiable "brand" with which to market Austin and its music to a wider audience: Austin as a free-spirited, free-thinking, and music-centered community.[1]

The idea for Nelson's Fourth of July Picnics began with the Dripping Springs Reunion, a three-day country music festival organized by four Dallas-based promoters—Edward Allen, Michael McFarland, Peter B. Smith, and Don Snyder—at a ranch only twenty-four miles west of Austin in the small town of Dripping Springs, Texas, on March 17–19, 1972. As McFarland commented to reporters on the eve of the reunion, the promoters "just wanted to put on the best country and western show I'd ever seen and could ever hope to see."[2] To achieve this goal, the Reunion organizers turned to Nashville. While a few of Nashville's more radical and youth-oriented songwriters, including Kris Kristofferson and Billy Joe Shaver, performed at the Reunion, most of the musicians on the program represented the latest trends emerging from Nashville's Music Row (including Waylon Jennings, Tom T. Hall, Loretta Lynn, and Roger Miller) or were long-established members of the Nashville country music establishment such as Roy Acuff and Hank Snow. Yet, while this assemblage of mainstream country artists brought significant star power to the Dripping Springs Reunion, the promoters also needed to augment the program with a few Austin-based acts to fill the twelve-hour bill. As a result, a few local artists, among them yodeler Kenneth Threadgill, also performed at the Reunion.[3]

The Dripping Springs Reunion attracted countercultural adherents of the emerging progressive country music scene and an older, more conservative white population alike, and the event carried clear political significance for both groups. For the politically conservative audience in attendance, the Dripping Springs Reunion was a potentially potent symbol of conservative strength in the same way that the large rock festivals of the late 1960s, such as Woodstock and, more locally, the Texas International Pop Festival of 1969, had mobilized the youth countercul-ture politically and socially.[4] As *Los Angeles Times* music critic Robert Hilburn noted, some audience members interviewed at the Reunion expressed their hope that high attendance figures would demonstrate "the strength of the silent majority" to the world. Additionally, Hilburn observed that organizers of the Dripping Springs Reunion promoted the event as a wholesome affair that would conform to the expectations of the "typical" country music fan: "What the promoters wanted was a sort of family Woodstock featuring country music, giving adults a chance to participate in a celebration of their music (and no doubt life-style) just the way the younger rock fans had done at so many festivals."[5]

While the Reunion may have been conceived as a celebration of conservative cultural and political values, it also offered the growing community of countercultural country music fans in nearby Austin an opportunity to partake of a wide variety of country music in the familiar venue of the rock festival, a venue that was in many ways safer than the honky-tonks and dance halls in which this music was typically presented. Many observers in the Austin underground press expressed great consternation over the potential interaction of the city's hippies and its "straight" country music fans. John Lash, writing for *The Gar*, worried that the cross-cultural collision of the Dripping Springs Reunion might result in violence:

> As is quite obvious, the type of people that will be attracted [to Dripping Springs] will be different, not only in relation to income and age but also attitudes, politics, morals, and life-style. Here you'll have a crowd that will take a cold beer over a joint any day, and that sort of digs [Spiro] Agnew. It will be very interesting to see how 60,000 country music fans will react to the whole situation.[6]

Apparently, the Reunion's promoters were also concerned about the potential for violent conflicts between its audience's countercultural and conservative constituents. As "stroud," a regular contributor to *The Rag*, observed in his postmortem of the event:

> This first country and western festival, supposedly designed to do for C&W music what rock festivals do for rock (read—make money), was indeed a strange scene. The first thing to strike one's notice was the incredible number of security men—most of them Hays County deputies and most of them armed. While no incidents occurred, it is truly frightening to think of at least 200 armed men running around in a beer drinking crowd (no dope-smoking). In addition to security people there were hordes of "officials" running around—most of them, including apparently most of the population of Dripping Springs, honorary. Out of a first day crowd of about 3000, probably twenty per cent had on "security," "official," or "press" badges.[7]

Perhaps fortunately, attendance fell far short of the initial estimates, and many of the initial fears of violence and disorderly conduct were not realized. As Jan Reid recalled in *The Improbable Rise of Redneck Rock*, however, there were a few memorable incidents as Austin's long-haired cosmic cowboys engaged with their "cedar-chopper" counterparts: "Dope-smoking gate-crashers were taken aback by the sight of uniformed security guards toting shotguns, and a Veteran of Foreign Wars trinket vendor was equally taken aback by a young man who flipped his Frisbee in the air and remarked, 'If we'd quit having wars we wouldn't have any veterans.'"[8] These conflicts were also played out onstage; as Reid noted:

> Tex Ritter sang awhile, then emceed awhile too long, cracking lame Black Panther jokes and trying to bar Tom T. Hall from the microphone though the crowd was bellowing for an encore. Roy Acuff declared that he was the by-God king of country music, then crowed in triumph when an emcee announced that Merle Haggard was in a state of collapse and wouldn't make his scheduled appearance. "If that had happened to me or one of the boys in my band," Acuff claimed, "we'd a *been* here."[9]

Many Reunion participants may well have expected to witness performances by the stars of the Grand Ole Opry and to celebrate their conservative social values, but the sights and sounds of long-haired young performers likely stood as a direct affront to their core social values and their musical tastes. Furthermore, Acuff's criticism of Merle Haggard reveals ideological conflicts even within mainstream country music and most likely extends beyond a simple criticism of Haggard's lack of professional decorum. Although Haggard's "Okie from Muskogee" and "The Fightin' Side of Me" led progressive country musicians (and liberals in general) to view him as the musical embodiment of the Silent Majority, he was nothing of the sort to Acuff, a supporter of Alabama governor George Wallace. Rather, Haggard's contemporaneous work as a champion of the American working class in songs such as "Workin' Man's Blues" and "Hungry Eyes" had aligned him with the political Left in the eyes of many people along Music Row.[10] That Haggard, the paragon of conservatism to many members of the counterculture, would be viewed as too liberal a figure is particularly shocking in light of the many virulent reactions to his music. At the same time, it further underscores the Silent Majority's distrust of countercultural figures and rhetoric.

By most accounts, the Dripping Springs Reunion was a failure. Prior to the festival, promoters projected a daily attendance of around 60,000 people, but most estimates suggested that between 10,000 and 17,700 people attended the three-day festival. Because of poor advertising, the Reunion lost at least $75,000, and local newspaper headlines asked "What If They Gave a Festival . . . and Nobody Came?"[11] Yet, despite the physical and verbal conflicts between audience members and the featured musicians, many fans believed that, if the Reunion were to be mounted again with appropriate financing, the youth audience for country music would support country music festivals in central Texas. As one fan observed at the festival's conclusion, country music "is our music. . . . All we ever hear about is rock 'n' roll, rock 'n' roll. I hope this [reunion] can become an annual event so that people can see how beloved country music is."[12]

While McFarland, Snyder, Smith, and Allen decided to discontinue the Dripping Springs Reunion following their initial attempt, Willie Nelson, one of the featured artists at the 1972 Reunion, resurrected it as an event that featured the most exciting acts from Austin alongside some of Nashville's more radical artists. The Dripping Springs Reunion had been a particularly effective gathering for many emerging progressive country artists. Fiddler Alvin Crow, who was living in Amarillo and playing with the recently formed Pleasant Valley Boys, was enticed to move to Austin later that year, and Waylon Jennings, then an established Nashville recording artist, was introduced there to the music of the then unknown Texan songwriter Billy Joe Shaver, whose work would later form the basis of Jennings's landmark 1973 album, *Honky Tonk Heroes*, and the "outlaw" movement that flourished in Nashville in the mid-1970s.[13]

As the emerging leader of Austin's progressive country scene, Nelson was keenly aware of his audience's political goals and musical tastes and harbored a deep concern for their physical and ideological well-being. Nelson's experiences as a performer at the 1972 Dripping Springs Reunion allowed him to see firsthand the challenges associated with hosting an event that catered to two disparate audiences. He sought, therefore, not to try to bridge the generational and ideological divisions of the time. Instead, he chose to host a gathering at which fans of progressive country music, including not only Austin's cosmic cowboys but also older musicians who, like Nelson, were sympathetic to their cause, could gather to hear the latest music developed in Austin. At the same time, Nelson envisioned a festival that could capitalize on the progressive country movement's commercial potential, provide a venue for emerging talent, offer casual fans a concentrated exposure to the sounds of progressive country music, and develop a statewide or even national market for the music. As Nelson recalled:

In the spring [of 1972] some promoters had put together an outdoor concert called the Dripping Springs Reunion on a ranch west of Austin. They had bluegrass, Loretta Lynn, Tex Ritter, Roy Acuff, Kris Kristofferson, Waylon Jennings, Billy Joe Shaver, Leon Russell, and me—with [University of Texas coach] Coach [Darrell] Royal onstage. The promotion lost a bundle, but it had the seed of a sort of country Woodstock and got me wondering if I could do it better.[14]

With the failed Dripping Springs Reunion serving as a model of what not to do, Nelson set out to stage a festival that could both encapsulate the diverse sounds of Austin's progressive country scene and provide a safe space for Austin's cosmic cowboys to enjoy them.

After securing the Dripping Springs Reunion site from rancher Burt Hurlbut for $2,850, the control of all concessions sold on the premises, and money for capital improvements to the facilities, Nelson's first gathering was scheduled to occur on July 4, 1973. Having performed at the Dripping Springs Reunion, Nelson knew that the first step to organizing an event of such magnitude would be to hire a well-organized planner to assist with the project. He obtained the services of Michael Price, a businessman whom Nelson had met while in New York for his *Shotgun Willie* sessions at Atlantic. Price immediately went to work, asking François de Menil, a filmmaker and friend of his from New York, to arrange to film version of Nelson's 1973 gathering, hoping to follow the Woodstock model by capitalizing on postfestival marketing opportunities as well. De Menil, the son of French oil prospectors living in Houston, obtained $15,000 to finance the film and stipulated that Nelson must secure permission from all of the artists involved. Unfortunately, Nelson could not (or did not) secure the necessary releases, and, despite proposing that the releases be obtained after the festival, as was done at Woodstock, de Menil withdrew his funding for the film only days before the Picnic was scheduled to take place. To further complicate matters, Price, who believed that he was Nelson's sole legal representative, grew wary of the influence that Nelson's manager exerted on him and withdrew from the project as well.[15]

While Price and de Menil had exerted most of their energies in planning for the postpicnic marketing, Nelson was occupied with booking acts to fill the one-day program. Being rooted in both the Austin and Nashville scenes, Nelson was in a strong position to entice the strongest performers from both scenes to appear at the Picnic. The notion that Nelson was inviting his closest friends for a celebration of this music was quite prevalent in Austin. As Austin-based rock journalist Ed Ward noted in an October 1975 feature article in *Creem*:

> The favored type of music around town [Austin] was something called "progressive country," and Willie, in both his music and his lifestyle, sort of epitomizes what that term is all about. So when Willie made it

known that he wanted to get some of the top progressive country artists together for a little bash, some of his friends set it up, and in 1973 was born the first annual Willie Nelson 4th of July Picnic.[16]

Waylon Jennings remembered that Nelson exerted an almost inexplicably powerful influence on musicians in Austin and Nashville alike:

> Independence Day, 1973.
>
> Willie has called a gathering of the tribes to this dusty patch of ranch twenty miles west of Austin. He's roped in Sammi Smith, who's just had a big hit with Kris's [Kristofferson] "Help Me Make It through the Night," and myself to help him bring it off.
>
> Naturally it's pure chaos. We've got Ernest Tubb, Hank Cochran, Charlie Rich, Kris Kristofferson and Rita Coolidge, Ray Price, Loretta Lynn, Johnny Bush, the whole Austin scene with Jerry Jeff Walker and Doug Sahm, and yours trulys [sic] milling backstage.[17]

As Jennings's comments indicate, Nelson's first Fourth of July Picnic did feature a few elder statesmen of country music, yet the inclusion of Ernest Tubb and Hank Cochran on this program should not be a great surprise. Given the revivalist spirit that shaped much of the music

FIGURE 6.1. The audience at Willie Nelson's 1973 Fourth of July Picnic, Dripping Springs, Texas. Photograph by Alan Pogue, used by permission.

making in Austin, Tubb's and Cochran's presence not only provided a connection to an earlier generation of musicians and the honky-tonk styles that they helped to popularize but also offered a distinctly Texan connection to the past. Unlike Roy Acuff, whose musical style was emblematic of the string band traditions of the Southeast, Tubb's and Cochran's honky-tonk music was born and popularized in southwestern dance halls between the 1940s and the 1960s.

Nelson's 1973 Fourth of July Picnic was a boon to the Austin progressive country music scene. It brought national artists and Austin's local stars into close contact with one another, and speculations that Bob Dylan, who had recently been working with Austin fixture and Nelson confidant Doug Sahm, might even perform at the festival confirmed that the scene was becoming increasingly important.[18] The 1973 Picnic also offered an opportunity for Austin's entertainment entrepreneurs to demonstrate their skills as promoters, booking agents, and businesspersons to national artists who had been bypassing Austin in favor of Dallas and Houston. When Price and de Menil left Nelson's operation in mid-June 1973, Nelson turned to Eddie Wilson, proprietor of the Armadillo World Headquarters, to promote the event and make certain that all of the bills were paid on time. Beginning on June 23, less than two weeks prior to the event, Wilson and his team— including an accountant, a site manager, a lawyer, and a clerical staff— organized a promotional campaign to encourage Austin's young people to make the short trek to Dripping Springs for the Picnic. While Wilson and his team were paid handsomely for their efforts (more than 10 percent of the reported gross revenue of $111,398.60), the real benefit of the Wilson-Nelson alliance was in securing the Armadillo's future.[19] By July 4, 1973, the Armadillo had been open for nearly three years, but it had endured almost constant financial struggles as Wilson and his staff sought ways to entice Austin's young people to spend their disposable income at the Armadillo.[20] Moreover, Wilson had been working to develop the Armadillo as a venue suitable for national touring acts, noting that, although such musicians demand higher costs, they also generate more revenue from casual fans. By 1974, Wilson was planning to expand his operation at the Armadillo into a multimillion-dollar recording facility and media production center with the hope of bringing both local and national musicians there to make records.[21] Although a rushed affair, the opportunity to work with Nelson on the Fourth of July Picnic allowed Wilson to demonstrate both his efficiency and his hospitality as a promoter and businessman and set the stage for future developments at the Armadillo.

In addition, Wilson's assistance may well have worked to secure the notion of Austin as a unified musical community in the minds of many national artists. Whereas the presence of New York-based promoters like Michael Price very clearly demonstrated Nelson's links to the national music industry, Wilson was an unmistakable representative of the Austin scene. As such, when the artists arrived in Dripping Springs on July 4, 1973, they were greeted not by New York agents but by Texans. Moreover, these Texans appeared to have focused their attention exclusively on celebrating progressive country music and developing Austin as a center for new music. During a time when many artists on both the local and the national level were openly distrustful of the machinations of large music corporations, Wilson and the "Armadillos" displayed a marked parochialism that obscured the role of the music industry in Austin and at the Picnic. As a result, Nelson's Fourth of July Picnic permitted musical exchange between national artists and lesser-known Texan artists and forged connections that provided Austin's musicians new energy, motivation, and musical direction that encouraged further expansion of the scene's activities and the local music industry.

Nelson's 1973 Fourth of July Picnic also elicited strong audience response. Unlike the poorly attended Dripping Springs Reunion, fans of progressive country music flocked to Hays County to witness Nelson's picnic, causing a Woodstock-like traffic jam outside the festival grounds. Reid described Nelson's Picnic as "a traffic jam in the wilderness," invoking pastoral tropes that were central to the progressive country scene.[22] Although Dripping Springs is just a few miles west of Austin, this journey outside of Austin appears to have satisfied a collective desire to escape into rural Texas. In fact, the difficulty of the trip imbued the Picnic with a degree of importance that a painless commute could not. Traveling on foot in the final miles, the cosmic cowboys became Texan pioneers of a sort, forging new musical and social paths through physical sacrifice. Yet, at the same time, once they arrived at Burt Hurlbut's ranch, the concertgoers could feel safe and free to celebrate the shared musical and social values of the Austin progressive country music scene within the bounded spaces of the picnic grounds.

Nelson's attempts to stage subsequent events were marked by confrontations with local authorities who, like those people who protested the Kerrville Folk Festival, wished to prevent a mass gathering of young people. Following the relative success of the Dripping Springs event, Nelson decided to take the program on the road, appearing at venues throughout the state of Texas and venturing ever farther from the safe spaces around Austin. After hosting a three-day event at College Station (1974) and a one-day festival in Liberty Hill (1975), Nelson sought to stage the 1976 Picnic near the town of Gonzales, Texas, sixty miles south of Austin and seventy miles east of San Antonio. Under the Texas Music Festival Act, a law that governed music festivals lasting longer than one day, Nelson was required to request written permission from the Gonzales County Commissioners' Court to stage the event. However, Citizens for Law, Order, and Decency (CLOD), a local citizens' group led by Gonzales minister James Darnell, protested the event, observing the following in an April 1976 advertisement in the Gonzales *Inquirer*:

> To allow this invasion is to invite [the] anti-American, anti-Christian, hippie subculture right into our homes. Drinking and drunkenness (already a terrible problem in our schools), illegal sale and use of marijuana and hard drugs, nudity and immorality, lawlessness and total disrespect for law officers, anti-patriotism and crude music that stirs up the viler impulses of the human psyche will all characterize this "Bicentennial event."[23]

After CLOD petitioned the Gonzales County commissioners, the court decided to withhold approval of the event.[24] Friends of Willie, a counterorganization composed of local fans and promoters, then circulated a petition to reverse the decision, collecting more than two thousand names in little more than one week.[25] In late May, Nelson filed a new permit application under the Texas Mass Gathering Act, which had jurisdiction over events lasting twelve hours or less, because, unlike the Texas Music Festival Act, the application needed only the approval of the county judge. The application was approved, and Nelson booked acts for a shorter, one-day festival that would feature only eighteen artists.[26]

The language of Darnell's April advertisement lays bare the core issues at stake in the battle between Austin's cosmic cowboys and rural Texans. First, his use of the word "invasion" to describe the arrival of Nelson's fans in Gonzales indicates that Darnell (and presumably most of the congregation of his Daystar Fellowship Church) saw the Picnic as an assault on a purportedly innocent Texan town and perceived progressive country musicians and their fans as dangerous outsiders. Moreover, Darnell's diatribe echoes the sentiments of Merle Haggard's "Okie from Muskogee" by positioning the long-haired youths in opposition to core middle-American values. Yet the mass of young people who might attend Nelson's 1976 Picnic differed in one significant way from the hippies of San Francisco mentioned in Haggard's song. Whereas Haggard's hippies existed in a distant and exotic California, the hippies of Nelson's Picnics were perhaps more threatening to conservative Texans because they actually resided there, alongside the congregation of Darnell's church. Echoing the rhetoric of the parents who protested the influence of rock 'n' roll on their children during the 1950s, Darnell and the more than twelve hundred people who signed a petition opposing the Gonzales Picnic feared the complete dissolution of their community at the hands of the "crude music" that would be performed at the event. Although Nelson and his colleagues presented their positive construction of the Austin scene and its concomitant youth culture in the Fourth of July Picnics, Darnell's protests—and the Texas Music Festival Act—helped to fortify the boundaries that separated the "anti-American, anti-Christian hippie subculture" from more conservative rural and small-town Texans.[27] Moreover, as journalist Mike Reynolds reported in *Crawdaddy* in May 1977, the Gonzales Picnic "was more akin to [the] Altamont [Speedway Free Festival, where, in December 1969, Hell's Angels murdered an audience member within feet of the stage], though no one was murdered. From whoever keeps such statistics, eighteen overdoses, fifteen stabbings and seven rapes kept people on their toes for the two days out on the dust-choked sprawl of Gonzales. To take up the slack there was the pastime of piss-on-the-prone, musical fistfights and general falling down and coughing."[28] Willie Nelson's Fourth of July Picnics, therefore, represented both a psychological and a tangible threat to the security and sanctity of small-town Texan life, threats that many members of the progressive country movement appeared to dismiss.

To rebuff critics like Darnell and to direct public attention away from the overdoses and violence of the Picnics, Nelson, like most contemporaneous festival promoters, portrayed the Fourth of July Picnics as peaceful celebrations in his public interviews. Nelson also financed a feature-length film that, in addition to providing additional postfestival revenue, depicted the Picnic as a positive social event and challenged the protesters' claims. While the first Picnic at Dripping Springs in 1973 was supposed to be filmed, the financial and logistical arrangements never came through. So, for the 1974 Picnic, held at the Texas World Speedway in College Station, Nelson hired director Yabo Yablonski and producers Michael Jay Jones and Gary Kratochvil to film the three-day affair. The resulting film, *Willie Nelson's 4th of July*

Picnic, was released by La Paz Productions in 1977 and depicts the occasion as a nonviolent event in which the distinction between audience and performer was blurred and all of the participants celebrated the progressive country movement.[29]

Yablonski portrayed the communality of the Picnic by combining shots of the audience's reactions to the musical events with images of the musicians' interactions both onstage and in the wings. The sequence that accompanies "Whiskey River," the opening musical number in the film, is particularly indicative of how this idealized notion is constructed throughout the film. Yablonski begins by highlighting the diversity of Nelson's audience, a group including not only college students and other young people but also a few older fans, among them a heavy-set man in his late thirties or early forties seen dressed only in patterned overalls dancing and drinking from a bottle of whiskey. In the same sequence, Yablonski also focuses on a group of young people dancing in a circle and sharing alcoholic beverages. These shots are spliced together with images of Nelson's entire band—not Nelson himself, who, as both the bandleader and the festival's impresario and namesake, certainly deserved and could have demanded close-up shots—performing as a cohesive and collective unit, drawing attention to the group effort necessary for the success of the Picnic and the scene itself. This three-and-a-half-minute segment breaks down the boundaries between the audience and the performers onstage; everyone appears to be enjoying the music. Furthermore, this sequence's placement at the very beginning of the film indicates that the ideas of community and communality are central elements of the Picnic's success and suggests that these ideas should frame viewers' perception of the remaining eighty minutes of performances and the 1974 Picnic as a whole.

The conclusion of *Willie Nelson's 4th of July Picnic* further underscores Yablonski's construction of Austin's progressive country music scene as a unified community. In the film's final fifteen minutes, all of the performers who had appeared onstage throughout the festival come together for an extended jam session. Michael Murphey, the artist onstage at the time, invites Nelson, Leon Russell, the Nitty Gritty Dirt Band, David Allan Coe, and many others to perform alongside him, noting that "These people *are* the cosmic cowboys." By 1974, therefore, the term *cosmic cowboy* had already transcended Austin and become a broader phenomenon applicable to non-Austin bands, Nashville songwriters, and internationally renowned session musicians, producers, and impresarios. Moreover, the song had recently been recorded by the Nitty Gritty Dirt Band for their album *Stars & Stripes Forever*.[30]

The assemblage performs two songs: Michael Murphey's "Cosmic Cowboy" and "Goodnight, Irene," a folksong written by Leadbelly and made popular by the Weavers in 1950. The choice of these compositions to conclude the film is of particular interest for a number of reasons. First, each of these songs represents the core musical and cultural values of the progressive country movement. "Cosmic Cowboy" addresses the idealization of the American West, while "Goodnight, Irene" hearkens to the movement's origins in the folk-singing groups at Threadgill's and the University of Texas. Moreover, because of their repetitive refrains and the ubiquity of Murphey's song on local radio stations, both are easily adaptable to group singing, allowing both the musicians displayed onstage and the now invisible audience, hidden by the cover of darkness, to contribute their voices to the mix. Murphey's studio recording of "Cosmic Cowboy" displays the same type of imprecise background singing found at the live performance at Nelson's picnic. However, perhaps most important, this concluding scene offers a unifying vision of the progressive country music movement by drawing together the wide variety of musicians who performed in the three-day 1974 Willie Nelson Fourth of July Picnic in a single performance. Just as music festivals bring together a heterogeneous body of fans for a single, intense musical experience, so, too, by Yablonski's estimation, do they galvanize a community of musicians through their shared musical and cultural values.

While the film presents an image of Nelson's Picnics as a positive and socially uplifting cultural happening, *Willie Nelson's 4th of July Picnic* does not directly attempt to rebut the charges of immorality, drunkenness, and drug use that protesters like Darnell feared. Rather, several shots prominently feature blatantly illegal—and in the eyes of many of the Picnics' detractors, immoral—acts, including the consumption of alcohol and marijuana, public nudity, and fondling. Such behavior was as much a part of the Picnic as was the performance of music itself, but the film implies that the Picnic's community-building efforts made such immorality forgivable, if not permissible. Like many other contemporary concert films, *Willie Nelson's 4th of July Picnic* focused on the centrality of music and community to the festival experience and challenged the notion that music festivals are violent and debauched events.

Just as the film selectively presented the activities of the picnic attendees in order to highlight their positive efforts and quiet concerns about moral turpitude, it—like the Dripping Springs Reunion and the annual picnics themselves—displayed a very selective program representing a narrow perspective of the Austin progressive country music scene. Nelson's 1974 picnic in College Station, Texas, lasted three days and featured no fewer than thirty-six artists and groups, including representatives of Austin's local club scene, the local stars of progressive country music, and national country stars (table 6.1). The portrait of Austin's progressive country music scene in *Willie Nelson's 4th of July Picnic* was, however, necessarily limited. Yablonski could not capture the full breadth of the three-day festival in a two-hour feature film. The film instead offers performances of only eight of the festival's thirty-six acts: Nelson, B. W. Stevenson, Waylon Jennings, Leon Russell, Doug Kershaw, Jerry Jeff Walker, the Lost Gonzo Band, and Michael Murphey. This reduced program offers a slightly different understanding of progressive country music in Austin than the Picnic from which the footage was culled. The elimination of nearly all of Austin's local bands, with the sole exception of the Lost Gonzo Band,

TABLE 6.1.   Artists who performed at Willie Nelson's 1974 Fourth of July Picnic, College Station, Texas.[31]

Local Artists with No Connections to the National Record Industry	Austin Artists with Connections to the National Record Industry	National Artists with Connections to Austin
Milton Carol Band	Asleep at the Wheel	Barefoot Jerry
		Moe Bandy
Alvin Crow	Guy Clark	Jimmy Buffett
Freda and the Firedogs	Doug Kershaw	Lee Clayton
Greezy Wheels	Michael Murphey	Hank Cochran
Ray Wylie Hubbard	Tracy Nelson and Mother Earth	David Allan Coe
Lost Gonzo Band	Willis Alan Ramsey	Larry Gatlin
Augie Meyers	B. W. Stevenson	Tompall Glaser
Fanni Smith	Jerry Jeff Walker	Linda Hargrove
Spanky and Our Gang	Rusty Wier	Alex Harvey
Kenneth Threadgill		John Hartford
		Waylon Jennings
		Dee Moeller
		Rick Nelson
		Willie Nelson
		Leon Russell
		Red Steagall

and the inclusion of artists with major-label recording contracts validate the progressive country music movement. At once, this representation depicts Austin's connections to the Nashville music industry, marking it as being of national interest, and portrays it as a free-spirited oasis, isolated from the rest of the country, in which the stars of country music can collaborate with each other outside the influence of Music Row.

Progressive country music developed within the many venues for live musical performance located throughout Austin. The daily interactions of musicians, promoters, and audiences in the city's clubs and dance halls facilitated the constant renegotiation of Austin's musical and social identities. Festivals like Willie Nelson's Fourth of July Picnics, on the other hand, offered audiences fixed representations of the progressive country music movement, reinforced the scene's core musical and social values, and distilled and commodified the complex daily interactions of Austin's progressive music scene. Nelson's Picnics were carefully composed snapshots of the progressive country music movement that permitted, for a relatively low admission fee, the music's passionate fans and casually committed audiences alike to connect to Austin's musical community through their participation in an intense live musical experience.[32] As a result, Nelson's Picnics solidified Austin's reputation as an alternative hotbed for live music where musicians could collaborate and liberal audiences could celebrate their collective difference.

The progressive country music scene that flourished in Austin during the 1970s was built upon the contradictions and orthodoxies that became most evident during the frenzy of the scene's music festivals. Fueled by grassroots entrepreneurialism and an anticorporate attitude, the sustainability and growth of the scene were as dependent upon the material and financial support of the Nashville and Los Angeles music industries—which supplied recording studios, publishing houses, distribution networks, publicity, and financial capital—as it was upon the daily efforts of Austinites. Furthermore, because festivals concentrated the scene's activities and brought the diverse and often fragmented constituencies of the progressive country music scene together for a single event, these gatherings demonstrated the political and economic power of the events, thereby encouraging corporations and local politicians to take the scene participants seriously and, as a result, garnering increased support from internal and external sources.

The progressive country music scene, like the Picnics, witnessed a constant flow of "local" musicians between the national music industry and the local scene. Yet, unlike those scenes in which a local artist who finds success with a regional or national record label, Austin's progressive country music scene became a site in which artists who were deeply entrenched in the national industry could safely perform an anti-industrial critique and become de facto local musicians. Local lore suggests, for instance, that Waylon Jennings was closely associated with the progressive country music movement, but, with the exception of occasional performances in Austin and his participation in Nelson's Picnics, he was actually fully imbricated within the Nashville music scene, where he maintained his recording contract with RCA Records and resided. Yet, Jennings's participation in the scene's music festivals allowed him to be perceived as making the same kind of significant contributions to the scene as Michael Murphey, Marcia Ball, Jerry Jeff Walker, or Ray Benson.

More important, the music festivals that were supported by members of the progressive country music scene allowed the scene participants to publicly perform their collective identity and Texas-centric values and to proclaim their difference from a perceived cultural mainstream. It is striking that, although the festival stages were not spacious enough to represent the full spectrum of musics that were created and enjoyed in Austin, the festival organizers did, in fact, make certain that equal time was granted to musicians who, like Kenneth Threadgill, embodied the roots of Austin music, as well as to more mainstream acts such as Nashville outlaw David Allan Coe. The resultant portrait captured the inclusive musical attitudes of progressive country music audiences. Yet, by focusing on musicians who either hailed from Texas or were recasting themselves as Texan, it also articulated an oppositional message that recast the familiar festival format as a vibrant and distinctly Texan (and therefore exclusionary) event.

At the core of these music festivals—as with nearly all events within Austin's progressive country music scene—was a collective desire to share musical experiences and to join together to create something that transcended the individuals. Through these shared musical experiences, the scene participants found, at least for the duration of these events, a space within which they could reconcile their own complicated relationships with the white working-class culture and celebrate their collective experience through music.

Notes

Preface

1. George Lipsitz, "Foreword," in Susan D. Crafts, Daniel Cavicchi, and Charles Keil, *My Music: Explorations of Music in Daily Life*, Music in Daily Life Project (New Hanover: Wesleyan University Press, 1993), xiii.

2. Richard A. Peterson and Andy Bennett, "Introducing Music Scenes," in *Music Scenes: Local, Translocal, and Virtual* (Nashville: Vanderbilt University Press, 2004), 2–3.

3. For scholarship representing this approach to music scenes, see Kruse, *Site and Sound*; Hebdige, *Subculture*; Wallach, "Living the Punk Lifestyle in Jakarta"; Melanie Lowe, "'Tween' Scene: Resistance within the Mainstream," in *Music Scenes: Local, Translocal, and Virtual*, ed. Richard A. Peterson and Andy Bennett (Nashville: Vanderbilt University Press, 2004), 80–95; Straw, "Communities and Scenes in Popular Music," 494; Shank, *Dissonant Identities*.

4. See, for instance, Finnegan, *Hidden Musicians*; Sara Cohen, "Men Making a Scene"; Huq, "Raving, Not Drowning"; Middleton, "DC Punk and the Production of Authenticity."

5. McClary and Walser, "Start Making Sense!" 281–283; Brackett, *Interpreting Popular Music*, 19.

6. Schilt, "'Riot Grrrl Is . . .'"

7. As Barry Shank has suggested, "a scene itself can be defined as an overproductive signifying community; that is, far more semiotic information is produced than can be rationally parsed" (Shank, *Dissonant Identities*, 122).

8. See, for instance, Spring, "Behind the Rave"; Laird, *Louisiana Hayride*; Sara Cohen, *Decline, Renewal and the City*, 95–123.

1. Porterfield, "Introduction," in *Exploring Roots Music*, ix–xxiv; Pecknold, *That Selling Sound*, 189–199.

2. Rodnitzky, "Decline of Contemporary Protest Music," 46; Lund and Denisoff, "Folk Music Revival and the Counter Culture," 403–404; Denisoff, *Sing a Song of Social Significance*, 178–179; DiMaggio, Peterson, and Esco Jr., "Country Music: Ballad of the Silent Majority," 44–46; Lund, "Fundamentalism, Racism, and Political Reaction in Country Music," 88–91; Fox and Williams, "Political Orientation and Music Preferences among College Students," 370–371; Cobb, "From Muskogee to Luckenbach"; Averill, "Esoteric-exoteric Expectations of Redneck Behavior and Country Music"; Malone, *Don't Get above Your Raisin'*, 237–244; Cusic, "Politics and Country Music, 1963–1974"; LaChapelle, *Proud to Be an Okie*, 138–148.

3. Kemp, *Dixie Lullaby*, 20–34.

4. Gracey, "City Audiences Honest, Picky."

5. Ball, email communication with author, 25 January 2007.

6. For a more complete discussion of this phenomenon within the broader context of American culture, see Lytle, *America's Uncivil Wars*, 269–315.

7. Kuhlman, "Direct Action at the University of Texas," 550–566; Russell, "*Sweatt v. Painter* Archive."

8. Herrera, "TIME for a Change," 13; Gutiérrez, *Making of a Chicano Militant*, 109–110.

9. Gracey, email communication with author, 5 April 2007. See also Kleinman, "Street Noise"; Coppage, "Is Country Going to the Dogs?"

10. Martin, "Time Is a Pivotal Issue," 10.

11. Ball, interview with author, 18 January 2007.

12. Butch Hancock, qtd. in Dawidoff, *In the Country of Country*, 305.

13. "Texas Stompin' " 11; Kleinman, "Street Noise," 5; Valentine, "Street Noise," 28. See also Tucker, "Progressive Country Music, 1972–1976," 96; Turley, "Social and Ecological Determinants," 133.

14. Jason Dean Mellard, "Cosmic Cowboys, Armadillos and Outlaws: The Cultural Politics of Texan Identity in the 1970s," Ph.D. dissertation, The University of Texas at Austin, 2009, 1.

15. Archie Green, "Midnight and Other Cowboys," 150, 152; Archie Green, "Austin's Cosmic Cowboys," 66–68; Malone, "Myth, Media, and the Making of Texas Music," 9; Spitzer, "Romantic Regionalism and Convergent Culture," 90; Lock, "Counterculture Cowboys," 15; Michael Allen, " 'I Just Want to Be a Cosmic Cowboy,' " par. 3.

16. Sepulvedo and Burks, "Texas."

17. Flippo, "Splash," 21.

18. Simon, "Vulcan Gas Company."

19. Patoski, interview with author, 1 April 2008; Menconi, "Music, Media, and the Metropolis," 26–27.

20. "Broken Spoke Legend"; Smith, interview with author, 2 June 2007; Murphey, interview with Jack Bernhardt, 5 June 1993; Shank, *Dissonant Identities*, 46.

21. Agnew, *Back from the Land*.

22. Wilson, interview with Robert Heard, 26 June 1974.

23. Austin's underground press provided extensive coverage of the changing face of the city throughout this period of transition. See, for instance, Smith, "Urban Renewal"; Rainbow, "Tour of a Commercial Slum"; "Open City"; Plumb, "'Progress' and Destruction in South Austin"; Plumb, "Are You In on the Planning for Austin?"; Elder, "Austin Neighborhoods"; "Obituary: West Mall"; Foxx, "Hippy Hollow"; Wylie, "University Hills Saves Park"; Cravey, "Barton Springs"; Gouldy, "God Bless City Hall"; Moriarty, "90-Story Highrise"; Rislier, "1 Million People in Austin"; Shrake, "Screwing Up of Austin"; "Editorial: We Already Have Dallas and Houston"; Neff, "MOPAC: The Monster That Ate Austin"; Schweers, "What a Bore!" See also Orum, *Power, Money & the People*, 267–305.

24. Orum, *Power, Money & the People*, 307–348; "City Aims at Record in Building."

25. In 1970, the full-year population of Austin stood at 251,808, while in 1980, 345,496 people resided there. This increase continued a trend that had been mounting since around 1920. Interestingly enough, to that point, Austin had never enjoyed less than a 16-percent increase in population since it was founded (*Texas Almanac and State Industrial Guide, 1980–1981*).

26. The growth of the student body at the University of Texas actually happened in spite of a trend toward smaller incoming freshman classes throughout the decade between 1968 and 1977. In fact, it appears as though UT's student body grew as older students returned to their studies after some time off. Whereas the size of incoming freshman classes decreased steadily from 9,165 in 1968 to 7,689 in 1977, the senior class nearly doubled from 5,911 in 1968 to 10,642 in 1977. Similarly, the university's graduate and professional programs were a source of growth as more women entered graduate schools in the 1970s.

27. Cody, "Austin Movement"; Cody, "Notes on the Movement,"; Cumquat, "Sign on the Line, $5," 14. This communal approach was a central part of much counter-cultural activity in the late 1960s and early 1970s and found its most public (and perhaps most widely accepted) expression through music. See, for instance, Weber, "'Could Be an Illusion, but I Might as Well Try,'" 141–142, 144–146.

28. Wilson, interview with Robert Heard, 26 June 1974; Capri, "View of Shelter-Vision"; Groenenwegen and Bentley, "From San Antonio to Mars"; Wexler and Ritz, *Rhythm and the Blues*, 18, 20; 268–269, 273–276; Ball, interview with author, 18 January 2007; Smith, interview with author, 2 June 2007; Livingston, interview with author, 25 June 2007; Patoski, *Willie Nelson*, 243–287.

29. Nightbyrd, "Highway 71 Revisited"; Gross, "Something's Right in Austin"; Axthelm, "Songs of Outlaw Country"; Reynolds, "Hook 'Em Horns"; "In the Heart of Honky-Tonk Rock."

30. Dailey, "Michael Murphey"; Draper, "Rocky Mountain Special"; Flippo, "Austin: The Hucksters are Coming"; Neff, "Big Commotion in Austin."

1. Oakes, "Thousands Turn Out for Threadgill," 17.
2. Haworth, "Threadgill, Kenneth."
3. Malone, email communication with author, 7 March 2008. See also: Malone, *Country Music, U.S.A.*, ix.
4. Reid, *Improbable Rise of Redneck Rock*, 18.
5. Shank, *Dissonant Identities*, 40.
6. Ibid. Similarly, folklorist Archie Green, who served as the faculty advisor of the Campus Folksong Club at the University of Illinois at Urbana-Champaign, recalled that, "although our club grew to more than five hundred members, sober leaders know that they formed but a tiny enclave within a huge campus geared to elite and popular culture" (Green, "Campus Folksong Club," 64).
7. Friedman, *Buried Alive*, 40.
8. Hartman, *History of Texas Music*, 209–210; Koster, *Texas Music*, 99–100.
9. Reid, *Improbable Rise of Redneck Rock*, 20–21.
10. Landau, "Newport Folk Festival," 17.
11. Kennedy, interview with Jan Reid, 1 January 1970; Murphey, interview with Jack Bernhardt, 5 June 1993; Raphael, interview with author, 6 June 2007; Livingston, interview with author, 25 June 2007.
12. Malone, email communication with author, 7 March 2008.
13. "Old Gas Station Is Center for Weekly Folk Sessions."
14. Porterfield, *Jimmie Rodgers*, 201, 432; Green, *Singing in the Saddle*, 37–38; Specht, "Blue Yodeler Is Coming to Town"; Mazor, *Meeting Jimmie Rodgers*, 131–154.
15. Neal, *Songs of Jimmie Rodgers*, 69–77, 194–199.
16. Olds, "Threadgill: Country Music King Gets His Day."
17. Olds, "Jimmie Rodgers: The First Hillbilly Star."
18. Olds, "Threadgill: Country Music King Gets His Day"; Lash, "Interview: Threadgill," 6; "Threadgill Unifies Cultures with Yodels."
19. Landau, "Newport Folk Festival," 17.
20. Neely, "Blackland Farm," *Austin's Original Singer-Songwriter* (Lost Art Records LAR 101G, 2002).
21. Spitzer, "Jimmie Rodgers in Texas," 2.
22. Lash, "Interview: Threadgill," 6–7.
23. Spitzer, "Jimmie Rodgers in Texas," 2. See also Neal, *Songs of Jimmie Rodgers*, 264–267.
24. Olds, "Threadgill: Country Music King Gets His Day."
25. "Threadgill Unifies Cultures with Yodels, Rodgers Style"; Mays, "Old Is Beautiful—in Music or on Threadgill," 14.
26. "Thousands Turn Out for Threadgill," 19.
27. "Threadgill: Country Music King Gets His Day."
28. Malone, email communication with author, 7 March 2008.
29. Smith, interview with author, 2 June 2007.

30. See, for instance, Wiemers, "Joplin Called Him Daddy."

31. Gracey, email communication with author, 5 April 2007.

32. Ibid.; Pecknold, *That Selling Sound*, 143–152.

33. Reid, *Improbable Rise of Redneck Rock*, 78.

34. Pecknold, *That Selling Sound*, 168–169.

35. Gracey, email communication with author, 5 April 2007.

36. Historian Eric Hobsbawm has observed that "we should expect [the invention of traditions] . . . to occur more frequently when a rapid transformation of society weakens or destroys the social patterns for which 'old' traditions had been designed, producing new ones to which they were not applicable, or when such old traditions and their institutional carriers and promulgators no longer prove sufficiently adaptable and flexible, or are otherwise eliminated: in short, when there are sufficiently large and rapid changes on the demand or the supply side" (Hobsbawm, "Introduction: Inventing Traditions," 4–5).

37. Historian Gary Hartman has argued that the unique circumstances of Texan ethnic diversity and comingling have resulted in innumerable musical hybrids: "Not only has the Lone Star State served as a crossroads for so many different ethnic groups, but the particular social, political, and economic forces that have shaped the area have helped make the Southwest one of the most complex and diverse regional societies in the country. Nowhere is this tremendous diversity more apparent than in Texas music. An astounding variety of musical genres have thrived in the region, often cross-pollinating to create new subgenres" (Hartman, "Roots Run Deep," 3–4).

38. Malone, "Myth, Media, and the Making of Texas Music," 9. Historian Edward Shils has observed similarly that:

> *there are two pasts.* One is the sequence of occurred events, of actions which were performed and of the actions which they called forth, moving through a complex sequence of actions until the presence is reached. . . . There is another past. This is the perceived past. This is a much more plastic thing, more capable of being retrospectively reformed by human beings living in the present. It is the past which is recorded in memory and in writing, formed from encounters with "the hard facts," not just from inescapable but also from sought-for encounters. (Shils, *Tradition*, 195)

39. Meinig, *Imperial Texas*, 124; Nackman, *Nation within a Nation*, 3–6.

40. Ethnomusicologist Fabian Holt offers an extensive discussion of the roles that discourse about music play in shaping conceptions of genre, noting that "naming a music is a way of recognizing its existence and distinguishing it from other musics. The name becomes a point of reference and enables certain forms of communication, control, and specialization into markets, canons, and discourses. This process also involves exclusionary mechanisms, and it is often met with resistance" (Holt, *Genre in Popular Music*, 3–4). See also Blaustein, "Rethinking Folk Revivalism," 272; Glassie, "Tradition," 395.

41. Sterling and Keith, *Sounds of Change*, 102–105, 108–112.

42. Ibid., 129–130.

43. McLuhan, *Understanding Media*, 7–23.

44. "Sonobeat-KAZZ Connection," 1.

45. "Austin Music Scene: Bill Josie," 11; "Sonobeat Records: Austin in the '60s," 8.

46. "Austin Music Scene: Bill Josie," 11.

47. "Sonobeat Discography"; "Sonobeat Records: Austin in the '60s," 7–9.

48. This was especially true for the 13th Floor Elevators, one of the pioneers of psychedelic rock, who used KAZZ-FM and the New Orleans Club to develop their on-stage act, work out repertoire, and build an audience. Later, after an unsuccessful trip to San Francisco, they came back to KAZZ-FM and the New Orleans Club to regroup. See Drummond, *Eye Mind*, 112–113; "Local Rock 'n' Roll Band Back from Successful Tour."

49. "Sonobeat-KAZZ Connection," 4.

50. Moyer, interview with author, 4 December 2009.

51. Gracey, email communication with author, 5 April 2007.

52. Allen, "KOKE-FM," 7.

53. Menconi, "Music, Media and the Metropolis," 60–64.

54. Wilson, interview with Robert Heard, 26 June 1974.

55. Reid, *Improbable Rise of Redneck Rock*, 62–63.

56. Wilson, interview with Robert Heard, 26 June 1974. Jim Franklin actually took up residence backstage.

57. Business records for the Armadillo World Headquarters are spotty (Armadillo World Headquarters Collection, CAH).

58. Wilson, interview with Robert Heard, 26 June 1974.

59. Menconi, "Music, Media and the Metropolis."

60. Wilson, interview with Robert Heard, 26 June 1974.

61. In a 1974 article for the *American-Statesman*, Wilson estimated that, while the club began with regular audiences of around four hundred people per night, "around 150,000 in town will probably attend Armadillo at one time or another" (White, "Armadillo World Headquarters Celebrates 4th Year").

62. Gracey, email communication with author, 5 April 2007.

63. Ibid.

64. Endres, *Austin City Limits*, 13.

65. This approach to various types of Texan music, which are discussed further in chapter 5, is exemplified in the work of Doug Sahm and Willie Nelson, both of whom drew regularly upon a vast array of Texan musical traditions in their recorded work, including conjunto, rhythm and blues, western swing, rock and roll, and honky-tonk.

66. Joe Gracey, qtd. in Endres, *Austin City Limits*, 13.

67. Endres, *Austin City Limits*, 28–33; McKenzie, "Mediatin' Music," 1.

68. Clark, interview with Art Young, 14 January 1977, transcript, 25–26.

69. Gilzow, "Austin Country Radio," 20; "History of 1200 WOAI!"

70. Gilzow, "Austin Country Radio," 47.

71. Ibid., 20.

72. Pecknold, *That Selling Sound*, 200–235.

73. Gilzow, "Austin Country Radio," 42.

74. Ibid., 43–44.

75. The Drake system was developed in 1966 at San Francisco radio station KYA-AM by program director Bill Drake, who created narrow playlists, limited the disc jockey's on-air banter, and used extensive market research to make changes to the station (Coleman, *Playback*, 83–85).

76. Moyer recalled that the station occasionally did live, in-studio broadcasts with artists such as Willie Nelson (Moyer, interview with author, 4 December 2009).

77. Gilzow, "Austin Country Radio," 21, 42; Gracey, email communication with author, 5 April 2007.

78. It is worth noting that Austin's public radio station, KUT-FM, was making use of this practice daily at the time this book was written.

79. Gilzow, "Austin Country Radio," 42.

80. For a more detailed discussion of the ways in which the notion of musical authenticity is used to validate one's sense of self, see Moore's discussion of "second-person authenticity" in "Authenticity as Authentication," 218–220.

81. Moyer, interview with author, 4 December 2009.

Chapter 2

1. Murphey, interview with Jack Bernhardt, 5 June 1993; Cusic, "Michael Martin Murphey."

2. Green, "Austin's Cosmic Cowboys," 91–92; Livingston, interview with author, 25 June 2007.

3. Green, "Austin's Cosmic Cowboys," 77–79; Spitzer, "Romantic Regionalism and Convergent Culture."

4. Green, "Austin's Cosmic Cowboys," 65–67.

5. Allen, "'I Just Want to Be a Cosmic Cowboy,'" par. 11.

6. Wilson, interview with Robert Heard, 26 June 1974.

7. Friedman, *Great Psychedelic Armadillo Picnic*, 92–94.

8. A&M SP-4388.

9. Murphey, *Geronimo's Cadillac*.

10. De León, "Region and Ethnicity," 270–273.

11. This performance was captured in the feature-length film *Willie Nelson's 4th of July Picnic* (La Paz Productions, 1977).

12. Parallels to the escapism of the cosmic cowboy may be found in any number of other musical styles from roughly the same era. The glam rock of David Bowie, T. Rex, and Alice Cooper, among others, witnessed artists exploring androgynous performance attire as a way of examining contemporaneous definitions of masculinity, while funk bands such as George Clinton's Parliament/Funkadelic and jazz musicians such as Sun Ra exploited science fiction and space exploration in their stage shows, rhetoric, and music as a way of expressing utopian landscapes for racial equality.

13. The unnamed character in the first verse is probably Clark's wife, Susanna, who is addressed directly in the song's third verse, in which the speaker chides "Oh, Susanna, don't you cry, babe." Such references reinforce the autobiographical nature of the song.

14. Clark, interview with Jack Bernhardt, 7 November 1988.

15. Ibid. See also Bernhardt, "Guy Clark"; Clark, interview with Jack Bernhardt, 24 October 1988; Clark, "Handmade Gifts."

16. Walker, *Jerry Jeff Walker*. Clark later recorded "L.A. Freeway" for his 1975 RCA Records album, *Old No. 1* (RCA 1303).

17. Jacket of Walker, *Jerry Jeff Walker*, Decca DL7–5384 (1972).

18. *Heartworn Highways*, dir. James Szalapski (Warner Bros. Domestic Cable, 1981).

19. Furthermore, by implying that Christ is part of the translocal music scene of Austin and heaven, "Alleys of Austin" resonates with Kris Kristofferson's 1972 song "Jesus Was a Capricorn" (Monument 31909), which posits that Christ would have been ridiculed by mainstream culture because his appearance and ideology more closely resembled those of the hippie counterculture than of mainstream Christianity.

20. "Rag Man of the Week: John Clay," 6.

21. "John Clay: Plastic Plowboy," 16.

22. Ibid.

23. Clay and the editors of *The Rag* employed a similar strategy in June 1968, when they published Clay's "Fratrats Gonna Take Your Place," an invective against privileged University of Texas students (Clay, "Fratrats Gonna Take Your Place").

24. Clay also spoke out about the social detriments of marijuana usage in "Fratrats Gonna Take Your Place": "More and more I hear people say/Fratrats gettin' potted in a brand new way./Police gonna come knockin' down the frathouse door/And it never happened to them before."

25. Rossinow, "New Left in the Counterculture," 90–91.

26. See, for instance, Zar, "Place in the Country."

27. Moreover, this commentary may have been directed toward the pastoralism of the organic food cooperatives that were springing up in Austin and other countercultural centers at the time, many of which espoused lofty ideals but often struggled as a result of horticultural ignorance. For a nuanced treatment of the organic food movement and its relationship to the counterculture, see Belasco, "Food and the Counterculture," 273–292.

28. Kruppa, email communication with author, 24 May 2006.

29. Kruppa, "New Hicks," statement 1.

30. Ibid., statement 83.

31. Ibid., statement 7–8.

32. Ibid., statement 3.

33. Ibid., statement 75–77; emphasis in original.

34. Ibid., statement 80.

35. Ibid., statements 48–61. Barry Shank, in his ethnographic study of the Austin punk scene, which flourished during the early 1980s, presents an argument

similar to Kruppa's, noting that the progressive country music scene was built around a dual notion of sincerity that drew upon the perceived sincerity of country music and the scene's public critique of the mainstream music industry: "The sincere performance of country and western music in Austin indicates a doubled and ironic articulation of an antimodern romanticism, celebrating the productivity of capitalist modernity while simultaneously critiquing the increasing influence of marketplace duplicity and 'instrumental reason' " (Shank, *Dissonant Identities*, 147). Similarly, Michael Dunne has remarked that:

> because the largest percentage of contemporary outlaw music [a subgenre of progres-
> sive country music that originated in Nashville and was promulgated by Waylon
> Jennings, Willie Nelson, Tompall Glaser, and Jessi Colter], these writers and performers
> substituted equally sentimental but merely self-reflexive form[s] of romantic expres-
> sion. . . . As a result of this development, the cowboy of song became merely a persona,
> a rhetorical device by which the songwriter and performer sought to exploit the lis-
> tener's habitual sympathetic disposition toward the genre of the cowboy. In place of the
> cowboy's plausibly occasioned physical and emotional suffering, these outlaw songs
> offered thinly disguised accounts of the supposed rigors of the country music business.
> Instead of blood on the saddle, these songs offered frustration on Music Row. Instead
> of the prospect of premature and violent death, they recounted the agonies of unrecog-
> nized musical genius. Instead of Western stoicism, they professed pathetic whining.
> (Dunne, "Romantic Narcissism in 'Outlaw' Cowboy Music," 228)

36. Kruppa, "The New Hicks," statements 32-42.
37. Flippo, "Austin: The Hucksters Are Coming," 24.
38. Flippo, "Hill Country Sound," 20.
39. Dailey, "Michael Murphey: More than a Cosmic Cowboy."
40. Murphey, interview with Jack Bernhardt, 5 June 1993.
41. Reid, *Improbable Rise of Redneck Rock*, 211; Flippo, "Austin: The Hucksters Are Coming," 24.

Chapter 3

1. Reid, *Improbable Rise of Redneck Rock*, 9–10.
2. See, for instance, Lanham, "Houston Hippies Harassed," 11; Dreyer, "Houston: High Price of Hip."
3. Haggard, "Okie from Muskogee/If I Had Left It Up to You."
4. Malone, *Don't Get above Your Raisin'*, 46. "Mama Tried" and "Sing Me Back Home" were the title tracks of Capitol ST-2972 and ST-2848, respectively.
5. Di Salvatore, "Merle Haggard," 223; Malone, *Country Music, U.S.A.*, 319. On 21 March 1972 Haggard received a letter expunging and pardoning Haggard's criminal record from then California governor Ronald Reagan, and on 13 July 1973 he played a concert at the White House at the request of First Lady Pat Nixon. This performance took place, on the same day that the press implicated Nixon in the Watergate scandal (Haggard with Carter, *Merle Haggard's My House of Memories*, 227–230; Malone, *Country Music, U.S.A.*, 373). For a more thorough

treatment of the Silent Majority, see Lassiter, *Silent Majority*, and LaChapelle, *Proud to Be an Okie*.

6. Tichi, *High Lonesome*, 198–200; Malone, *Country Music, U.S.A.*, 319; Malone, *Don't Get above Your Raisin'*, 45–46, 241–243; Di Salvatore, "Merle Haggard," 223; Lund and Denisoff, "Folk Music Revival and the Counter Culture," 404; Ching, *Wrong's What I Do Best*, 43–44.

7. R. Serge Denisoff has characterized this type of protest as "rhetorical." As opposed to the "magnetic" protest song, which seeks to build consensus among listeners to undertake a concrete action, the "rhetorical" protest song is a song that "stressed individual indignation and dissent but did not offer a solution in a movement. The song was a statement of dissent which said, 'I protest, I do not concur,' or just plain 'damn you' " ("The Evolution of the American Protest Song," 18).

8. Moreover, as Jerome L. Rodnitzky has observed, "Okie from Muskogee" represents a direct rebuttal to the purported protests of the hippie counterculture by modifying "the simple unvarnished Guthrie-Seeger style . . . [to create] country-and-western topical ballads that appeal to the prejudices of older, middle-America" (Rodnitzky, "Decline of Contemporary Protest Music," 46). The prejudices to which Rodnitzky alludes are clarified by Paul DiMaggio, Richard A. Peterson, and Jack Esco Jr. in a 1972 article titled "Country Music: Ballad of the Silent Majority," which cites "Okie from Muskogee" as presenting a "contrast [between] Godless, unclean, foul-mouthed, dope-taking, unconventional, educated, complex, urban youths . . . [and] their virtuous small town counterparts" (DiMaggio, Peterson, and Esco Jr., "Country Music: Ballad of the Silent Majority," 46).

9. Hemphill, *Nashville Sound*, 90–91; Carter, *From George Wallace to Newt Gingrich*, 34.

10. LaChapelle, *Proud to Be an Okie*, 180–207.

11. Lund, "Fundamentalism, Racism, and Political Reaction in Country Music," 88. Among the songs Lund lists under this rubric are Pat Boone's "Wish You Were Here, Buddy" and Stonewall Jackson's "The Minute Men Are Turning in Their Graves."

12. Ibid., 91. Yet, Rodnitzky observed that songs like "Okie from Muskogee" and "The Fighting Side of Me" marked a significant change in the purpose of working-class protest songs: "These new protest songs on the right are destroying another folk-protest myth—*specifically, the legend that topical songs appealing to the discontented common 'folk' were almost by definition ballads sympathetic to social reform*" (Rodnitzky, "Decline of Contemporary Protest Music," 46 [emphasis added]).

13. DiMaggio, Peterson, and Esco Jr., "Country Music: Ballad of the Silent Majority," 44.

14. Hubbard, interview with author, 6 July 2005; Reid, *Improbable Rise of Redneck Rock*, 105–106; Koster, *Texas Music*, 43.

15. This interpretation is supported by Hubbard's recollection of the song's genesis. Hubbard, interview with author, 6 July 2005.

16. Walker, *¡Viva Terlingua!*; Nelson, *Austin City Limits* (17 October 1974); Nelson, Panther Hall, Fort Worth, Texas (26 February 1975); Nelson, Ebbets Field,

Denver, Colorado (2 September 1975); Nelson and Coe, KAFM-FM 92.5 Broadcast (1 July 1974).

17. Note especially the performance at Panther Hall, Fort Worth (26 February 1975).

18. Ching, *Wrong's What I Do Best*, 43.

19. Leo Feist, 1915.

20. Hubbard, interview with author, 6 July 2005.

21. Ironic performance of "Okie from Muskogee" and "The Fighting Side of Me" was quite common in contemporaneous folk music circles as well. See, for instance, Nelson, *Austin City Limits* (17 October 1974); Nelson, Panther Hall, Fort Worth, Texas (26 February 1975); Nelson, Ebbets Field, Denver, Colorado (2 September 1975); Nelson and Coe, KAFM-FM 92.5 Broadcast (1 July 1974).

22. Reid, *Improbable Rise of Redneck Rock*, 179–186; Friedman, *Sold American*. Responses to "The Ballad of Charles Whitman" were understandably negative, given the short amount of time that had passed between the event and the release of *Sold American*. Friedman defended his decision to write the song in a radio interview in June 1975: "I would like to leave it in the song format because it says it better than I could articulate it otherwise, except that what it really is, is a—just that if you get blown away out of 27,000 people, I mean your number is up, you know, I mean so you, your number's up" (Friedman and Friedman, interview with Art Young, transcript, 17–19).

23. "New Acts: Kinky Friedman," 248.

24. Benarde, *Stars of David*, 205–206.

25. Flippo, "Ride 'Em Jewboy," 20.

26. Ibid.

27. Sloman, "Kinky and the Money Changers," 31.

28. "Figure" is pronounced so as to rhyme with "nigger."

29. Fox, *Real Country*, 37–41.

30. Walker, *¡Viva Terlingua!*.

31. Hudson, *Telling Stories, Writing Songs*, 188.

32. Nightbyrd, "Cosmo Cowboys," 13.

33. Ibid.

34. Ibid., 14.

35. Wilson, interview with Robert Heard, 28 June 1974.

36. Green, "Midnight and Other Cowboys," 137–138.

Chapter 4

1. Martin, "Time Is a Pivotal Issue," 10.

2. Neff, "Big Commotion in Austin."

3. Axthelm, "Songs of Outlaw Country."

4. Nightbyrd, "Highway 71 Revisited," 25.

5. Ward, "Review of *The Lost Gonzo Band* (MCA 487) and *Juz Loves Dem Ol' Greezy Wheels* (London PS 657)," 49.

6. Katz, *Capturing Sound*, 1–47.

7. Sociologist Andy Bennett, in his work on the film *Woodstock* (1970), explains the effects of such mediated representations of a musical community on subsequent understandings and interpretations of that community even among the people who were active participants (Bennett, "'Everybody's Happy, Everybody's Free'").

8. Thomas Porcello has suggested, based on his experience as a recordist in Austin during the early 1990s, that the "textural participatory discrepancies" that result from live performance are an essential component of the "Austin sound" (Porcello, "Music Mediated as Live in Austin," 107–108).

9. I would like to thank one of the anonymous readers of this manuscript for suggesting this connection.

10. "Mr. Bojangles" b/w "Round and Round."

11. Hall, "Mr. Bojangles' Dance," 9.

12. For a more detailed discussion of the recording process, see Zak, *Poetics of Rock*.

13. Livingston, interview with author, 25 June 2007.

14. Reid, *Improbable Rise of Redneck Rock*, 98.

15. Murphey, interview with Jack Bernhardt, 5 June 1993.

16. Walker, *Jerry Jeff Walker*, liner notes.

17. Livingston, interview with author, 25 June 2007.

18. Raphael, interview with author, 6 June 2007.

19. Gay Jr., "Acting Up, Talking Tech."

20. Walker, *Jerry Jeff Walker*, liner notes.

21. Ibid.

22. Reid, *Improbable Rise of Redneck Rock*, 92.

23. Livingston, interview with author, 25 June 2007. Apparently, Crouch himself used the word "imagineer," a term associated with Walt Disney's escapist theme parks, to describe himself. An account of this appears in an anonymous 1976 *Newsweek* article covering his "Non-buycentennial Day" celebration ("Texas: Hondo's Jamboree").

24. Livingston, interview with author, 25 June 2007.

25. Raphael, interview with author, 6 June 2007.

26. Liner notes for Walker, *¡Viva Terlingua!*

27. Livingston, interview with author, 25 June 2007.

28. Ibid.; Raphael, interview with author, 6 June 2007.

29. Livingston recalled, "We were not on the stage. The drummer was up there, but we were all set on the ground. They put a bunch of bales of hay for baffles" (Livingston, interview with author, 25 June 2007).

30. S. Alexander Reed has argued that crowd noise is perhaps the most essential component of a live album:

> It is of course naïve to suppose that the capacity for crowd noise to advertise a performance's value lies simply in the bandwagon approach that a hundred thousand fans can't be wrong. Its deliberate use as an identifiable but integrated sign to which attention is drawn both in the recording process . . . [and] also on final recordings by virtue of its selective placement and volume helps to argue that crowd noise need not be auxiliary human buzzing but that it assumes a foreground role woven through many records. (Reed, "Crowd Noise and the Hyperreal")

31. Flippo, "Splash," 22.

32. Flippo, "Hill Country Sound," 22.

33. Gracey, "City Audiences Honest, Picky," 20.

34. Jennings, "Luckenbach, Texas (Back to the Basics)" b/w "Belle of the Ball."

35. Murphey, *Cosmic Cowboy Souvenir*.

36. Moman and Emmons, "Luckenbach, Texas (Back to the Basics of Love)."

37. Hartman, *History of Texas Music*, 175.

38. Whitburn, *Joel Whitburn's Top Country Singles, 1944–2001*, 170; Whitburn, *Joel Whitburn's Top Pop Singles, 1955–2002*, 356.

39. Jennings with Kaye, *Waylon: An Autobiography*, 271.

40. Livingston, interview with author, 25 June 2007; Hall, "Mr. Bojangles' Dance," 20. Walker's *Collectables* (MCA 450 [1974]) was also recorded at Odyssey.

Chapter 5

1. Townsend, *San Antonio Rose*, 317.

2. Benson, interview with author, 31 May 2005; Domino, interview with author, 25 June 2007.

3. Townsend, *San Antonio Rose*, 318–321.

4. Benson, interview with author, 31 May 2005.

5. Townsend, *San Antonio Rose*, 1–22, 38.

6. Specht, "Put a Nickel in the Jukebox," 78.

7. Ginnell, *Milton Brown and the Founding of Western Swing*, 108; Lieberson, "Swing Guitar," 90; Townsend, *San Antonio Rose*, 151.

8. Ginnell, *Milton Brown and the Founding of Western Swing*, 26; Townsend, *San Antonio Rose*, 151–152; Philips, "History of Western Swing Fiddling," 10.

9. Townsend, *San Antonio Rose*, 61.

10. As western swing historian Jean A. Boyd has explained, western swing bands were innovators in the development of the swing "feel" found in most swing music, having been among the first to "abandon . . . the 2/4 meter common in ragtime and Dixieland in favor of a looser, freer swing-four" (Boyd, *Jazz of the Southwest*, 12).

11. Both Bob Wills and Milton Brown arrived in Fort Worth for this reason, and, as historian Gerald W. Haslam has explained, this same process of migration reinforced country music traditions already in place in California during the 1930s (Haslam, *Workin' Man Blues*). See also Ginnell's discussion of post–World War I Fort Worth (Ginnell, *Milton Brown and the Founding of Western Swing*, 12–14) and Evans's detailed exploration of how these influences shaped the life and career of Bob Wills (Evans, "Bob Wills," 16–21).

12. Boyd, *Jazz of the Southwest*, 7–9.

13. Pinson, "Bob Wills Recordings: A Comprehensive Discography," in Townsend, *San Antonio Rose*, 355–359.

14. Townsend, *San Antonio Rose*, 284; Pecknold, *That Selling Sound*, 199.

15. Sleeve notes to Haggard, *A Tribute to the Best Damn Fiddle Player in the World (or, My Salute to Bob Wills)*.

16. Qtd. in Gracey, untitled article (1975), 1; "Crow Plays 'Southwestern Folk,' " 15.

17. Patoski, untitled article, 15.

18. "Crow Plays 'Southwestern Folk.' " See also Davis, "Alvin Crow's Honky Tonk Way of Knowledge," 56; Austex Records, "Biography: Alvin Crow & the Pleasant Valley Boys"; Moser, "Whole Bow," para. 5.

19. Benson, interview with author, 31 May 2005.

20. Patoski, "Alvin Crow . . . 6 Days on the Road," 5.

21. Benson, interview with author, 31 May 2005.

22. Domino, interview with author, 25 June 2007.

23. Ibid.

24. Moser, "Whole Bow."

25. Benson, interview with author, 31 May 2005.

26. Moser, "Whole Bow."

27. Benson, interview with author, 31 May 2005.

28. Green, "Austin's Cosmic Cowboys," 78. Green observes that, by the early 1970s, "the richest single setting for musical convergence was Austin."

29. Benson, interview with author, 31 May 2005; "Happy Birthday America! With Good Old Country Music."

30. Domino, interview with author, 25 June 2007.

31. Patoski, "Alvin Crow . . . 6 Days on the Road."

32. Gracey, "Johnny Gimble," 19.

33. Long Neck LN-001.

34. Ginnell, *Milton Brown and the Founding of Western Swing*, 70, 96–97; Townsend, *San Antonio Rose*, 55; Coffey, "Jesse Ashlock," 18.

35. This arranging practice may also be found in Asleep at the Wheel's 1976 recording of "Blues for Dixie," written by Bob Wills's former business manager, O. W. Mayo. The recording features three former Playboys: Gimble, electric mandolinist Tiny Moore, and rhythm guitarist Eldon Shamblin (only Gimble and Moore take solos). The solo sections begin after all of the lyrics have been presented, and Benson also introduces the soloists in the style of Bob Wills. Moreover, this song concludes the first side of the record, just as Ashlock's solos with the Pleasant Valley Boys appear in the middle of the record.

36. Ashlock died on 9 August 1976. Coffey, "Jesse Ashlock," 18.

37. Allsup produced *Comin' Right at Ya*, *Texas Fold*, and *Wheelin' and Dealin'*; Wilson produced the group's 1974 eponymous release.

38. This discourse of authenticity was, as ethnomusicologist Mark Slobin reminds us, one of the key characteristics of the folk revivalism of the 1970s and 1980s (Slobin, *Subcultural Sounds*, 21).

39. Cantwell, *When We Were Good*, 38.

40. Katz, *Capturing Sound*, 14–18, 24–31.

41. Goldsmith, interview with author, 23 May 2005.

42. Ball, interview with author, 18 January 2007; Smith, interview with author, 2 June 2007.

43. Benson, interview with author, 31 May 2005; Domino, interview with author, 25 June 2007; Goldsmith, email communication with author, 12 April 2007.

44. Columbia KG 32416 (1973).

45. Journalist Joe Nick Patoski reviewed *The Bob Wills Anthology* for the independent *Austin Sun* on 15 May 1975, just two days after Wills's death. He noted that Wills's unrelenting individualism and perseverance tapped into the romantic regionalism that had helped shape Anglo-Texan identities since the Texas Revolution and that his music could help young Texans reconnect with that collective understanding of Texanness: "At best I'm a second, more likely third, generation Texas Playboy fan. Others, I'm sure, have sentiments that run deeper. But Bob Wills did me right. More than anything this side of Pleasure, Bob gave me a real Texas soul to carry on home" (Patoski, untitled review of *The Bob Wills Anthology*).

46. Oceans, email communication with author, 24 April 2008.

47. Pinson, "The Bob Wills Recordings: A Comprehensive Discography," in Townsend, *San Antonio Rose*, 364; Patoski, "Alvin Crow . . . 6 Days on the Road," 5.

48. Asleep at the Wheel, *Comin' Right at Ya*.

49. Asleep at the Wheel, *Asleep at the Wheel*.

50. One needs only to look at the physical layout of the Armadillo World Headquarters to witness changing attitudes toward listening and dancing in the progressive country music scene. While the concert space included an open floor for dancing, the dance floor was located at the back of the hall, behind the large seating area for the listening audience.

51. Taruskin, "Pastness of the Present and the Presence of the Past," 152; Butt, *Playing with History*, 54.

52. Benson, interview with author, 31 May 2005; Ginnell, *Milton Brown and the Founding of Western Swing*, 108–113; Coffey, "Steel Colossus," 48–49.

53. Patoski, "Alvin Crow . . . 6 Days on the Road," 5.

54. Domino, interview with author, 25 June 2007.

55. For a longer meditation on sound recording's effects on musical composition and performance, see Katz, *Capturing Sound*.

56. *Alvin Crow and the Neon Angels*, Big Wheel BW 1003, 1979.

57. Pinson, "The Bob Wills Recordings: A Comprehensive Discography," in Townsend, *San Antonio Rose*, 347.

58. Ibid.

59. Green, "Austin's Cosmic Cowboys," 78.

Conclusion

1. For a more extended discussion of the role of festivals in music scenes, consult Dowd, Liddle, and Nelson, "Music Festivals as Scenes"; King, "Blues Tourism in the Mississippi Delta."

2. "C&W Rock Festival."

3. Ibid.; Hilburn, "'Woodstock' of C&W: Pride, but No Money."

4. The Texas International Pop Festival was held in the Dallas suburb of Lewiston only two weeks after Woodstock (30 August–1 September 1969). While most newspaper reports of the festival indicate only minor problems with illegal drug consumption, public nudity, and illicit sex, many local residents protested against the event because they believed it had a negative influence on their community. The Texas Music Festival Act was passed in order to regulate the hours of operation and to set standards for facilities management for music festivals (Acts of the Texas Legislature 1971, 62nd Legislature, 1867, ch. 552; amended Acts 1973, 63rd Legislature, 995, ch. 399). See also Tatum, "Pop Show Promoters Insuring [*sic*] against Another Muddy Mess"; Overton, "Lewisville Worries Bit"; Ewell, "Patrol Worried: Festival to Create Traffic Woes"; Johnson and Tatum, "Drugs Mar Pop Festival"; Schwartz, "Thousands Tell Their Message of Peace, Love"; Tatum, "Crackdown on Drugs Ordered: Lewisville Mayor Says Law Violators at Festival Face Arrest"; Schwartz, "Youngsters Draw Praise: Lewisville Merchants Find Visitors Warm, Friendly"; Johnson, "Wilson Blasts Lax Drug Law Enforcement"; Tatum, "Lewisville's Police Chief Will Resign"; Johnson, "Suit Asks $175,000 after Pop Festival".

5. Hilburn, "'Woodstock' of C&W." Hilburn goes on to describe the audience as "a mixture of young and old, sometimes bringing together three generations of a family. They sat around on the dirt in picnic fashion with blankets, lawn chairs, [and] coolers of beer."

6. Lash, "Dripping Springs Reunion," 6.

7. stroud, "Country to Popular Belief . . . ," 10.

8. Reid, *Improbable Rise of Redneck Rock*, 245.

9. Ibid. (emphasis in original).

10. Haggard, *Portrait of Merle Haggard*. See also Malone, *Don't Get above Your Raisin'*, 45–46.

11. Hilburn, "'Woodstock' of C&W"; Lash, "What If They Gave a Festival . . . and Nobody Came?"

12. Hilburn, "'Woodstock' of C&W."

13. Moser, "Whole Bow"; Jennings with Kaye, *Waylon: An Autobiography*, 32–33.

14. Nelson with Shrake, *Willie: An Autobiography*, 171.

15. Ibid., 252–255.

16. Ward, "Willie Nelson," 40.

17. Jennings with Kaye, *Waylon: An Autobiography*, 204.

18. Reid, *Improbable Rise of Redneck Rock*, 256.

19. Ibid., 255–256.

20. See, for instance, White, "Armadillo World Headquarters Celebrates 4th Year," 45: "'At the outset we had 300 to 500 people who would come here under any circumstances,' Wilson mused." See also Menconi, "Music, Media, and the Metropolis."

21. Wilson claimed to employ a market analyst who specialized in youth markets in order to develop marketing strategies to reach Austin's ubiquitous community of young people (Wilson, interview by Robert Heard, 26 June 1974).

22. Reid, *Improbable Rise of Redneck Rock*, 246, 248, 250. Ed Ward, discussing the 1975 Picnic in Liberty Hill, Texas, echoed Reid's description: "I'm glad I left Austin early because people wound up parking as far as five miles from the site and walking under the 95 degree sun (usually lugging a Styrofoam cooler of beer) right through downtown Liberty Hill, the small town that played host to the festival, to the site, a flat, grassless plain just outside of town" (Ward, "Rednecks, Thai Sticks, and Lone Star Beer," 76).

23. Qtd. in Patoski, "Rednecks Frying in the Sun," 12. Nelson had experienced similar local opposition when he organized the Spring Fever Festival in Prairie Hill, Texas, on 8 May 1976, but District Judge Clarence Ferguson ruled that the festival could take place despite local protests (Oppel, "Hearing Clears Way for Festival").

24. "Gonzales County Rejects Nelson Music Fest."

25. Hershorn, "Friends Don't Forget Willie."

26. Patoski, "Rednecks Frying in the Sun," 12; Oppel, "Picnic to Feature Mixed Bag." The program featured, in addition to Nelson, Waylon Jennings, Leon Russell, Kris Kristofferson, Jerry Jeff Walker, Roger Miller, Rusty Wier, Steve Fromholz, George Jones, Bobby Bare, Ray Wylie Hubbard, David Allan Coe, Tompall Glaser, Billy Joe Shaver, B. W. Stevenson, Asleep at the Wheel, Jessi Colter, and Rita Coolidge.

27. Patoski, "Rednecks Frying in the Sun," 12.

28. Reynolds, "Hook 'Em Horns!" 31.

29. Some fans found the presence of a camera crew to be an intrusion on the picnic. Townsend Miller, music critic for the *Austin American-Statesman*, observed in his review of the 1974 picnic: "Someone said the Picnic seemed to be staged for the TV filming of a 'Midnight Special' rather than for the crowd. Often this seemed true, because camera stands as well as moving crews interfered with the crowd's vision throughout" (Miller, "Not Much C-W Music at Willie's Picnic").

30. United Artists UA-LA184-J2.

31. Miller, "Not Much C-W Music at Willie's Picnic"; McNeely, "Fireworks Show, and Willie, Too."

32. Admission fees for the Picnics were $5.50 for the 1973 Picnic in Dripping Springs, $8 per day or $20 for a three-day pass at the 1974 Picnic, and $10 for the 1976 Picnic in Gonzales. "Willie Nelson's 4th of July Picnic at Dripping Springs"; "Willie Nelson July 4 Picnic"; Oppel, "Picnic to Feature Mixed Bag." Dowd, Liddle, and Nelson observe "varying degrees of commitment displayed by festival attendees and expected by festival organizers" (Dowd, Liddle, and Nelson, "Music Festivals as Scenes," 163).

Works Cited

Interviews and Personal Communications

Ball, Marcia. Interview with author. 18 January 2007.

———. Email communication with author. 25 January 2007.

Benson, Ray. Interview with author. 31 May 2005.

Clark, Guy. Interview with Jack Bernhardt. 24 October 1988. Jack Bernhardt Collection #20061, Southern Folklife Collection, Wilson Library, University of North Carolina at Chapel Hill.

———. Interview with Jack Bernhardt. 7 November 1988. Southern Folklife Collection, Wilson Library, University of North Carolina at Chapel Hill.

———. Interview with Art Young. 14 January 1976. Oral History Collection, Austin History Center, Austin Public Libraries.

Domino, Floyd. Interview with author. 25 June 2007.

Friedman, Richard "Kinky," and Jeffrey Mark Friedman. Interview with Art Young. 10 June 1975. Oral History Collection, Austin History Center, Austin Public Libraries.

Gracey, Joe. Email communication with author. 5 April 2007.

Goldsmith, Tommy. Interview with author. 23 May 2005.

———. Email communication with author. 12 April 2007.

Hubbard, Ray Wylie. Interview with author. 6 July 2005.

Kruppa, Joe. Email communication with author. 24 May 2006.

Livingston, Bob. Interview with author. 25 June 2007.

Malone, Bill C. Email communication with author. 7 March 2008.

Moyer, Ken. Interview with author. 4 December 2009.

Murphey, Michael Martin. Interview with Jack Bernhardt. 27 May 1993. Jack Bernhardt Collection #20061, Southern Folklife Collection, Wilson Library, University of North Carolina at Chapel Hill.

———. Interview with Jack Bernhardt. 5 June 1993. Jack Bernhardt Collection #20061, Southern Folklife Collection, Wilson Library, University of North Carolina at Chapel Hill.

Oceans, Lucky. Email communication with author. 24 April 2008.

Patoski, Joe Nick. Interview with author. 1 April 2008.

———. Interview with author. 3 April 2008.

Raphael, Mickey. Interview with author. 6 June 2007.

Smith, Bobby Earl. Interview with author. 2 June 2007.

Wilson, Eddie. Interview with Robert Heard. 26 June 1974. Oral History Collection, Austin History Center, Austin Public Libraries.

Print Sources

Agnew, Eleanor. *Back from the Land: How Young Americans Went to Nature in the 1970s, and Why They Came Back*. Chicago: Dee, 2004.

Allen, Michael. "'I Just Want to Be a Cosmic Cowboy': Hippies, Cowboy Code, and the Culture of a Counterculture." *Western Historical Quarterly* 36(3) (Autumn 2005). http://www.historycooperative.org/journals/whq/36.3/allen.html (accessed 28 November 2005).

Allen, Nelson. "KOKE-FM." *Pickin' Up the Tempo: A Country Western Journal* 1 (April 1975): 7–8. Dolph Briscoe Center for American History, University of Texas at Austin, Vertical File (Subject): Music: Country and Western 2.

Austex Records. "Biography: Alvin Crow & the Pleasant Valley Boys." Dolph Briscoe Center for American History, University of Texas at Austin, Vertical File (General Bio.): Crow, Alvin.

"Austin Music Scene: Bill Josie." The *Rag* 7(23) (7 May 1973): 11.

Averill, Patricia. "Esoteric-exoteric Expectations of Redneck Behavior and Country Music." *Journal of Country Music* 4(2) (Summer 1973): 34–38.

Axthelm, Pete. "Songs of Outlaw Country." *Newsweek* 87 (12 April 1976): 79.

Belasco, Warren. "Food and the Counterculture: A Story of Bread and Politics." In *Food in Global History*, ed. Raymond Grew, 273–292. Boulder: Westview, 1999.

Benarde, Scott R. *Stars of David: Rock 'n' Roll's Jewish Stories*. Lebanon, N.H.: Brandeis University Press, 2003.

Bennett, Andy. "Subcultures or Neo-tribes? Rethinking the Relationship between Youth, Style, and Musical Taste." *Sociology* 33(3) (August 1999): 599–617.

———. "Consolidating the Music Scenes Perspective." *Poetics* 32(3–4) (2004): 223–234.

———. "'Everybody's Happy, Everybody's Free': Representation and Nostalgia in the *Woodstock* Film." In *Remembering Woodstock*, ed. Andy Bennett. Aldershot: Ashgate, 2004. 43–54.

———, and Richard A. Peterson, eds. *Music Scenes: Local, Translocal, and Virtual*. Nashville: Vanderbilt University Press, 2004.

Bernhardt, Jack. "Guy Clark." In *The Encyclopedia of Country Music*, ed. Paul Kingsbury, 94. New York: Oxford University Press, 1998.

Blaustein, Richard. "Rethinking Folk Revivalism: Grass-roots Preservationism and Folk Romanticism." In *Transforming Tradition: Folk Music Revivals Examined*, ed. Neil V. Rosenberg, 258–274. Chicago: University of Illinois Press, 1993.

Boyd, Jean A. *The Jazz of the Southwest: An Oral History of Western Swing*. Austin: University of Texas Press, 1998.

Brackett, David. *Interpreting Popular Music*. New York: Cambridge University Press, 1995. Paperback ed., Berkeley: University of California Press, 2000.

"The Broken Spoke Legend." http://www.brokenspokeaustintx.com/legend.htm (accessed 28 May 2009).

Butt, John. *Playing with History*. New York: Cambridge University Press, 2002.

"C&W Rock Festival: Pickin' and Singin' in Texas." *Los Angeles Times* (17 March 1972).

Capri, Lynn. "View of Shelter-Vision." *Austin Sun* 1(10) (22 January–4 February 1975): 16.

Cantwell, Robert. *When We Were Good: The Folk Revival*. Cambridge: Harvard University Press, 1997.

Carter, Dan T. *From George Wallace to Newt Gingrich: Race in the Conservative Counterrevolution, 1963–1994*. Baton Rouge: Louisiana State University Press, 1996.

Ching, Barbara. *Wrong's What I Do Best: Hard Country Music and Contemporary Culture*. New York: Oxford University Press, 2001.

"City Aims at Record in Building." *Austin American-Statesman*, morning ed. (17 November 1974), B27.

Clark, Shelton. "Handmade Gifts: A Conversation with Legendary Singer-songwriter-luthier Guy Clark." *Fretboard Journal* 3 (Fall 2006): 46–53.

Clay, John. "Fratrats Gonna Take Your Place." The *Rag* 2(28) (13 June 1968): 6.

Cobb, James C. "From Muskogee to Luckenbach: Country Music and the 'Southernization' of America." *Journal of Popular Culture* 16(2) (Winter 1982): 81–91.

Cody, James. "The Austin Movement." The *Gar* 1(9–10) (June 1972): 8–9.

———. "Notes on the Movement; or, the Revolutionary Times." *The Gar* 1(11) (July 1972): 11, 22–23.

Coffey, Kevin. "Steel Colossus: The Bob Dunn Story." *Journal of Country Music* 17(2) (1995): 46–56.

———. "Jesse Ashlock." In *The Encyclopedia of Country Music*, ed. Paul Kingsbury, 18. New York: Oxford University Press, 1998.

Cohen, Sara. "Men Making a Scene: Rock Music and the Production of Gender." In *Sexing the Groove: Popular Music and Gender*, ed. Sheila Whiteley, 17–36. London: Routledge, 1997.

———. *Decline, Renewal, and the City in Popular Music Culture: Beyond the Beatles*. Aldershot: Ashgate, 2007.

Cohen, Ronald D. *Rainbow Quest: The Folk Music Revival & American Society, 1940–1970*. Boston: University of Massachusetts Press, 2002.

Coleman, Mark. *Playback: From Victrola to MP3, 100 Years of Music, Machines, and Money*. New York: Da Capo, 2005.

Coppage, Noel. "Is Country Going to the Dogs?" *Stereo Review* 41 (November 1978): 99–104.

Covach, John. "We Won't Get Fooled Again: Rock Music and Musical Analysis." *In Theory Only* 13(1–4) (September 1997): 117–141.

Cravey, Robin. "Barton Springs: Will Special Interests Mean Its Ruin?" *Austin Sun* 1(11) (5–19 February 1975): 6–7.

"Crow Plays 'Southwestern Folk.' " *Music City News* 15(2) (August 1977): 15. Dolph Briscoe Center for American History, University of Texas at Austin, Vertical File (Subject): Music: Country & Western 1.

Cumquat, Lillian. "Sign on the Line, $5." *Austin Sun* 1(19) (29 May 1975): 14.

Cusic, Don. "Michael Martin Murphey." In *The Encyclopedia of Country Music*, ed. Paul Kingsbury, 360. New York: Oxford University Press, 1998.

———. "Politics and Country Music, 1963–1974." In *Country Music Annual 2002*, ed. Charles K. Wolfe and James E. Akenson. 161-185. Lexington: University Press of Kentucky, 2002.

Dailey, David. "Michael Murphey: More than a Cosmic Cowboy." *Daily Texan* (22 March 1974).

Davis, John T. "Alvin Crow's Honky Tonk Way of Knowledge." *Third Coast* (November 1982): 52–59. Dolph Briscoe Center for American History, University of Texas at Austin, Vertical File (General Bio): Crow, Alvin.

Dawidoff, Nicholas. *In the Country of Country: People and Places in American Music*. New York: Pantheon, 1997.

De León, Arnoldo. "Region and Ethnicity: Topographical Identities in Texas." In *Many Wests: Place, Culture, and Regional Identity*, ed. David M. Wrobel and Michael C. Steiner, 259–274. Lawrence: University Press of Kansas, 1997.

Denisoff, R. Serge. "The Evolution of the American Protest Song." In *The Sounds of Social Change: Studies in Popular Culture*. Eds. R. Serge Denisoff and Richard A. Peterson. Chicago: Rand McNally & Co., 1972. 15–25.

Sing a Song of Social Significance. Bowling Green: Bowling Green University Popular Press, 1972.

DiMaggio, Paul, Richard A. Peterson, and Jack Esco Jr. "Country Music: Ballad of the Silent Majority." In *The Sounds of Social Change: Studies in Popular Culture*, ed. R. Serge Denisoff and Richard A. Peterson, 38–55. Chicago: Rand McNally, 1972.

Di Salvatore, Bryan. "Merle Haggard." In *The Encyclopedia of Country Music*, ed. Paul Kingsbury, 223. New York: Oxford University Press, 1998.

Dowd, Timothy J., Kathleen Liddle, and Jenna Nelson. "Music Festivals as Scenes: Examples from Serious Music, Womyn's Music, and SkatePunk." In *Music Scenes: Local, Translocal, and Virtual*, ed. Andy Bennett and Richard A. Peterson, 149–167. Nashville: Vanderbilt University Press, 2004.

Draper, Sheila. "A Rocky Mountain Special with Folks like Michael Murphy." *Picking Up the Tempo: A Country Western Journal* 15 (February 1976): 1–3, 18.

Dreyer, Thorne. "Houston: High Price of Hip." The *Rag* 2(13) (5 February 1968): 1, 8–9.

Drummond, Paul. *Eye Mind: The Saga of Roky Erickson and the 13th Floor Elevators, the Pioneers of Psychedelic Sound.* Los Angeles: Process, 2007.

Dunne, Michael. "Romantic Narcissism in 'Outlaw' Cowboy Music." In *All That Glitters: Country Music in America*, ed. George H. Lewis. 226-238. Bowling Green: Bowling Green University Press, 1993.

"Editorial: We Already Have Dallas anzd Houston." *Austin Sun* 1(13) (6 March 1975): 3.

Elder, Steve. "Austin Neighborhoods." The *Rag* 7(22) (1 May 1973): 5.

Endres, Clifford. *Austin City Limits: The Story behind Television's Most Popular Country Music Program.* Austin: University of Texas Press, 1987.

Evans, Rush. "Bob Wills: The King of Western Swing." *Journal of Texas Music History* 2(2) (2002): 16–29.

Ewell, James. "Patrol Worries: Festival to Create Traffic Woes." *Dallas Morning News* (27 August 1969).

Filene, Benjamin. *Romancing the Folk: Public Memory and American Roots Music.* Chapel Hill: University of North Carolina Press, 2000.

Finnegan, Ruth H. *The Hidden Musicians: Music-making in an English Town.* New York: Cambridge University Press, 1989.

Flippo, Chet. "Splash." *Texas Observer* 65 (19 January 1973): 21–22.

———. "Ride 'Em Jewboy: Kinky Friedman's First Two Premieres." *Rolling Stone* 134 (10 May 1973): 20.

———. "Hill Country Sound." *Texas Parade* 34(11) (April 1974): 16–23.

———. "Austin: The Hucksters Are Coming." *Rolling Stone* 158 (11 April 1974): 24.

Fox, Aaron A. *Real Country: Music and Language in Working-class Culture.* Durham, N.C.: Duke University Press, 2004.

Fox, William S., and James D. Williams. "Political Orientation and Music Preferences among College Students." *Public Opinion Quarterly* 38(3) (Autumn 1974): 352–371.

Foxx, Ed. "Hippy Hollow." *Glyptodon News* 1(4) (7–21 May 1973): 4–5.

Friedman, Kinky. *The Great Psychedelic Armadillo Picnic: A "Walk" in Austin.* Crown Journeys. New York: Crown, 2004.

Friedman, Myra. *Buried Alive: The Biography of Janis Joplin.* New and rev. ed. New York: Harmony, 1992.

Gay, Leslie C., Jr. "Acting Up, Talking Tech: New York Rock Musicians and Their Metaphors of Technology." *Ethnomusicology* 42(1) (Winter 1998): 81–98.

Gilzow, Rick. "Austin Country Radio." *Nashville West* 1(11) (July 1976): 20–21, 42–50. Dolph Briscoe Center for American History, University of Texas at Austin, Vertical File (Subject): Music: Country & Western 1.

Ginnell, Cary. *Milton Brown and the Founding of Western Swing.* Chicago: University of Illinois Press, 1994.

Glassie, Henry. "Tradition." *Journal of American Folklore* 108(430) (Autumn 1995): 395–412.

"Gonzales County Rejects Nelson Music Fest." *Dallas Morning News* (23 May 1976).

Gouldy, Robert. "God Bless City Hall and a Quick Overview of the Neighborhood Action Plan." The *Gar* 4(3) (February 1975): 7–9.

Gracey, Joe. "City Audiences Honest, Picky." *Austin American* (17 November 1973).

———. "Johnny Gimble." *Picking Up the Tempo: A Country Western Journal* 11 (October 1975): 18–19.

Gracyk, Theodore. *Listening to Popular Music, or, How I Learned to Stop Worrying and Love Led Zeppelin*. Ann Arbor: University of Michigan Press, 2007.

Green, Archie. "Commercial Music Graphics #34: Midnight and Other Cowboys." *JEMF Quarterly* 11(3) (Autumn 1975): 137–152.

———. "The Campus Folksong Club: A Glimpse at the Past." In *Transforming Tradition: Folk Music Revivals Examined*, ed. Neil V. Rosenberg, 61–72. Chicago: University of Illinois Press, 1993.

———. "Austin's Cosmic Cowboys: Words in Collision." In *Torching the Fink Books and Other Essays on Vernacular Culture*, 66–107. Chapel Hill: University of North Carolina Press, 2001.

Green, Douglas B. *Singing in the Saddle: The History of the Singing Cowboy*. Nashville: Country Music Foundation Press and Vanderbilt University Press, 2002.

Groenenwegen, Jim, and Bill Bentley. "From San Antonio to Mars: Sir Doug's Honky Blues." *Austin Sun* 1(27) (19 September–1 October 1975): 13–15, 18, 20–21.

Gross, Michael. "Something's Right in Austin: Commander Cody Live Armadillo LP Proclaims a Texas Renaissance." *Zoo World* (14 March 1974): 16.

Gutiérrez, José Angel. *The Making of a Chicano Militant: Lessons from Cristal*. Madison: University of Wisconsin Press, 1998.

Haggard, Merle, with Tom Carter. *Merle Haggard's My House of Memories: For the Record*. New York: HarperEntertainment, 1999.

Hall, Douglas Kent. "Mr. Bojangles' Dance: The Odyssey and Oddities of Jerry Jeff Walker." *Rolling Stone* 176 (19 December 1974): 9, 20.

"Happy Birthday America! With Good Old Country Music." Southern Folklife Collection Festival Files #30007, Southern Folklife Collection, Wilson Library, University of North Carolina at Chapel Hill.

Hartman, Gary. "The Roots Run Deep: An Overview of Texas Music History." In *The Roots of Texas Music*, ed. Lawrence Clayton and Joe W. Specht, 3–36. College Station: Texas A&M University Press, 2003.

———. *The History of Texas Music*. College Station: Texas A&M University Press, 2008.

Haslam, Gerald W. *Workin' Man Blues: Country Music in California*. Berkeley: University of California, 1999.

Haworth, Alan Lee. "Threadgill, Kenneth." In *The Handbook of Texas Music*, Ed. Roy E. Barkley, et al. 326. Austin: Texas State Historical Association, 2003.

Hebdige, Dick. *Subculture: The Meaning of Style*. London: Methuen, 1979. Repr., New York: Routledge, 1988.

Hemphill, Paul. *The Nashville Sound: Bright Lights and Country Music*. New York: Simon and Schuster, 1970.

Herrera, Frances. "TIME for a Change = The Improvement of Minority for Education." The *Gar* 1(8) (April 1972): 13.

Hershorn, Connie. "Friends Don't Forget Willie." *Dallas Morning News* (29 May 1976).

Hilburn, Robert. "'Woodstock' of C&W: Pride, but No Money." *Los Angeles Times* (21 March 1972).

"The History of 1200 WOAI!" http://radio.woai.com/pages/about.html (accessed 3 March 2009).

Hobsbawm, Eric. "Introduction: Inventing Traditions." In *The Invention of Tradition*, ed. Eric Hobsbawm and Terence Ranger, 1–14. New York: Cambridge University Press, 1983.

Holt, Fabian. *Genre in Popular Music*. Chicago: University of Chicago Press, 2007.

Hudson, Kathleen. *Telling Stories, Writing Songs: An Album of Texas Songwriters*. Austin: University of Texas Press, 2001.

Huq, Rupa. "Raving, Not Drowning: Authenticity, Pleasure, and Politics in the Electronic Dance Music Scene." In *Popular Music Studies*, ed. David Hesmondhalgh and Keith Negus, 90–102. London: Arnold, 2002.

"In the Heart of Honky-tonk Rock: Going Back to the Basics in Austin." *Time* (19 September 1977): 86, 88.

Jennings, Waylon, with Lenny Kaye. *Waylon: An Autobiography*. New York: Warner, 1996.

"John Clay: Plastic Plowboy." *The Rag* (4 September 1973): 16.

Johnson, Tom. "Wilson Blasts Lax Drug Law Enforcement." *Dallas Morning News* (2 September 1969).

———. "Suit Asks $175,000 after Pop Festival." *Dallas Morning News* (22 October 1969).

———, and Henry Tatum. "Drugs Mar Pop Festival." *Dallas Morning News* (31 August 1969).

Katz, Mark. *Capturing Sound: How Technology Has Changed Music*. Berkeley: University of California Press, 2004.

Keil, Charles, and Steven Feld. *Music Grooves: Essays and Dialogues*. Chicago: University of Chicago Press, 1994.

Kemp, Mark. *Dixie Lullaby: A Story of Music, Race, and New Beginnings in a New South*. New York: Free Press, 2004. Paperback ed., Athens: University of Georgia Press, 2006.

King, Stephen A. "Blues Tourism in the Mississippi Delta: The Functions of Blues Festivals." *Popular Music and Society* 27(4) (2004): 455–475.

Kleinman, Michael. "Street Noise." The *Gar* 3(3) (February–March 1974): 4–5.

Koster, Rick. *Texas Music*. New York: St. Martin's Griffin, 2000.

Kruppa, Joe. "The New Hicks: Mellow, Righteous, Sincere." Typescript, Archie Green Collection, Southern Folklife Collection, Wilson Library, University of North Carolina at Chapel Hill.

Kruse, Holly. *Site and Sound: Understanding Independent Music Scenes*. New York: Lang, 2003.

Kuhlman, Martin. "Direct Action at the University of Texas during the Civil Rights Movement, 1960–1965." *Southwestern Historical Quarterly* 98(4) (April 1995): 550–566.

Lacasse, Serge. "'Listen to My Voice' The Evocative Power of Vocal Staging in Recorded Rock Music and Other Forms of Vocal Expression." PhD diss., University of Liverpool, 2000.

LaChapelle, Peter. *Proud to Be an Okie: Cultural Politics, Country Music, and Migration to Southern California*. Berkeley: University of California Press, 2007.

Laird, Tracey E. W. *Louisiana Hayride: Radio and Roots Music along the Red River*. New York: Oxford University Press, 2004.

Landau, Jon. "The Newport Folk Festival." *Rolling Stone* 16 (24 August 1968): 16–17.

Lanham, Connie. "Houston Hippies Harassed." The *Rag* 2(12) (29 January 1968): 11.

Lash, John. "Dripping Springs Reunion: Country Music Country, USA." The *Gar* 1(7) (March-April 1972): 6.

———. "What If They Gave a Festival . . . and Nobody Came?" The *Gar* 1(8) (April 1972): 2–3.

———. "Interview: Threadgill." The *Gar* 2(1) (September 1972): 6–7.

Lassiter, Matthew D. *The Silent Majority: Suburban Politics in the Sunbelt South*. Princeton: Princeton University Press, 2006.

Lieberson, Richard. "Swing Guitar: The Acoustic Chordal Style." In *The Guitar in Jazz: An Anthology*, ed. James Sallis. 89–112. Lincoln: University of Nebraska Press, 1996.

Livingston, Tamara E. "Music Revivals: Towards a General Theory." *Ethnomusicology* 43(1) (Winter 1999): 66–85.

"Local Rock 'n' Roll Band Back from Successful Tour." *Austin American-Statesman* (7 January 1967). Reprinted in *Not Fade Away: The Texas Music Magazine* 1(2) (1977): 14.

Lock, Cory. "Counterculture Cowboys: Progressive Texas Country of the 1970s & 1980s." *Journal of Texas Music History* 3(1) (Spring 2003): 14–23.

Lund, Jens. "Fundamentalism, Racism, and Political Reaction in Country Music." In *The Sounds of Social Change: Studies in Popular Culture*, ed. R. Serge Denisoff and Richard A. Peterson, 79–91. Chicago: Rand McNally, 1972.

———, and R. Serge Denisoff. "The Folk Music Revival and the Counter Culture: Contributions and Contradictions." *Journal of American Folklore* 84(334) (October–December 1971): 394–405.

Lytle, Mark Hamilton. *America's Uncivil Wars: The Sixties Era from Elvis to the Fall of Richard Nixon*. New York: Oxford University Press, 2006.

Malone, Bill C. "Myth, Media, and the Making of Texas Music." *Texas Humanist* 7(6) (July–August 1985): 8–10.

———. *Country Music, U.S.A.*, 2d rev. ed. Austin: University of Texas Press, 2002.

———. *Don't Get above Your Raisin': Country Music and the Southern Working Class*. Chicago: University of Illinois Press, 2002.

———. "'The Music Came Up from His Soul': From Western Swing to Classic Nashville Sessions, Johnny Gimble Has Fiddled His Way through the History of Country." *No Depression* 42 (November–December 2002): 96–102.

Martin, Kim. "Time Is a Pivotal Issue: Texas Artists Just Can't Run on L.A. Time, That's All." The *Gar* 3(5) (June–July 1974): 10.

Mays, Prissy. "Old Is Beautiful—in Music or on Threadgill." *Alcade* (May 1973). Dolph Briscoe Center for American History, University of Texas at Austin, Vertical File (General Bio): Threadgill, Ken.

Mazor, Barry. *Meeting Jimmie Rodgers: How America's Original Roots Music Hero Changed the Pop Sounds of a Century*. New York: Oxford University Press, 2009.

McClary, Susan, and Robert Walser. "Start Making Sense! Musicology Wrestles with Rock." In *On Record: Rock, Pop, and the Written Word*, ed. Simon Frith and Andrew Goodwin. 237–249 New York: Pantheon, 1990.

McKenzie, Marty. "Mediatin' Music." *Austin Sun* 2(6) (25 March–7 April 1976): 1, 20.

McLuhan, Marshall. *Understanding Media*. London: Routledge Classics, 2005.

McNeely, David. "Fireworks Show, and Willie, Too." *Dallas Morning News* (4 July 1974).

Meinig, D. W. *Imperial Texas: An Interpretive Essay in Cultural Geography*. Austin: University of Texas Press, 1969.

Mellard, Jason Dean. "Cosmic Cowboys, Armadillos and Outlaws: The Cultural Politics of Texan Identity in the 1970s." Ph.D. dissertation, The University of Texas at Austin, 2009.

Menconi, David L. "Music, Media, and the Metropolis: The Case of Austin's Armadillo World Headquarters." Master's thesis, University of Texas at Austin, 1985.

Middleton, Jason. "DC Punk and the Production of Authenticity." In *Rock over the Edge: Transformations in Popular Music Culture*, ed. Roger Beebe, Denise Fulbrook, and Ben Saunders, 335–356. Durham, N.C.: Duke University Press, 2002.

Mihelich, John, and John Papineau. "Parrotheads in Margaritaville: Fan Practice, Oppositional Culture, and Embedded Cultural Resistance in Buffett Fandom." *Journal of Popular Music Studies* 17(2) (May 2005): 175–202.

Miller, Matt. "Rap's Dirty South: From Subculture to Pop Culture." *Journal of Popular Music Studies* 16(2) (May 2004): 175–212.

Miller, Townsend. "Not Much C-W Music at Willie's Picnic." *Austin American-Statesman* (12 July 1974): 47.

Moore, Allan. "Authenticity as Authentication." *Popular Music* 21(2) (2002): 209–223.

Moriarty, J. David. "90-Story Highrise: Let Them Give Us New York." *Austin Sun* 1(12) (20 February–5 March 1975): 1, 11.

Moser, Margaret. "The Whole Bow: Alvin Crow Plays It His Way, Always Has." *Austin Chronicle* (12 November 2004). http://www.austinchronicle.com/gyrobase/Issue/story?oid-oid%3A237280 (accessed 14 August 2006).

Nackman, Mark E. *A Nation within a Nation: The Rise of Texas Nationalism*. London: Kennikat, 1975.

Neal, Jocelyn R. *The Songs of Jimmie Rodgers: A Legacy in Country Music.* Bloomington: Indiana University Press, 2009.

Neff, James. "MOPAC: The Monster That Ate Austin." *Austin Sun* 1(29) (16–29 October 1975): 1, 9.

———. "A Big Commotion in Austin." *Country Style* 26 (December 1977): 5, 66–67.

Nelson, Willie, with Bud Shrake. *Willie: An Autobiography.* New York: Simon and Schuster, 1988.

"New Acts: Kinky Friedman." *Variety* 270 (9 May 1973): 248.

Nightbyrd, Jeff. "Highway 71 Revisited." *Crawdaddy* 22 (March 1973): 25–26.

———. "Cosmo Cowboys: Too Much Cowboy and Not Enough Cosmic." *Austin Sun* 1(15) (3 April 1975): 13, 19.

Oakes, Wayne. "Thousands Turn Out for Threadgill: But He's Still Waiting for Ships that Never Come In." *Texas Observer* (7 August 1970): 17–19.

"Obituary: West Mall." The *Rag* 7(31) (23 July 1973): 4.

"An Old Gas Station Is Center for Weekly Folk Sessions." *Daily Texan* (13 December 1964). Dolph Briscoe Center for American History, University of Texas at Austin, Vertical File (General Bio): Threadgill, Ken.

Olds, Greg. "Threadgill: Country Music King Gets His Day." *Austin-American Statesman* (5 July 1970). Dolph Briscoe Center for American History, University of Texas at Austin, Vertical File (General Bio): Threadgill, Ken.

———. "Jimmie Rodgers: The First Hillbilly Star." *Austin Sun* 1(25) (21 August–3 September 1975): 25, 28, 30–31.

"Open City." The *Rag* 6(18) (20 March 1972): 10–11.

Oppel, Pete. "Hearing Clears Way for Festival." *Dallas Morning News* (29 April 1976).

———. "Picnic to Feature Mixed Bag." *Dallas Morning News* (29 June 1976), C6.

Orum, Anthony M. *Power, Money, & the People: The Making of Modern Austin.* Austin: Texas Monthly Press, 1987.

Overton, James. "Lewisville Worries Bit." *Dallas Morning News* (27 August 1969).

Patoski, Joe Nick. "Alvin Crow . . . 6 Days on the Road." *Picking Up the Tempo: A Country Western Journal* 1 (April 1975): 4–5. Dolph Briscoe Center for American History, University of Texas at Austin, Vertical File (Subject): Music: Country & Western 2.

———. Untitled review of *The Bob Wills Anthology. Austin Sun* 1(18) (15 May 1975): 15.

———. "Rednecks Frying in the Sun: Willie Nelson's Picnic Is On." *Rolling Stone* 217 (15 July 1976): 12.

———. *Willie Nelson: An Epic Life.* New York: Little, Brown, 2008.

Pecknold, Diane. *That Selling Sound: The Rise of the Country Music Industry.* Durham, N.C.: Duke University Press, 2007.

Peña, Manuel. *The Texas-Mexican Conjunto: History of a Working-class Music.* Austin: University of Texas Press, 1985.

Philips, Stacy. "Johnny Gimble: Western Swing Innovator." *Strings* 7(1) (1992): 27–30.

———. "The History of Western Swing Fiddling." *Fiddler Magazine* 2(2) (Summer 1995): 10–14.

Plumb, Mary Lee. "'Progress' and Destruction in South Austin." The *Gar* 2(5) (February 1973): 11–12.

———. "Are You in on the Planning for Austin?" The *Gar* 2(6) (March–April 1973): 10–11.

Porcello, Thomas. "Music Mediated as Live in Austin: Sound, Technology, and Recording Practice." In *Wired for Sound: Engineering and Technologies in Sonic Cultures*, Eds. Paul D. Greene and Thomas Porcello. 103–117. Middletown, Conn.: Wesleyan University Press, 2005.

Porterfield, Nolan. *Jimmie Rodgers: The Life and Times of America's Blue Yodeler*. Chicago: University of Illinois Press, 1979.

———. "Introduction." In *Exploring Roots Music: Twenty Years of the* JEMF Quarterly, ed. Nolan Porterfield, ix–xxviii. Lanham, Md.: Scarecrow, 2004.

"Rag Man of the Week: John Clay." The *Rag* 2(28) (13 June 1968): 6.

Rainbow, Arthur. "A Tour of a Commercial Slum." The *Gar* 1(6) (March 1972): 8–9.

Reed, S. Alexander. "Crowd Noise and the Hyperreal." In *The Proceedings of the First Art of Record Production Conference, 17–18 September 2006, University of Westminster, London*. http://www.artofrecordproduction.com (accessed 25 April 2006).

Reid, Jan. *The Improbable Rise of Redneck Rock*. New ed. Austin: University of Texas Press, 2004.

Reynolds, Mike. "Hook 'Em Horns." *Crawdaddy* 72 (May 1977): 28–33.

Rislier, Dave. "1 Million People in Austin." *Austin Sun* 1(12) (20 February–5 March 1975): 1, 9.

Rodnitzky, Jerome L. "The Decline of Contemporary Protest Music." *Popular Music and Society* 1(1) (Fall 1971): 44–50.

Ronström, Owe. "Revival Reconsidered." *World of Music* 38(3) (1996): 5–20.

Rosenberg, Neil V. "Starvation, Serendipity, and the Ambivalence of Bluegrass Revivalism." In *Transforming Tradition: Folk Music Revivals Examined*, ed. Neil V. Rosenberg, 194–202. Chicago: University of Illinois Press, 1993.

Rossinow, Doug. "The New Left in the Counterculture: Hypotheses and Evidence." *Radical History Review* 67 (1997): 79–120.

Russell, Thomas D. "*Sweatt v. Painter* Archive." http://www.houseofrussell.com/legalhistory/sweatt/ (accessed 30 July 2009).

Savage, Steve. "Lipsmacks, Mouth Noises, and Heavy Breathing." Paper presented at the Art of Record Production Conference, London, 18 September 2005. http://www.artofrecordproduction.com/content/view/26/52 (accessed 15 October 2007).

Schilt, Kristen. "'Riot Grrrl Is . . .': The Contestation over Meaning in a Music Scene." In *Music Scenes: Local, Translocal, and Virtual*, ed. Richard A. Peterson and Andy Bennett, 115–130. Nashville: Vanderbilt University Press, 2004.

Schochet, Gordon. "Tradition as Politics and the Politics of Tradition." In *Questions of Tradition*, ed. Mark Salber Phillips and Gordon Schochet, 296–322. Toronto: University of Toronto Press, 2004.

Schwartz, Marlyn. "Thousands Tell Their Message of Peace, Love." *Dallas Morning News* (31 August 1969).

———. "Youngsters Draw Praise: Lewisville Merchants Find Visitors Warm, Friendly." *Dallas Morning News* (2 September 1969).

Schweers, D. "What a Bore! Skunk Hollow: Undermining Conservation." *Austin Sun* 1(33) (11–17 December 1975): 6.

Sepulvado, Larry, and John Burks. "Texas." *Rolling Stone* 23 (7 December 1968): 16–19.

Shank, Barry. *Dissonant Identities: The Rock 'n' Roll Scene in Austin, Texas.* Hanover, N.H.: Wesleyan University Press, 1994.

Shils, Edwards. *Tradition.* Chicago: University of Chicago Press, 1981.

Shrake, Bud. "The Screwing Up of Austin." *Austin Sun* 1(12) (20 February–5 March 1975): 8–9.

Simon, Cheryl L. "Vulcan Gas Company." In *The Handbook of Texas Online.* http://www.tshaonline.org/handbook/online/articles/VV/xdv1.html (accessed 29 May 2009).

Slobin, Mark. *Subcultural Sounds: Micromusics of the West.* Hanover, N.H.: Wesleyan University Press, 1993.

Sloman, Larry. "Kinky and the Money Changers." *Crawdaddy* (April 1975): 30–31.

Smith, Judy. "Urban Renewal: The Home You Save May Be Your Own." The *Rag* 3(1) (14 October 1968): 3, 15.

"The Sonobeat-KAZZ Connection." http://sonobeatrecords.com/kazzconnection1.html (accessed 28 September 2009).

"Sonobeat Records: Austin in the '60s." *Not Fade Away: The Texas Music Magazine* 1(2) (1977): 6–9.

Specht, Joe W. "The Blue Yodeler Is Coming to Town: A Week with Jimmie Rodgers in West Texas." *Journal of Texas Music History* 1(2) (Fall 2001): 1–6.

———. "Put a Nickel in the Jukebox: The Texas Tradition in Country Music, 1922–50." In *The Roots of Texas Music,* ed. Lawrence Clayton and Joe W. Specht, 66–94. College Station: Texas A&M University Press, 2003.

Spitzer, Nicholas R. "Jimmie Rodgers in Texas." *Picking Up the Tempo: A Country Western Journal* 11 (October 1975): 1–3. Dolph Briscoe Center for American History, University of Texas at Austin, Vertical File (Subject): Music: Country & Western, 2.

———. "Romantic Regionalism and Convergent Culture in Central Texas." In *All That Glitters: Country Music in America,* ed. George H. Lewis, 87–93. Bowling Green: Bowling Green State University Press, 1993.

Spring, Ken. "Behind the Rave: Structure and Agency in a Rave Scene." In *Music Scenes: Local, Translocal, and Virtual,* ed. Richard A. Peterson and Andy Bennett, 48–64. Nashville: Vanderbilt University Press, 2004.

Sterling, Christopher H., and Michael C. Keith. *Sounds of Change: A History of FM Broadcasting in America.* Chapel Hill: University of North Carolina Press, 2008.

Straw, Will. "Communities and Scenes in Popular Music [1991]." In *The Subcultures Reader,* ed. Ken Gelder and Sarah Thornton, 494–505. New York: Routledge, 1997.

stroud. "Country to Popular Belief . . ." The *Rag* 6(20) (3 April 1972): 10.

Taruskin, Richard. "The Pastness of the Present and the Presence of the Past." In *Authenticity and Early Music*, ed. Nicholas Kenyon, 137–210. New York: Oxford University Press, 1988.

Tatum, Henry. "Pop Show Promoters Insuring [*sic*] against Another Muddy Mess." *Dallas Morning News* (20 August 1969).

———. "Crackdown on Drugs Ordered: Lewisville Mayor Says Law Violators at Festival Face Arrest." *Dallas Morning News* (1 September 1969).

———. "Lewisville's Police Chief Will Resign." *Dallas Morning News* (3 September 1969).

Texas Almanac and State Industrial Guide, 1980–1981. Dallas: Belo, 1981.

"Texas: Hondo's Jamboree." *Newsweek* (8 March 1976): 35.

"Texas Stompin'." *Glyptodon News* 1(2) (3–17 April 1973):

"Threadgill Unifies Cultures with Yodels, Rodgers Style." *Daily Texan* (21 September 1972). Dolph Briscoe Center for American History, University of Texas at Austin, Vertical File (General Bio): Threadgill, Ken.

Tichi, Cecilia. *High Lonesome: The American Culture of Country Music*. Chapel Hill: University of North Carolina Press, 1994.

Townsend, Charles R. *San Antonio Rose: The Life and Music of Bob Wills*. Chicago: University of Illinois Press, 1976.

Tucker, Stephen R. "Progressive Country Music, 1972–1976: Its Impact and Creative Highlights." *Southern Quarterly* 22(3) (Spring 1984): 93–110.

Turley, Alan Craig. "The Social and Ecological Determinants of the Production of Original Rock Music in Austin, Texas." PhD diss., University of Texas at Austin, 1997.

Valentine, Michael. "Street Noise." The *Gar* 4(2) (November–December 1974): 28–29.

Wallach, Jeremy. "Living the Punk Lifestyle in Jakarta." *Ethnomusicology* 52(1) (Winter 2008): 98–116.

Ward, Ed. "Review of *The Lost Gonzo Band* (MCA 487) and *Juz Loves Dem Ol' Greezy Wheels* (London PS 657)." *Rolling Stone* 193 (14 August 1975): 49.

———. "Willie Nelson: Rednecks, Thai Sticks, and Lone Star Beer." *Creem* 7(5) (October 1975): 40, 76–77.

Weber, Kai. "'Could Be an Illusion, but I Might as Well Try': Ideals and Practices of the Grateful Dead and the Woodstock Nation." In *The Sixties Revisited: Culture, Society, Politics*, ed. Jürgen Heideking, Jörg Helbig, and Anke Ortlepp, 139–148. Heidelberg: Universitätsverlag Winter, 2001.

Wexler, Jerry, and David Ritz. *Rhythm and the Blues: A Life in American Music*. New York: Knopf, 1993.

Whitburn, Joel. *Joel Whitburn's Top Country Singles, 1944–2001*. Menomonee Falls, Wis.: Record Research, Inc., and Billboard, 2003.

White, Susan. "Armadillo World Headquarters Celebrates 4th Year." *Austin American-Statesman*, morning ed. (14 August 1974), 45.

Wiemers, Carl. "Joplin Called Him Daddy." *Summer Texan* (31 July 1973). Dolph Briscoe Center for American History, University of Texas at Austin, Vertical File (General Bio): Threadgill, Ken.

Williams, Raymond. *The Country and the City*. New York: Oxford University Press, 1973.

"Willie Nelson July 4 Picnic." *Dallas Morning News* (2 July 1974), A12.

"Willie Nelson's 4th of July Picnic at Dripping Springs." The *Rag* 7(29) (4 July 1973): 12.

Wylie, Caroline Cates. "University Hills Saves Park." *The Gar* 2 (8) (August-September 1973): 4.

Zak, Albin, III. *The Poetics of Rock: Cutting Tracks, Making Records*. Berkeley: University of California Press, 2001.

———. "Editorial." *Journal on the Art of Record Production* (Academic) 1(2) (October 2007) http://www.artofrecordproduction.com/component/option.com_docman/task,doc_view/gid,52 (accessed 19 July 2008).

Zar, Rubin. "A Place in the Country." The *Gar* 2(5) (February 1973): 19.

Discography

Asleep at the Wheel. *Comin' Right at Ya*. United Artists 038F, 1973.

———. *Asleep at the Wheel*. Epic KE-33097, 1974.

———. *Texas Gold*. Capitol ST-11441, 1975.

———. *Wheelin' and Dealin'*. Capitol ST-11546, 1976.

———. *The Wheel*. Capitol ST-11620, 1977.

———. *Collision Course*. Capitol SW-11726, 1978.

———. *Served Live*. Capitol ST-11945, 1979.

Bridger, Bobby. *Merging of Our Minds*. RCA Victor LSP-4792, 1972.

———. *And I Wanted to Sing for the People*. RCA Victor APL1-0182, 1973.

Clark, Guy. *Old No. 1*. RCA Victor APL1-1303, 1975.

———. *Texas Cookin'*. RCA Victor APL1-1944, 1976.

Commander Cody and His Lost Planet Airmen. *Live from Deep in the Heart of Texas*. Paramount PAS-1017, 1973.

Crow, Alvin, and the Neon Angels. *Alvin Crow and the Neon Angels*. Big Wheel BW 1003, 1979.

Crow, Alvin, and the Pleasant Valley Boys. *Alvin Crow and the Pleasant Valley Boys*. Long Neck LN-001, 1976.

———. *High Riding*. Polydor PD-1-6102, 1977.

The Flatlanders. *More a Legend than a Band*. Rounder CD SS34, 1990.

———. *Live '72*. New West NW 6052, 2004.

For the Records: Austin Country, 1973–1978. Maverick Records LP-001, 1980.

Freda and the Firedogs. *Freda and the Firedogs*. Plug Music PM 0004-2, 2002.

Friedman, Kinky. *Sold American*. Vanguard VSD 79333, 1973.

———. *Kinky Friedman*. ABC-Paramount ABCD 829, 1974.

———. *Lasso from El Paso*. Epic PE 34304, 1976.

———, and the Texas Jewboys. *Mayhem Afterthought: August 19, 1973, You Are There*. Sphincter Records SRI 00712D, 2005.

Fromholz, Steven. *Come on Down to Texas for Awhile: The Anthology, 1969–1991.* Raven RVCD-116, 2001.

Haggard, Merle. *A Tribute to the Best Damned Fiddle Player in the World, or, My Salute to Bob Wills.* Capitol ST-638, 1970.

The Lost Gonzo Band. *The Lost Gonzo Band.* MCA 487, 1975.

———. *Thrills.* MCA 2232, 1976.

———. *Signs of Life.* Capitol SW-11788, 1978.

Meyers, Augie, and the Western Head Band. *Live at the Longneck.* Texas Re-Cord LP-1002, n.d.

Murphey, Michael. *Geronimo's Cadillac.* A&M SP-4358, 1972.

———. *Cosmic Cowboy Souvenir.* A&M SP-4388, 1973.

———. *Michael Murphey.* Epic KE-32835, 1974.

———. *Blue Sky/Night Thunder.* Epic KE-33290, 1975.

Neely, Bill. *Austin's Original Singer-Songwriter.* Lost Art Records LAR 101G, 2002.

Nelson, Willie. *Shotgun Willie.* Atlantic SD-7262, 1973.

———. *Phases and Stages.* Atlantic SD-7291, 1974.

———. *Red Headed Stranger.* Columbia KC-33482, 1975.

New Riders of the Purple Sage. *Austin, Texas, June 13, 1975.* Kufala KUF0125, 2005.

Nitty Gritty Dirt Band. *Stars and Stripes Forever.* United Artists UALA-184J2, 1974.

Ramsey, Willis Alan. *Willis Alan Ramsey.* Shelter SW 8914, 1972.

Sahm, Doug. *Doug Sahm and Band.* Atlantic SD-7254, 1973.

———. *Groover's Paradise.* Warner Bros. BS-2810, 1974.

Shaver, Billy Joe. *Old Five and Dimers Like Me.* Monument KZ 32293, 1973.

Stevenson, B. W. *B. W. Stevenson.* RCA Victor LSP-4685, 1972.

———. *Lead Free.* RCA Victor LSP-4794, 1972.

———. *Calabasas.* RCA Victor APL1-0410, 1973.

———. *My Maria.* RCA Victor APL1-0088, 1973.

———. *We Be Sailin'.* Warner Bros. WBS-2901, 1975.

———. *Lost Feeling.* Warner Bros. WBS-3012, 1977.

Viva! Terlingua! Nuevo!: Songs of Luckenbach, Texas. Palo Duro PDR-4201, 2006.

Walker, Jerry Jeff. *Mr. Bojangles.* Atco SD-33259, 1968.

———. *Bein' Free.* Atco SD-33336, 1970.

———. *Jerry Jeff Walker.* Decca SD-33259, 1972.

———. *¡Viva Terlingua!* MCA 382, 1973.

———. *Walker's Collectables.* MCA 450, 1974.

———. *Ridin' High.* MCA 2156, 1975.

Wier, Rusty. *Don't It Make You Wanna Dance?* 20th Century Records T-469, 1975.

———. *Rusty Wier.* 20th Century Records T-495, 1975.

Wills, Bob, and His Texas Playboys. *San Antonio Rose: The Bob Wills Recordings, 1932–1947.* Bear Family BCD 15933-LL, n.d.

———. *The Bob Wills Anthology.* Columbia PG 32416, 1973.

———. *For the Last Time.* United Artists LA 216-J2, 1975.

Filmography

Szalapski, James, dir. *Heartworn Highways*. Warner Bros. Domestic Cable, 1981.
Wadleigh, Michael, dir. *Woodstock: 3 Days of Peace and Music*. Warner Bros. 1970.
Yablonski, Yabo, dir. *Willie Nelson's 4th of July Picnic*. La Paz Productions. 1974.

Index

Made in the USA
Coppell, TX
02 June 2020